ANTHONY GIDDENS

is contro-
takes up
oncept of
ttempted
structure.

of world
cities in
construc-
in a new
onalism,"
lens.

iversity.

ANTHONY GIDDENS

The last modernist

Stjepan G. Meštrović

London and New York

First published 1998
by Routledge
11 New Fetter Lane, London EC4P 4EE

Simultaneously published in the USA and Canada
by Routledge
29 West 35th Street, New York, NY 10001

Typeset in Garamond by Routledge
Printed and bound in Great Britain by MPG Books Ltd,
Bodmin, Cornwall

British Library Cataloguing in Publication Data
A catalogue record for this book is available from the British Library

Library of Congress Cataloging in Publication Data
Meštrović, Stjepan Gabriel.
Anthony Giddens: the last modernist / Stjepan G. Meštrović.
Includes bibliographical references and index.
1. Giddens, Anthony. 2. Sociology–Methodology.
3. Postmodernism. 4. Social structure. 5. Sociology–Great
Britain. I. Title.
HM22.G8G546 1998
301'.01–dc21

ISBN 0–415–09572–7 (hbk)
ISBN 0–415–09573–5 (pbk)

TO JOEL AND CHARLOTTE

CONTENTS

PREFACE AND
ACKNOWLEDGMENTS

I believe that humankind is caught in some interesting conceptual lacunae at this *fin de millennium*. Postmodernism, as a concept, is dead or dying and is being replaced by a vocabulary based on culture, nationalism, secessionism, Balkanization, and social fission. Modernism, too, is expiring in the West and has expired in formerly Communist nations. Yet the West is trying to export more modernism (talk of human rights, free markets, democracy) and more postmodernism (Disney products, McDonaldization, the Internet, *Barney and Friends*, etc.) to the rest of the world even as these two phenomena are dead or dying, and the West itself is Balkanizing rapidly.

I enter this interesting discussion vis-à-vis Anthony Giddens, who denies the existence of postmodernism and urges us to stay on the course of what he calls "high modernity." His nemesis, Jean Baudrillard, is also treated in the pages of the present discussion. Baudrillard believes that a radical break has occurred with modernity and that we are living in an era dominated by rootless, circulating fictions. I disagree with both Giddens and Baudrillard, though I hold considerable sympathy for Baudrillard. This is because Giddens's vocabulary is the empty, anachronistic vocabulary used by today's politicians, bureaucrats, and professionals: freedom, agency, globalization, security, democracy, etc. For example, NATO, which used to be a military alliance, is fast becoming a democratic club of supposedly like-minded nations that will not threaten nor be threatened by Russia. Who really believes this fiction, given the many signs that Russia is about to become more belligerent? On the other hand, Baudrillard's emphasis on virtual reality and hyperreality is more believable: NATO does come across as hyperreality, and Western soldiers, whose mandate is *not* to die for any cause, really are becoming virtual soldiers. Yet I'm not completely satisfied with this assessment either because "real" money – billions of dollars – is being spent to prop up these and other fictions, and millions of "real" people go along with the fictions. Mass society is not virtual.

Thus in this book I criticize both Giddens and his nemesis, Baudrillard, vis-à-vis forgotten or misunderstood voices from over a century ago, especially Émile Durkheim and Arthur Schopenhauer. I believe that Durkheim and

Schopenhauer had the vision to foresee many of the conceptual dilemmas that afflict our present era. And Giddens, like most other social theorists, either amputates or denatures sociology's legacy, especially Durkheim's legacy. By re-examining this neglected legacy, and by using it to criticize Giddens (and his nemesis), I hope to open up new avenues for discussion.

I would like to thank my colleagues for encouraging me and discussing this work with me: Chris Rojek, Keith Tester, David Riesman, Slaven Letica, and Thomas Cushman.

Some of the themes in chapter 3 were originally developed in "Searching for the Starting Points of Scientific Inquiry: Durkheim's *Rules of Sociological Method* and Schopenhauer's Philosophy," *Sociological Inquiry* 59(3), 1989: 267–86; and some of the themes in chapter 7 were originally developed in "Anomia and Sin in Durkheim's Thought," *Journal for the Scientific Study of Religion*, 24(2), 1985: 119–36.

1

INTRODUCTION

This is not a book about Giddens and his work in the conventional sense of introducing the reader to the major tenets of structuration theory or the other aspects of Giddens's thought. Such aims are achieved admirably in books written by Ian Craib (1992), Ira Cohen (1989), and others whose works are reviewed briefly in chapter 2. Rather, this book uses the work of Anthony Giddens as a vehicle to engage in a broad discussion of modernity, postmodernity, culture, and the relevance of classical social theory for contemporary times. In sum, I treat Giddens's work as representative of what I consider to be wrong with modern sociology. Some readers might expect my criticisms to come from a sympathetic reading, for example that Giddens's ambiguities and contradictions would be noted, but that his statements would then be accorded the best reasonable interpretation and only problems that still remain be seriously criticized. But mine is not a sympathetic reading. Instead, it is polemical, but it is not aimed at Giddens personally as much as at Giddens as representative of tendencies that I find objectionable in modern sociology. Let me note that good examples of the sort of work I offer here are to be found in David Riesman's *Thorstein Veblen* (1995), Douglas Kellner's *Jean Baudrillard* (1989), and C. Wright Mills's *The Sociological Imagination* (1959), books that range far beyond Veblen, Baudrillard, and Parsons in their respective discussions. The authors of these polemics admit that they are not overly fond of the vehicles they use for their discussions (Veblen, Baudrillard, Parsons), and I hereby confess that I am not overly fond of Giddens's work either. Nevertheless, I hope to fill a needed gap in the existing literature on Giddens as well as these other topics by:

1 focusing on theorists whom and theories that Giddens and other contemporary theorists tend to neglect, such as the works of David Riesman, Wilhelm Wundt, Georg Simmel, and Thorstein Veblen;
2 examining these neglected theories and theorists in a *cultural context*, namely, taking into account the people, habits of the heart (popularized admirably by Bellah *et al.* 1985), traditions, customs, and intellectual currents that surrounded them;

1

3   juxtaposing Giddens's concept of "high modernity" with Jean Baudrillard's writings on postmodernity;
4   challenging Giddens's assumption that classical social theory must be overhauled radically in order to be useful;
5   challenging Giddens's claims that the ghost of Auguste Comte animated the defunct version of sociology that he hopes to revivify;
6   challenging Giddens's assumption that sociology is the study of modern Western societies only – an assumption that seems to fairly represent the discipline of sociology today;
7   exposing the many contradictions in Giddens's writings concerning the nation-state, the creation of synthetic traditions, and human agency.

The present book should be read as a logical development of my previous works, each of which stands at loggerheads with core assumptions, presuppositions, and arguments made by Giddens as well as much of contemporary sociology. At this point I confront the question why I bother with Giddens in discussing these many other topics, for I have written extensively on them while making minimal or no reference to Giddens at all. In addition, several contemporary theorists have also addressed some of these topics in ways that I find commendable, including Akbar Ahmed (1992), Zygmunt Bauman (1991), Douglas Challenger (1994), Thomas Cushman (1995), Keith Doubt (1996), Mike Featherstone (1995), Chris Rojek (1995), and Keith Tester (1992), among others. None of these theorists are as centrally concerned with Giddens as I am in this book. Yet they share some common assumptions with me that run against the grain of Giddens's sociology, namely: modernity leads to order as well as disorder; modernity co-exists in curious ways with traditionalism and what might be called postmodernity; modernity is enabling as well as disabling; and the classical social theorists (Durkheim, Weber, Marx, Simmel, and so on) are still relevant and useful to contemporary social theorizing.

In this book, I challenge Giddens directly because his popularity represents what is wrong with much of contemporary sociology. Much like Baudrillard has been referred to as the "high priest" of postmodernity, Giddens should be regarded as the "high priest" of modernity. Like so many of his contemporaries, Giddens claims that modernity leads to new forms of social order; modernity represents a radical disjunction with previous forms of social order; modernity carries some risks but is enabling overall; and the classical social theorists are mostly obsolete, or if they are to be used, "their ideas must be radically overhauled today" (Giddens 1979: 1). For Giddens, sociology is the study of modern societies only.

Giddens's attitude toward the social theorists who precede him is not unlike the collective hubris among many if not most contemporary sociologists who believe that nobody had seriously addressed society in a systematic way before them. Parsons is much closer to Giddens historically than

Durkheim and other classical social theorists, yet Giddens claims that he is the first to work out a theory of human agency. But are Parsons and Giddens really very different in their attitudes or assumptions despite Giddens's public repudiation of Parsons? In the 1990s, it is fashionable to criticize Parsons, but the more interesting point is that many sociologists tried to imitate Parsons, from Robert K. Merton to Jürgen Habermas and, ironically, even Giddens. I will argue throughout this book that Giddens stays in the shadow of Parsons despite his many criticisms of him. Perhaps more importantly, the entire discipline of contemporary sociology stays in the shadow of Parsons. For example, Giddens as well as most contemporary sociologists reject postmodernism out-of-hand; misunderstand anomie; neglect emotions and culture in analyses; are *still* obsessed with the problem of social order; view the self as excessively cognitive; assume rather than investigate the nature of human agency.

Furthermore, both Giddens and the contemporary sociologists whom he represents do not seem to be overly concerned with glaring paradoxes in their positions. The most important paradox is Giddens's thrust on human agency and his view of modernity as a juggernaut. Other related paradoxes include the concepts of globalization and the nation-state with rigid boundaries; his overemphasis on the knowledgeable agent who must passively accept the creation of synthetic traditions; and the contradiction in believing one is an effective agent locally (at home, neighborhood, or office) who feels powerless globally.

Despite my criticisms, Giddens and I converge in recognizing the dawning of a new era in which "synthetic traditions" as well as synthetic emotions are created as a rational, planned substitute for the role previously served by spontaneous "habits of the heart" (from Tocqueville). But in my book *Postemotional Society* (1997), I view this development negatively, as a new form of enslavement, whereas Giddens views it (in *Beyond Left and Right* [1994] as well as *Modernity and Self-Identity* [1991a]) positively, as a vehicle for democratized life politics. It is not that reinvented traditions are inherently dangerous, but they *can* be dangerous, and Giddens, as well as most contemporary sociologists, fails to investigate the possible dangers of synthetic traditions. An apparent contradiction in Giddens's work must be repeated here for the sake of emphasis: on the one hand, he advocates agency, individual power, and emancipation, but, on the other, he advocates what seems to be the opposite of agency, the submission to rationally planned and synthetically created traditions in the name of democratization. One cannot have it both ways.

My lack of fondness for Giddens's work stems from the conviction that his writings are representative of a more general tendency in contemporary social theorizing that I believe is damaging to sociology. By this I mean the following:

1   Most sociologists seem to accept the incorrect depiction of sociology as rooted in Comtean positivism that supposedly led to Durkheimian and Parsonian functionalism.

2   Most sociologists seem to go along with Giddens in *The Constitution of Society* (1994) regarding the claim that sociology is the study of modern societies. Sociology thereby jettisons the idea of continuity with the past.

3   The general respect ascribed to Giddens has occurred in an era in which it is fashionable to write and speak about the alleged death of sociology. Giddens has the dubious distinction of being perceived as a major social theorist by "mainstream" colleagues at a time when sociology majors are shrinking, sociology departments are being closed, and sociology is largely seen as irrelevant to everyday life by many non-sociologists.

Thus, my criticisms of Giddens should be more properly construed as criticisms of Giddens *as a vehicle* and representation of more general trends in contemporary sociology.

I should add that I find the notion of "mainstream sociology" problematic. While many contemporary sociologists refer to something called mainstream sociology, one could argue that no such entity exists. Sociology is so diverse and uncultivated in contrast to neighboring disciplines such as psychology and economics that one could argue that it makes more sense to refer to many little streams in sociology all going in different directions. On the other hand, it is also true that elite journals such as *The American Journal of Sociology* and *The American Sociological Review* seem to self-consciously promote "mainstream sociology" as an accepted view of the discipline that is supposed to bring order to the perceived chaos of so many different views in sociology. In this sense, Giddens is a popular, mainstream sociologist even though many sociologists go about their business without paying much attention to him.

It is important to note that Giddens, as a social theorist, is a man for *this*, current season, and is not a theorist for all seasons. His glib optimism, popular sociology rhetoric, and shallow treatment of theory resonate with the current climate of feel-good-optimistic ideology in sociology. For example, he recognizes that modernity causes many people to feel disembedded, to which he replies, glibly, that they can be re-embedded. I realize that this will not be perceived as a reproach by most of my colleagues. What is wrong with optimism – even a shallow optimism?

The automatic response will be that nothing is wrong with it. But a more thoughtful response will be that a sociology built upon unrealistic optimism in the face of mounting social problems is not serious, and in its present form is fated to become extinct because it is increasingly seen as useless. Giddens and many other mainstream sociologists have been singing a merry tune of global democratization even as genocide raged in Bosnia, Russians expressed a nostalgia for Communism, the European Community began unravelling almost as soon as it was formed, and "ethnic cleansing" became a metaphor for our times – to borrow Akbar Ahmed's (1995) phrase – among many other disturbing developments. And it is worth noting that not a single article on Hitler's rise to power or crimes was published in so-called mainstream sociology journals. For the most part, as noted by Bauman (1989), mainstream sociologists ignored the Holocaust. I do not feel indifferent to sociology's indifference to urgent moral questions of the day. Arthur Schopenhauer may have had a point when he wrote, over a century ago, that when conceived as a response to human suffering, optimism is really a wicked and heartless doctrine.

This does not mean that a more pessimistic response is necessarily nihilistic nor that it promotes hopelessness. It could well be that pessimism finds the real paths to hope and faith whereas, as Nietzsche taught us, optimism may be nihilistic. Sociology's great pessimists – who include Thorstein Veblen, Émile Durkheim, and Max Weber – certainly pointed to hopeful alternatives even as they exhibited strong social criticisms. Yet they come across as *serious* scholars who were willing to confront real social problems. This is illustrated, for example, by Veblen's writings on the dominance of the machine metaphor for comprehending modernity, Durkheim's gloomy assessment of anomie as a condition of unlimited desires that can never be satiated, and by Weber's writings on the iron cage. By contrast, Giddens simply fails to confront these and other negative aspects of modernity. His treatment of "risks" in "high modernity" is a shallow response to modernization, and deserves to be appraised critically.

WHY GIDDENS AND NOT HABERMAS?

Some readers will wonder why I did not write a book entitled *Habermas: The Last Modernist*. Habermas has left social science and returned to philosophy, enabling Giddens to take over sociology. An interesting irony is that Giddens has co-opted American sociology much like Parsons co-opted European sociology. In any event, Jürgen Habermas is widely perceived as the heir to Theodor Adorno and the Frankfurt School. His explicit goal is that of his predecessors, to "complete the Enlightenment project" despite all of its faults. That is, indeed, a modernist goal. And there is no doubt that all of the critical theorists end their treatises in the standardized fashion of calling for "pure" rationality to save us from the perils of "instrumental" rationality. Neither Habermas nor his predecessors come across as shallow or glib. On the contrary, their works are serious and earnest. Yet the critical theorists are also considered passé.

This is because, as most everyone knows in the West, we have already reasoned too much. How much more reasoning must we undergo before we get it "right"? Moreover, Adorno and other critical theorists are widely perceived as elitist. They imply that they hold the key to "pure" reasoning and could guide mass society to the promised land. Such elitism is distasteful in an other-directed era that is much more egalitarian and oriented toward tolerance than the inner-directed era of the critical theorists. The critical theorists never entertain the notion that feelings in general or compassion in particular might remedy some of the ills of the Enlightenment project. Emotions, for the critical theorists, are *irrational* and threatening to their project. For all these reasons, Habermas and the critical theorists are old-fashioned, inner-directed modernists, of historical and nostalgic interest to many, but not directly relevant to the present. Had it not been for Anthony Giddens, Habermas might have been the last modernist.

Giddens recognizes the limitations of the Enlightenment project *somewhat* – he is certainly not a deep philosopher – and he appreciates the importance of emotions (albeit synthetic emotions) for self-identity and the existence of social life. He could have taken the approach of some postmodernists and concluded that emotions make self-identity and social life *chaotic*. This is a conclusion that Giddens resolutely opposes, as I demonstrate later in the book. Instead, Giddens comes up with a truly ingenious twist to modernism: he calls for the rationalization, mechanization, colonization, and synthetic creation of the emotions. Neither the critical theorists nor the postmodernists could have conceived such a move.

The novelty of Giddens's approach to the modernity–postmodernity debate helps to explain much of his appeal. I confess that I am also unhappy with the alternatives of modernity versus postmodernity. In some ways, I share Giddens's disdain for postmodernity. On the other hand, if forced to choose allegiance to Giddens's theory versus Baudrillard's so-called postmodernism, I would choose postmodernism. (One must keep in mind that Baudrillard denies being a postmodernist even though he is hailed as the "high priest" of postmodernism. In the end, Baudrillard may turn out to be an anti-modernist.) This is because Baudrillard's disturbing vision of the present seems to ring true whereas Giddens's theory has the feel of Disney World about it. Baudrillard seems principled because he confronts the pessimistic, chaotic, and unruly aspects of social life. On the other extreme, like the critical theorists and Parsons, Giddens tries too hard to make one believe in the power of reflexivity even as the world does seem to be characterized by what Baudrillard calls rootless, circulating fictions.

Giddens never addresses the potentially dark side of a program for creating synthetic emotions. Any such contrived emotions must be pseudo-real and must be manipulated by an elite whose moral goals are open to doubt. Traditionally, emotions arose spontaneously from a natural, *cultural* milieu. Instead of arguing for or against the traditional notion of culture, Giddens seeks to establish a synthetic culture of sorts. In these regards, he betrays the modernist spirit of colonization, imperialism, system-building, and social engineering. Modernists used to colonize peoples, continents, time, and space. As Veblen and other theorists have noted (especially Henry Adams and George Orwell), modernity worships the machine as the system *par excellence* that organizes and tames Nature. In Giddens's system, modernists will colonize the last bastion of Nature – the emotions. Modernists have been perceived rightly as imperialists, always thinking in terms of empires, federations, and world conquest. Giddens does not write in these old-fashioned and distasteful terms, but he does write about global democracy based on the control of emotions. Previously, modernists got as far as Fordism and the assembly line in applying the machine model to social life. Giddens goes a step further: in *The Transformation of Intimacy* (1992b) and other works, he advocates the self-diagnosis of emotional problems and the remedy to such problems in much the same manner that one would fix a faulty carburetor.

Similarly, in *The Nation-State and Violence* (1987) Giddens overplays the modernist card in insisting that nationalism could not have existed in traditional societies. Contemporary nationalism holds many distinctive features in contrast to the past, but it is far-fetched to sever any and all linkages to historical forms of nationalism. Giddens amputates the past in discussing present-day nationalisms, and he amputates the past also in discussing contemporary sociological theory (especially in *The Constitution of Society* [1984]).

For these reasons, Giddens deserves to be called the last modernist. And again, his popularity suggests that he is representative of a general trend in contemporary social life in the West. The current *fin de siècle* is one in which most Westerners seem to live in the present cut off from the past, do not really care about the non-Western world, are willing to manipulate and be manipulated regarding their emotional lives, and wish to preserve the status quo despite heightened awareness concerning the ills of the modernist project. The critical theorists were completely off the mark in depicting the beginnings of this process as one leading to mass society that could be remedied by individualism and rationalism. On the contrary, most Westerners today believe they are individuals endowed with agency even as they succumb willingly to emotional manipulation by governments, corporations, and organizations. In this regard, they mirror Giddens's contradiction in advocating human agency and general emancipation at the same time that he advocates the creation of synthetic emotions and traditions vis-à-vis a social system that will bind time and space.

This contradiction is fundamental to Giddens's work, and needs to be elaborated further here (even though I have mentioned it already and it is treated at length later in the present volume). Immanuel Kant's definition of enlightenment included the courage to think for one's self, to use one's own understanding. Now, if Giddens's synthetic traditions are going to be able to secure allegiance, and if they are going to have any experiential plausibility, then presumably the foundations of these synthetic traditions must precisely *not* be thought about reflexively – traditions cease to be traditions if they are reflexively deconstructed. This is another aspect of Giddens's hidden modernism: he cannot seem to accept that individuals or communities might have their own spontaneous meanings which work without the beneficent involvement of those who presumably know best. Ironically, this also implies that Giddens cannot be reflexive about himself or about sociology and the double hermeneutic that he proposes; after all, reflexive inquiry will deconstruct the plausibility of what Giddens proposes concerning synthetic traditions. In summary, Giddens seems to be claiming that there are some things about which we must not or cannot think for ourselves, and such a claim is absolutely counter to the Enlightenment. Yet, on the other hand, he is a typical Enlightenment thinker insofar as he believes that rationality (not emotions) in the form enshrined by a sociological elite can yield knowledge that should be used for social engineering. Again, this fundamental ambivalence concerning the relationship of rationality to emancipation is not peculiar to Giddens, but is found in the heart of the modernist "project," as expounded brilliantly by Zygmunt Bauman in *Modernity and Ambivalence* (1991).

This fundamental contradiction in Giddens's thought reappears in many forms throughout his work. Thus, his overemphasis on the surveillance that is essential to the modernist nation-state in *The Nation-State and Violence* (1987) really contradicts his rhetoric of modernist emancipation elsewhere in his writings. Similarly, his allegiance to the extreme position in *The Constitution of Society* (1984) that sociology is the study of only modern and primarily Western societies really comes across as ethnocentric, and contradicts his rhetoric elsewhere concerning the need for cosmopolitan globalism. Given that Giddens severs connections between the past and present, between "us" (in the West) and "them" (in the non-West), what can his theories really offer to those who take seriously his emancipatory and liberal rhetoric?

ON THE STYLE AND ARGUMENTATION OF THIS BOOK

1 *Redundancy*. Some readers will be irritated by the redundancy that will be found in certain portions of this work. This is unavoidable because Giddens's work itself is largely redundant: how many times does he restate, always in slightly different forms, his claims concerning the freedom of the knowledgeable agent? Much like the critical theorists harped tendentiously on pure rationality, Giddens is tendentious concerning democratization, high modernity, globalization, and other concepts. A modernist reader might

have expected me to catalogue Giddens's several different nuances of these terms and treat them all at once and once and for all in a specific section of my book. But such a factory approach would prohibit me from treating the ways that Giddens's concepts create an interlocking whole within his thought treated as a contradictory system. And if I were to treat his interlocking terms and contradictions systematically, my book would read like a manual, not a discussion. I refuse to write a manual. Moreover, I confess that my style represents my leanings toward postmodernity in the modernist–postmodernist debate. I seek to open up new alternatives and possibilities for interpretation and discussion, not to emulate a machine. For this reason, it is simply unavoidable that I will offend or irritate readers who hold a penchant for the mechanical aspects of modernist thinking. Finally, it could be that my own redundancy, already evident in this introduction, is meant to be a somewhat reflexive irony, given Giddens's tediousness.

2 *Giddens's work as a unified whole.* Similarly, some modernist readers might expect me to dissect Giddens's work into its logical components, including but not limited to structuration theory, globalization, theory of modernity, sociology of knowledge, and so on. In addition, I might distinguish between the "early Giddens" and the "late Giddens" – this is a fashionable approach to studying Marx, Freud, Durkheim, and other theorists. Again, I will disappoint these readers by my refusal to dissect, disjoin, and tear apart. Instead, I will treat structuration theory and other components of Giddens's thought as part of a larger whole and unity. My reasons for this approach are the same as above: I refuse to treat Giddens's thought as if it were a machine that can be taken apart. May I repeat: Giddens's contradictions, ambiguities, and ambivalence are representative of similar traits in the lives of contemporary modernists.

3 *Not a manifesto.* Other readers might expect me to present a manifesto of my own as an alternative to Giddens's self-proclaimed manifestos.[1] But again, these readers will be disappointed. I have been sympathetic for a long time to Nietzsche's warning that one should be wary of the great systematizers: "I mistrust all systematizers and I avoid them. The will to a system is a lack of integrity" (1968: 470). I do *not* mean to imply that Giddens's tendency toward systematization is that extreme. Nevertheless, as Nazism, Communism, and other, lesser-known totalitarian systems have taught us in this century, there is an important kernel of truth in Nietzsche's assessment. I simply want to let the reader know that I self-consciously refuse to systematize my criticisms of Giddens and of his own post-Parsonian tendency toward a grand theory. Instead, I follow David Riesman's admonition that there is something healthy and natural in sociology remaining a wilderness.

4 *Conversational writing style.* Thus, the writing style in this book (like so many of my other books) is conversational. My hope is to enter into a dialogue with the reader in imagination and to provoke discussion. Again, many of my colleagues are contemptuous of "conversational writing." But

then, I am hostile to writing (and lecturing) that is not conducive to discussion. This might well constitute an irreconcilable difference between some readers and this author. My aim is not just to argue that Giddens is wrong in many regards, but to open up sites for discussion that have remained closed for too long, including: What were the real origins of sociology? If Durkheim was not a positivist, what was his position? Are sociology's classical theorists really irrelevant to contemporary times? Is Giddens's advocacy of synthetic traditions a good or dangerous thing overall? Why is Giddens's feel-good sociology so popular despite the existence of serious moral and social issues today? Do the information media lead to democracy or new forms of enslavement? Is the nation-state really the final form of nationalism? And so on. Without questions of these and other sorts that challenge existing views, popular concepts used by Giddens and others are reduced to trivial clichés.

5 *More Schopenhauer?* Finally, I anticipate that those readers who are familiar with some aspects of my other books will moan, if they read further in this book: "What? He's still doing Schopenhauer? And this time in relation to Giddens!" It is true that in the present volume I rely, again, on the centrality of Arthur Schopenhauer's philosophy to the culture of the previous *fin de siècle*, even though this verifiable fact has fallen into a cultural amnesia in the present *fin de siècle*. But let me explain the following:

(a) I am not merely repeating my previous arguments in the present volume concerning Schopenhauer or the *fin de siècle*. There will be some redundancy, but I cannot assume that the reader is familiar with my previous works or with the importance of Schopenhauer.

(b) That Schopenhauer was *the* central philosopher in the culture of the previous *fin de siècle* is beyond dispute. This influence is documented, and I urge the skeptical reader to check into my documentation (Meštrović 1988, 1991, 1992, 1993a).

(c) I am not making a simple, cause and effect, mechanical argument concerning Schopenhauer's influence. That is, I do *not* mean to imply that Schopenhauer directly influenced Durkheim or anyone else. Instead, I claim that Schopenhauer's philosophical vocabulary became intertwined with the intellectual culture of the previous *fin de siècle* and thereby supplied the cultural resources and restraints for the golden age of sociology, specifically, works by Durkheim, Simmel, Mead, Veblen, and Weber.

(d) If the reader is still skeptical after reading my exposition of Schopenhauer's importance, I urge him or her to read Georg Simmel's *Schopenhauer and Nietzsche* ([1907] 1986). If the reader is still skeptical or hostile to my use of Schopenhauer, I would urge him or her to wonder why the use of Nietzsche as central to cultural discussions of the present as well as previous *fin de siècle* does *not* provoke such hostility. In 1995 alone, there were over thirty books published on Nietzsche. In other words, if the reader is hostile to my use of Schopenhauer after I present rational and reasonable documentation for my claims, the reader's reaction might well be irrational.

(e) So that the reader is not lost concerning my motives vis-à-vis Giddens, let me state explicitly: highlighting Schopenhauer's importance to the era in which sociology began exposes dramatically Giddens's misrepresentation of the origins and make-up of the sociological enterprise as derived from Comte, perverted by Parsonian functionalism, and redeemed by Giddens.

PARTING THOUGHTS

Perhaps the preceding comments will be helpful to some readers in orienting themselves toward this work, which is unusual in some regards, but also typical when read in the light of Riesman, Veblen, Kellner, Baudrillard, Mills, and other social critics and polemicists whom I admire. One final analogy might be helpful. As I was writing this book, I could not help thinking of Schopenhauer's contempt for Hegel, whom Schopenhauer called the great charlatan. Like so many philosophers, Schopenhauer reasoned that if he exposed Hegel's philosophical weaknesses and errors, people would abandon Hegel and flock to him. Schopenhauer even scheduled his lectures to coincide with Hegel's, but the anticipated switch of audience allegiance from Hegel to Schopenhauer never materialized. Instead, Schopenhauer remained obscure until well after his death, enjoying a posthumous fame in the 1880s and 1890s. In the previous *fin de siècle*, Schopenhauer finally triumphed over the great charlatan.

The analogy between Schopenhauer and Hegel and my treatment of Giddens is not exact, of course, but is instructive. For me to go against Giddens is something like Schopenhauer daring to criticize Hegel. The point is that, according to Schopenhauer, while people were listening to Hegel, they did not hear Hegel and they did not listen to or hear how Schopenhauer heard Hegel. It took half a century for people to finally hear Schopenhauer as a spokesperson for their most hidden thoughts and to finally hear Hegel as someone who had deceived them about the power of rationality. (Karl Popper agrees with Schopenhauer that Hegel was a charlatan, but I do not want to enter this polemic here.) Likewise, I contend that many people today listen to Giddens but do not seem to hear him – do not hear his contradictions, his authoritarianism, his arrogant disdain for the theorists who came before him. I am writing this book because I feel that Giddens needs to be heard rather than just listened to, even if this might be the last thing that he wants. Whether or when I will be heard remains an open question.

11

2

ANTHONY GIDDENS

The last modernist

Against that positivism which stops before phenomena saying,
"there are only *facts*," I should say: no, it is precisely facts that
do not exist, only *interpretations*.
                    – Friedrich Nietzsche (1968: 458)

At least since the fall of Communism in some portions of the world in 1989,
but prior to that event as well, the course of world events has been moving
steadily in a direction that seems to challenge Anthony Giddens's and other
contemporary sociologists' predictions and assessments concerning modernity. Specifically, against the assimilatory and globalizing tendencies
predicted by Giddens in *The Nation-State and Violence* (1987), nation-states
are splintering and undergoing a sort of *fission* process into ever-smaller
units. For example, new nations were born from the collapse of both the
Soviet and Yugoslav Empires, which in turn were dominated by Russia and
Serbia, respectively. This new form of nationalism tends toward the *implosion*
of nation-states that results in new nations seeking new states, as opposed to
the previous variety of nationalism that emerged in the nineteenth century
and which, until recently, led to imperialism, colonialism, and various feder-
alisms. And this new form of Balkanization is no longer confined to the
Balkans, but is afflicting the modern West as well (Meštrović 1994). Thus,
Quebec nearly seceded from Canada recently; Israel has been divided by the
assassination of Prime Minister Rabin in 1995; Scotland is seriously considering secession from Great Britain; the European Union seems unable to
speak in one voice on many issues, and so on. Quite apart from this literal
Balkanization, the dismal state of gender and ethnic relations in Western
countries has practically converted gender and ethnicity into group identifi-
cations that are so hostile to each other that civil society and the institution
of the family also seem to be imploding. An unconscious fear of
Balkanization of the West is so pervasive that President Clinton expressed it
almost as a matter of course in a televised speech to the US public on 27
November 1995:

As the cold war gives way to the global village, our leadership is needed more than ever because problems that start beyond our borders can quickly become problems within them. We're all vulnerable to the organized forces of intolerance and destruction, terrorism, ethnic, religious and regional rivalries, the spread of organized crime and weapons of mass destruction and drug trafficking. Just as surely as Fascism and Communism, these forces also threaten freedom and democracy, peace and prosperity.[1]

Another defect in Giddens's neat and tidy concept of the nation-state – a concept that is not unique to him, but is *courant* today – is that *submerged nations* have erupted out of previous nation-states whose borders were enshrined in the Helsinki Accords, and these new nations went in search of states, from Croatia, Slovenia, Bosnia-Herzegovina, Slovakia, Lithuania, Latvia, Estonia, and many former republics of the former Soviet Union to Kurdistan and Palestine to the Northwest Territories in Canada (and elsewhere, of course). The nationalist process exposes a fundamental ambiguity in the modernist "project" that is mentioned by Senator Daniel Patrick Moynihan in *Pandaemonium* (1993), namely, the emancipatory strand of modernism enshrined in Woodrow Wilson's principle of the self-determination of nations conflicts with the assimilatory strand of modernism enshrined in the Helsinki Accords. One cannot have it both ways, because emancipation leads to perceived chaos while the preservation of order must necessarily suppress the right to self-determination. Yet an unchecked right to self-determination leads to an anomic condition in which nations splinter into increasingly smaller units, while an unchecked tendency toward preserving the inviolability of borders degenerates into appeasement of brutal regimes who oppress nationalities and/or minorities within existing borders. This fundamental ambiguity and ambivalence should be added to the list of similar tensions that are inherent in modernity and that are exposed by Zygmunt Bauman in *Modernity and Ambivalence* (1991) and other writings. The trajectory of analysis established by Bauman and Moynihan is far more relevant to contemporary times than the somewhat quaint, one-sided, and incomplete image of globalization and assimilation offered by Giddens. The most accurate assessment of the contemporary scene seems to be that both processes – globalization and a sort of Balkanization – are working simultaneously. In the words of Akbar Ahmed and Chris Shore:

On the one hand, there is an increasing centralization of what the international business press calls a "de-facto world government" with its own institutions: the International Monetary Fund (IMF), World Bank, G-7, the General Agreement on Tariffs and Trade (GATT) . . . on the other hand, however, these tendencies have been matched by a revival of localism and ethnic chauvinism, and an increase in xenophobia and nationalism throughout Europe and beyond.

(1995: 13)

In *Undoing Culture*, Mike Featherstone (1995) offers another assessment of the contemporary scene that is in line with Ahmed and Shore yet exposes the limitations of Giddens's vision of the world. Featherstone argues that globalization and modernization each hold two contradictory aspects: one toward increasing order and the other toward change and chaos. Unlike Giddens, Featherstone focuses on the neglected aspect of modernization as a world culture of competing differences, power struggles, and culture wars. Against the unidimensional vision of globalization found in Anthony Giddens's writings, Featherstone takes into account a world-wide return to local cultures, the clash of pluralities, and the atomization of the world alongside globalization. Ultimately, he argues, the postmodern world becomes recentered as opposed to decentered. Featherstone's approach overlaps theoretically with Chris Rojek's *Decentring Leisure* (1995), in which Rojek also posits a modernist force that presses for order working in tandem with a modernist force that aims at disorder. In general, I believe that Ahmed, Shore, Featherstone, and Rojek represent a more accurate assessment of the political and cultural horizon in the present *fin de siècle* than that represented by the work of Giddens.

Against the overall and superficial optimism found in Giddens's works – which is reflected in the works of scores of Western academic sociologists – apocalyptic themes have emerged in some postmodern literature, especially as humanity becomes more conscious of approaching the end of the century and millennium (Meštrović 1991). Giddens (1990) admits to "risks" in modern life, but these risks have taken on catastrophic proportions, from the potential for all-out economic meltdown, the impossibility of coping with a billion-dollar-per-day deficit in the USA, and the complete destruction of the earth's ozone layer to the potential for race riots in Western nations and ever-increasing ethnic conflict throughout the world. Akbar Ahmed (1995) may have a point in claiming that ethnic cleansing has become a metaphor for our times, and that it can be found not only in Sarajevo but in Bombay, Los Angeles, London, and elsewhere in the world.

Against Giddens's perspective on increasing empowerment and emancipation in the modern world – what he calls life politics – one finds increasing cynicism, disenchantment, and exasperation in Western countries, captured by David Riesman's (1950) portrait of the other-directed inside-dopester who compensates for his or her feelings of powerlessness by exhibiting curdled indignation and a desire to have "inside" knowledge concerning world events. For Riesman, the inside-dopester wants to *know* precisely because he or she fears that it is *impossible to act* meaningfully. Only a few years ago, many persons in capitalist countries agreed with the sentiment, "We don't trust the Soviets." But in the years since the end of the Cold War, a new sentiment has emerged in capitalist countries: "We don't trust our own government." The recent televised coverage of the O.J. Simpson trial exposed a tremendous undercurrent of cynicism and distrust of the police and government in the USA. The Simpson trial was linked in popular culture to alleged US government misconduct at Waco, Ruby Ridge, the Oklahoma City bombing, and even the JFK and Martin Luther King assassinations. Another form that the new exasperation takes – in addition to anti-government sentiment – is the huge size of jury verdicts in the USA against any defendant thought to be insured or to have wealth. This is one reason among several for the huge increase in malpractice premiums in certain medical specialties.

As modernists become better informed than their ancestors could imagine, they are also becoming more confused and blasé from the information overload as well as "compassion fatigue." The information media supply so much negative information about famines, wars, genocide, and other disasters that many Westerners throw up their hands in despair when confronted with the question of what they can do to make the world a better place. Most people conclude, perhaps correctly, that since they cannot improve the world, they might at least concentrate on improving their families or other local sites of action. The problem with this minimalist faith in human agency is that global issues impact local ones, thereby making it difficult to make a difference even in one's family. For example, how can one fulfill the wishes and dreams of one's children if a global economy results in "downsizing" and being fired from one's job for reasons one cannot control?

Overall, Giddens's position in relation to these and other alarming developments could be compared with Talcott Parsons's cool contemplation of abstract social order in *The Structure of Social Action* in 1937, during the Great Depression and massive social upheaval in the USA. Of course, Giddens repudiates Parsons,[2] frequently, and especially with regard to the so-called problem of social order, but the analogy holds nonetheless, with the implication that Anthony Giddens clings to and defends modernity in the face of overwhelming challenges to it. He not only defends modernity – albeit, in an ambiguous and complex way (Giddens 1990) – his very approach to sociological issues is quintessentially modernist. For example, he severs sociology from the other social sciences by insisting that it is the study of modern societies, as opposed to an approach that might find commonalities among the various social sciences, including the anthropological study of traditional societies. To be sure, Giddens also notes that modernity is a juggernaut (yet makes reflexive self-identity possible), that it causes "disembedding" (which makes "re-embedding" possible), and leads to high risks, observations which make his thought appear to be complex. His ambivalence toward modernity will be taken up later in this chapter and throughout this book. Nevertheless, in the end, and despite his critiques of some aspects of modernity and of modernist thinkers such as Talcott Parsons, Giddens should be classified as a modernist because of his complete disdain for tradition, his dismissal of postmodernity, and his penchant for social engineering, among other attitudes. One should add that present-day social ills are far worse, and potentially more dangerous, than they were in 1937. One of the most combustible dangers is that of seemingly internecine ethnic conflict and the ultimate fate of nuclear weapons in the former Soviet arsenal (see Khazanov 1995).

In this book, I offer a serious criticism of Anthony Giddens's stand on modernity as reflected in his works vis-à-vis these dramatic and somewhat ominous contemporary world developments. Let me state from the outset that one could approach his structuration theory separately from his overall writings on modernity. But for reasons that were given in the introduction, I have chosen to read his structuration theory as part of his overall and ambivalent stand toward modernity. (And I will not offer an exegesis of structuration theory because this task has been performed by many other commentators on Giddens.) To lend meaning to the present analysis, Giddens's theory shall be analyzed in relation to the theories of selected founders of sociology – especially Émile Durkheim, the world's first professor of sociology – and also in relation to postmodern, cultural, and other theorists who are concerned with grand questions similar to the ones that concern him: What is the fate of modernity? Is the Enlightenment project bankrupt, finally? If the present-day version of the Enlightenment project as rational is not bankrupt, can it really continue on its existing path of glorifying rationality while eschewing emotions, or is a new synthesis of reason and emotion needed? Can society exist and persist without culture? Does postmodernity refer to a real rupture with modernity? Is the human agent as free and skilled as Giddens purports? And so on.

GIDDENS AND THE END OF SOCIOLOGY

But in making clear that I will be using Durkheim and other classical social theorists as foils with which to judge Giddens as well as those who accept his work uncritically, I encounter immediately Giddens's assumptions that Durkheim and other founders of the social sciences are mostly irrelevant to the present; that sociology is the study of modern societies; and that modernity represents a dramatic discontinuity with pre-modern or traditional modes of social relations. Let me note that in making these claims, Giddens (1984, 1987) is typically modernist and in tune with many similar discussions in the present *fin de siècle*. Intellectual discourse these days tends to refer to dramatic endings of many sorts: Fukuyama's (1992) *end of history*,

Baudrillard's (1986) *end of culture*, Brzezinski's (1989) *end of Communism* (which is staging a dramatic comeback in Russia), even the *end of the millennium* as well as the *fin de siècle* (Meštrović 1991), the *end of sociology*, and others. Giddens writes with a calm equanimity in the face of these tumultuous, menacing discourses. He clings to the trajectory in social thought that can be traced back to Auguste Comte and the Enlightenment, and seems not to take seriously Jean Baudrillard and the postmodernists. Regarding classical social theory, Giddens seems to make very little use of Georg Simmel's ([1900] 1990) stand against the rational Enlightenment and Simmel's complex treatment of emotions and culture. Similarly, it is worth noting that Giddens ignores completely Thorstein Veblen, regarded by many as one of America's greatest social theorists and social critics, whose notion of "conspicuous consumption" seems *more* relevant to the present *fin de siècle* than the previous *fin de siècle*. Is Giddens right that the classical social theorists are irrelevant to the present? I propose to challenge Giddens with regard to his rather glib acceptance of Enlightenment assumptions, his casual dismissal of the classical social theorists, and his equally casual attitude toward the postmodernists. To be sure, Giddens criticizes both Comte and the Enlightenment project, but as with his criticisms of Parsons, he identifies in large measure with the targets of his criticisms. (To repeat: I will have more to say on Giddens's maddening ambivalence later in this chapter and throughout this book.) This does not mean that I shall defend postmodern social theory, nor that I accept that Durkheim, Veblen, Simmel, and other classical social theorists can be understood without cultural translation between their cultural milieux and ours. First, there exist quite a few grounds for criticizing postmodernity apart from the criticisms made by Giddens. Specifically, I disagree with Jean Baudrillard's vision of the postmodern world as one of rootless, circulating fictions. Yet even if Giddens is correct that postmodernity is mostly an invented term that does not correspond to reality, the fact that postmodernity appeals to so many intellectuals in the 1990s suggests that even knowing, skilled agents perceive that something has gone wrong with modernity, albeit, they cannot yet articulate precisely what is amiss. One may, and perhaps should disagree with Baudrillard in many respects, yet he cannot be ignored, and he is an important social theorist (see Rojek and Turner 1993). Second, it should be obvious that many of the central concepts by the classical social theorists, from Simmel's blasé attitude and Veblen's notion of conspicuous consumption to Durkheim's notion of anomie as the infinity of desires, are still relevant today.

Let me illustrate my objections to Giddens's attitude toward the social sciences by taking up his commentary in chapter 12 of Ahmed and Shore's *The Future of Anthropology: Its Relevance to the Contemporary World* (1995). Giddens writes:

What justification actually is there for a continuing role for anthropology, and if there is indeed such justification what shape might the discipline henceforth assume – where would its distinctiveness lie? . . . Substantively, the distinctiveness of anthropology, particularly in relation to sociology, was normally thought of as bound up with its concern with the non-modern. *Sociology, by contrast, concerns itself with the nature and impact of modernity*. Today, however, as many of the contributors to the book note, modernity is everywhere. Sociologists might see their province as primarily that of the First World while anthropologists concentrate upon the Third World. Yet as globalization develops apace, divisions between First and Third World societies crumble; and in any case the Third World is the creation of modernity rather than simply standing outside it. To persist with a substantive definition of anthropology as about non-modern societies and cultures would mean turning the subject into a version of museum studies. The anthropologist would be a sort of curator of an historical past.

(1995: 273–4; my emphasis).

Giddens does not explain or justify his attitude, in this or his other works, that sociology is the study of the modern while anthropology is a study of the traditional. It is an assumption that animates all of his work. But in this volume, I will dissect and challenge Giddens on this point and counter him with the obverse assumption: modernity cannot be understood adequately if one does not take into account its continuities with the past and its relationship with traditional societies that persist in the present, not to mention traditions within modern societies. I claim that sociology and anthropology, as well as psychology and some other social sciences, were born out of *cultural concerns* that take into account the future, the present, as well as the past; moreover, that postmodernity, modernity, and tradition co-exist simultaneously, even within the same society.

Giddens elaborates on his modernist lack of appreciation for classical social theory:

Sociologists and anthropologists might both lay claim to Durkheim, for example, but otherwise the intellectual ancestries to which they look tend to diverge. How much continuing intellectual mileage is there in the traditions of theory that have dominated anthropology? The answer would seem to be only a limited amount. . . . We cannot just turn from anthropology towards sociology, because *orthodox sociological traditions have as much difficulty in grasping the changes now transforming local and global social orders as do those coming from anthropology.*

(ibid.; my emphasis).

Against Giddens, I tend to agree with Ahmed and Shore that it is ironic that as journalists and novelists tend to write in more anthropological and sociological veins, anthropologists and sociologists are succumbing to the illusion that their "forms of writing [are] not altogether very different from fiction" (1995: 24). My own position on the alleged death of sociology (as well as some other social sciences) is that even if present-day academic sociology does disappear, sociology will be revivified in a new form by those who are not considered to be sociologists today, including novelists and journalists. For example, regarding the war in Bosnia in the 1990s, some of the best social scientific analyses of the war were produced by journalists, not by sociologists (see Cushman and Meštrović 1996). Nor is this situation altogether different from the state of affairs in the nineteenth century in which Comte's sociology lay dormant after he alienated his followers with his religious fanaticism, and Durkheim revivified sociology in the previous *fin de siècle*. Sociology cannot become extinct because social issues are of passionate interest to nearly everyone. Moreover, the sort of sociology that is perceived to be relevant and interesting to laypersons and professionals alike is the one that takes into account tradition, modernity, and the future of modernity simultaneously. One of the best illustrations of this is David Riesman's *The Lonely Crowd* (1950), which has sold over a million copies since its publication: Riesman deals specifically with the continuities and overlap among the forces of tradition-directedness, inner-directedness, and modernist other-directedness. Such issues are directly relevant, for example, to the place of Islam and many traditional African cultures in the modernization process. It is ironic that Riesman's work, which has sold over a million copies world-wide and appealed to an audience that went beyond sociologists as well as academicians in general, is largely ignored by contemporary "mainstream" sociologists who treat Riesman as a marginal figure. On the other hand, the work of Giddens sells widely *within* sociological circles but is mostly irrelevant beyond the academy.

CRITICISMS OF GIDDENS

To be sure, in recent years, quite a few critical studies of Giddens have been published.[3] But these criticisms tend *not* to be along the lines that I have sketched in the introduction and thus far in this chapter. Instead, the general theme in criticisms of Giddens is that his theory does not lend itself to empirical research, that his prose is unclear, that he is evasive and "fox-like" in relation to issues, and that he offers rhetorical solutions to

19

theoretical problems. The edited volume by Held and Thompson (1989) contains important feminist critiques of Giddens to the effect that his theoretical abstractions fail to capture female experience. (And I agree, as I will make clear in chapter 4.) Despite the seriousness of these criticisms, his critics nevertheless tend to be overly deferential in tone toward him. Specifically, even most of his critics seem to accept his overly felicitous assumptions about human agency; they fail to address the larger, contextual issues that they criticize him for omitting; they accept uncritically his dismissal of nineteenth-century social theorists; they tend to accept his claim that sociology is the study of modern societies; and they usually conclude that despite his faults as a theorist, Giddens has served a useful purpose in integrating the seemingly chaotic field of social theory. In some journal articles and monographs about him and his theories, Giddens offers a reply to his critics in which he comes across as gracious and kind, yet his replies do not offer much substance. He basically restates his positions. This is convenient in writing about Giddens, because, for the most part, he is tediously consistent. For example, his remarks on sociology in Shore and Ahmed (1995) are not substantially different from his remarks in *The Constitution of Society* (1984) or *The New Rules of Sociological Method* (1993). Despite some exceptions, Giddens's critics give the impression of a closed-shop attitude, a circle of like-minded intellectuals who simply will not address issues that come from outside that intellectual circle. Similarly, over one hundred articles have been published in scholarly journals on Anthony Giddens and his work, yet few of them offer a serious challenge to him. Giddens has become almost a "sacred" icon, an object of idolatry to his followers. (The task of the present volume might be seen as an effort to desacrilize him.) A sociological explanation for this state of affairs might be that in addition to his skills as a social theorist, Giddens's writings flow *with* the social tide that exhorts modernist assumptions. Giddens is the last modernist.

Yet the social tide may be changing. Let me be specific about which aspects of Giddens's theory I intend to criticize. In *The New Rules of Sociological Method*, Giddens lists three concerns as "vital" to his "project as a whole":

> One is to develop a critical approach to the development of nineteenth-century social theory, and its subsequent incorporation as the institutionalized and professionalized "disciplines" of "sociology," "anthropology" and "political science" in the course of the twentieth century. Another is to trace out some of the main themes in nineteenth-century social thought which became built into theories of the formation of the advanced societies and subject these to a critique. The third is to elaborate upon, and similarly to begin reconstruction of, problems raised by the – always troubling – character of the social sciences as concerned with a "subject-matter,"

what those "sciences" themselves presuppose: human social activity and intersubjectivity.

(1993: vii)

Regarding his first concern, Giddens offers a rather superficial overview of nineteenth-century social theory as grounded in rational Enlightenment assumptions and as seeking to model itself after the natural sciences. He does not acknowledge the role of anti-Enlightenment social forces and philosophies, nor the spirit of the previous *fin de siècle*, which was decidedly anti-modernist (see Meštrović 1991). He relies on a Disneyesque vision of the Enlightenment as the worship of reason and science without acknowledging, for example, the importance of Auguste Comte's mystical tendencies, or the pessimistic strands found in Giovanni Vico's (1668–1744) Enlightenment philosophy. Flowing from the Enlightenment, there were also many racist theories cloaked in the jargon of science and reason. He assumes that nineteenth-century science was the same as it is today in its basic assumptions, but this supposition is open to doubt. He ignores completely the enshrinement of Arthur Schopenhauer's anti-Enlightenment philosophy during the previous *fin de siècle* and its importance for the establishment of sociology after Comte, who only gave sociology its name. Finally, he does not acknowledge the importance of Wilhelm Wundt, whose *Völkerpsychologie* was really an effort in what today passes as *cultural studies*, and who influenced anthropologists such as Franz Boas and sociologists such as Émile Durkheim. Let me repeat that with regard to all of these assumption, Giddens merely reflects the dominant assumptions of most contemporary sociologists.

Furthermore, those who cling to the stereotypes of how scientific sociology was conducted in the nineteenth-century conducted vis-à-vis the model of the natural sciences may be engaging in a form of historical revisionism, or what I call postemotionalism (Meštrović 1997). It is no longer self-evident that the logic which contemporary natural scientists *present* to the world in published reports and treatises is the same logic that (1) was used by nineteenth-century natural scientists, or (2) is actually *used* by contemporary natural scientists to make their discoveries. The widely promulgated view of science as a foolproof method actually reflects the McDonaldization of society (Ritzer 1992), and may not be accurate. Harking back to George Orwell ([1937] 1958), one could claim that this stereotypical view of science is part of modernity's love affair with the machine; modernists seek to comprehend science as a mechanical thing. (Consider also the criticisms of the culture of the machine made by Thorstein Veblen and Henry Adams.) Giddens adopts this stereotype of natural science as the straw man that he attacks in order to promote some contradictory aspects of his own thought. I agree with him that sociology needs to re-examine the problem of what it means to be a social science, but I disagree with his unoriginal and popular account of how sociology allegedly sought to emulate an outmoded and probably inaccurate model of the scientific method as it purportedly operated in the natural sciences. In my opinion, one of the best guides as to how to conduct a genuinely scientific, and not postemotional sociology, is to be found in Émile Durkheim's *The Division of Labor in Society*. Durkheim wrote:

> Beside this present-day [positivistic] science, consisting of what has already been acquired, there is another, which is concrete and living, which is in part still unaware of itself and still seeking its way: beside the results that have been obtained, there are the hopes, habits, instincts, needs, and presentiments that are so vague that they cannot be expressed in words, yet so powerful that occasionally they dominate the whole life of the scientist. All this is still science: it *is even the best and major part of it*, because the truths discovered are very few in number beside those that remain to be discovered, and, moreover, to master the whole meaning of the discovered truths and to understand all that is summarized in them, one must have looked closely at scientific life whilst it is still in a free state, that is, before it has been crystallized in the form of definite propositions. . . . Each science has, to speak, a soul that lives in the consciousness of scientists. Only a part of that soul takes on substance and palpable forms. The formulas that express it, being general, are easily transmissible. But the same is not true for that other part of science that no symbol translates externally. Here everything is personal, having to be acquired by personal experience.
>
> ([1893] 1933: 84; emphasis added)

As for his second concern, Giddens follows Parsons's mistaken lead in assuming that the main themes in nineteenth-century thought were positivism, agency, and social structure (although he repudiates Parsons's focus on the problem of social order, and claims that Parsons failed to achieve a theory of human agency). This is a reading of sociology's founders filtered through the lens of Parsons, and is typical of an entire generation of sociologists who still work in academia. Giddens fails to incorporate, for example, Durkheim's self-acknowledged concern with establishing a "science of morality," which is arguably still relevant in the twentieth century and especially in the current *fin de siècle*, but is incompatible with so-called value-free positivism. While I agree with Giddens's repudiation of positivism – along the lines of Nietzsche's aphorism with which I began this chapter – neither Giddens nor Nietzsche offers a satisfactory account of what happens after the social world becomes one of mere interpretation and hermeneutics. How should hermeneutics be grounded so that it does not lead to Baudrillard's vision of a social world constituted of rootless, circulating fictions? Giddens repudiates postmodernism, but he does not specify how his hermeneutically based and anti-positivistic theory avoids merging into postmodernism beyond some vague rhetoric concerning high modernity and the existence of structure as a duality tied to agency.

Finally, his third concern is to supersede these allegedly flawed, and in his eyes obsolete, past attempts at establishing a proper understanding of agency versus structure with his own structuration theory. Giddens's (1979) key claims for structuration theory are that human agents are skilled and knowledgeable, that they are not the cultural dupes they are made out to be by Parsons and Durkheim, and that social structure is not only constraining but also enabling. Most of Giddens's critics accept these claims without question, but upon closer scrutiny, these claims turn out to be problematic: they overlook the irrational forces at work in the psyche, the boundedness of the knowledge that agents possess, and, above all, the strict limits of where and how agents may behave like agents in a world that is becoming increasingly monitored, controlled, and controlling. Giddens's vision of human agency is so "nice," that it might seem uncharitable to criticize it. Yet charity should not preclude one from citing some immediate and rather obvious flaws in his vision.

Is the human agent really as free, knowledgeable, and skilled as Giddens claims? There are many agents who clearly are not. For example, the mentally retarded (or challenged, in today's politically correct lexicon), mentally ill, children, and uneducated are among those who are implicitly left out of Giddens's emancipatory vision. Arguably, these and others who are not as knowledgeable and skilled as Giddens might like them to be nevertheless find an important place in Durkheim's vision of society, which is based on rituals, collective effervescence, and emotion. How children form "child societies" among themselves is still a mystery as the twentieth century draws to a close, as is the process by which children add to the collective effervescence of the family and its emotional life, even if skilled human agents must watch over them almost every moment of every waking hour.

Quite apart from the many social categories of persons who are not and cannot be as skilled and knowledgeable as Giddens assumes, it is not self-evident that the "ideal type" (in Max Weber's sense) human agent is that skilled and knowledgeable either. Contrast, for example, Giddens's view of human agency with that of David Riesman's concept of autonomy found in *The Lonely Crowd* (1950). It is worth noting that Giddens concentrates on Talcott Parsons but neglects Riesman – whose office was down the hall from Parsons in William James Hall at Harvard University. This is not a small oversight, given the success of Riesman's *The Lonely Crowd*. In any event, Riesman posits the more believable claim that most people conform to the society in which they live most of the time. Autonomy thereby becomes a hard-won achievement in which a person is able to choose specific areas in social life in which he or she will be a non-conformist. The ability to choose presupposes an ability to conform, and differentiates the autonomous type from the deviant, who is more simply unable to conform. Riesman's view has a ring of truth to it given all that twentieth-century social science has taught us about mass movements, mass societies, and conformity even among modernists. If Giddens were correct and Riesman were wrong, there would be no way to explain the power and efficacy of mass advertisements, group psychology, political demagoguery, and nationalism to systematically and frequently rob human agents of their capacity for reflection. Of course, George Orwell's ([1937] 1958) writings crystallize Riesman's insight, but Giddens writes as if Orwell never existed.

In addition, I should note again that Riesman (1950) implies a continuity flowing from modern to traditional societies with his scheme of how tradition-directed, inner-directed, and other-directed social characters overlap even as societies tend toward other-directedness. This view stands in sharp relief to Giddens's claims that modern society represents a discontinuous break from the past and that sociology is "not a generic discipline to do with the study of human societies as a whole, but that branch of social science which focuses particularly upon the 'advanced' or modern societies" (1984: xvii).

Doyle Johnson (1990) offers another penetrating criticism of Giddens, claiming that Giddens overemphasizes security needs and social reproduction. Despite his rhetoric concerning agency and empowerment, there is very little room in Giddens's structuration theory for real autonomy or post-conventional (from Lawrence Kohlberg) thinking.

Consider, for example, how *little* skill and knowledge Americans are found to possess concerning the world. A recent report based on polls found that in the USA "many adults [22 percent] did not know who the United States fought against in World War II, and a majority did not know what D-Day refers to . . . a third of them could not find France on a map of Europe."[4] This particular report is not unusual in assessing the knowledge and skills of Americans with regard to domestic or international issues. "Don't Know Much 'Bout History" is a line from a popular song that captures an important reality:

> According to the Associated Press, "more than half of America's high-school seniors do not know the intent of the Monroe Doctrine or the chief goal of United States foreign policy after World War II". . . . [T]his is something like the 46,000th consecutive study showing that . . . young people are not cutting the academic mustard.[5]

The serious reader of Giddens must wonder how this state of affairs is possible given that most Americans have more access and exposure to information than their ancestors did.

But the most serious flaw in Giddens's theory is that his concept of structuration ignores the idea of *culture*. And this obfuscation of culture cuts across all three of Giddens's vital concerns. Slowly but steadily in recent years, culture is becoming an increasingly important concept in all of the social sciences, especially social psychology and sociology. A reorientation toward the cultural concerns of the founders of the social sciences casts a new light on Giddens's supposition that they are obsolete and irrelevant to present-day concerns. Giddens's attempt to construct a social theory on solely cognitive grounds and to leave out people's histories, habits, customs, feelings, and other aspects of non-agency – in a word, culture – is insufficient for understanding human behavior and social processes (see also Arnason 1987). Against the grain of Giddens's misunderstanding of the founders of the social sciences, Wilhelm Wundt, Émile Durkheim, Sigmund Freud, Thorstein Veblen, and Georg Simmel, among others, focused:

1   on the lived, non-rational aspects of individual and social behavior, and viewed as secondary the reflected, reasoned, rational aspects of human agency;
2   on feelings, not on cognition and skill;
3   on the historical baggage and various "habits of the heart" (from Alexis de Tocqueville) that are transmitted from generation to generation, not on abstractions that are cut off completely from the past;
4   on compassion, empathy, sympathy, and other derivatives of *caritas* as the "glue" that holds societies together, not rational self-interest;
5   on a philosophical stand in the object–subject debate in which this alleged distinction was treated as spurious, not on a rigid, Cartesian schism between subject and object, body and mind.

One has to confront the question: how can Giddens's or any other theory of constraint and subjective agency ignore the concept of culture given that culture is vital to understanding both agency and constraint? The most important, and most neglected, precursor to these cultural concerns of the founders of the social sciences in the previous century is to be found in *Völkerpsychologie*. *Völkerpsychologie* was established by two German Jewish scholars, Moritz Lazarus (1824–1903) and Heyman Steinthal (1823–99) and initially focused on myths and fairy tales.[6] It is important to note that Lazarus and Steinthal were among Georg Simmel's teachers in Berlin[7] because Simmel's sociology has been neglected severely by twentieth-century social theorists, including Parsons and Giddens. Lazarus and Steinthal drew their initial inspiration from Hegel, but focused more exclusively on the idea of custom as opposed to blood (genetics, racial factors) in explaining how culture is transmitted across generations. *Völkerpsychologie* was taken up by Wilhelm Wundt, who influenced Franz Boas, George Herbert Mead, Georg Simmel, Sigmund Freud, Émile Durkheim, and Carl Gustav Jung, among others. Wundt did not focus on problems of agency versus structure, but on language, ethics, myth, and religion. Wundt's influence cannot be underestimated. I assign to Wundt the importance that Giddens assigns to Comte. To pick one example out of many, Durkheim studied with Wundt from 1885 to 1886, and there can be little doubt that Durkheim's famous (and sometimes infamous) notion of the collective consciousness is a refraction of Hegel's *Volksgeist* as refined by Lazarus and Steinthal and Wundt. One should add that Durkheim made his intellectual debt to Wundt explicit (in Lukes 1982). Simon Deploige (1921) observed long ago, and correctly, that Durkheim's sociology is German in inspiration, and could not possibly have been inspired by either Comte or the French cultural milieu that overemphasized individualism.

Of course, this last point is debatable. One could argue that Tocqueville (with his concept of "habits of the heart") and Rousseau (with his notion of the "general will") represent a cultural strain of inquiry in French intellectual tradition. I have already mentioned the neglected possibility of the "other" Enlightenment, which focused on emotions and culture, and which ran concurrently with the rational Enlightenment enshrined by most twentieth-century social theorists, including Giddens. This is an interesting and important avenue for future analysis which would have to examine the possible influence of German Romanticism on the French Romanticism that inspired Tocqueville and Rousseau. The more important point is that counter-Enlightenment (or "other" Enlightenment) cultural traditions in France and elsewhere are not taken seriously by Giddens or most other contemporary social theorists.

Consider, for example, Giddens's superficial treatment of Wundt's influence on Durkheim. In *Durkheim*, Giddens writes that Durkheim "was much impressed by Wundt's psychological laboratory (he also included a lengthy analysis of the latter's more philosophical writings in his articles on German social thought)" (1978: 38). This is the extent of Giddens's "analysis" of this important intellectual link between Wundt and Durkheim! Giddens places Wundt's philosophy in parentheses, as if it were less important than Wundt's "laboratory," even though Wundt's writings on culture had much more of an impact on intellectuals than his laboratory. In *Capitalism and Modern Social Theory* as well, Giddens takes up Wundt and general German influence on Durkheim, but again in a most superficial manner. Giddens (1971: 66–70) notes that Durkheim wrote about German efforts to establish a "science of morality," but fails to make the obvious connection that Durkheim, too, sought to establish sociology as a science of morality. Giddens notes that Durkheim reviewed Wundt's *Ethics*, but does not comment on how Durkheim might have incorporated Wundt's views into his version of sociology. Instead, Giddens dismisses the role of German social theory in Durkheim's thought with the quip that the Germans were re-establishing what Comte already began (ibid.: 68). Moreover, Giddens writes: "It is difficult to assess precisely how far Durkheim was directly influenced by their [German] writings, and how far alternatively these simply reinforced conclusions which he had already reached from other sources" (1971: 71). And that is all that Giddens has to say about this subject! Elsewhere in his writings, Giddens works tendentiously to force Durkheim into the role of Comte's disciple. Let me repeat that Durkheim made his intellectual debt to the Germans explicit and that he castigates "other sources," most of them French, that might have led to the establishment of sociology as the science of morality (see Meštrović 1991).

In contrast to the scant literature on French counter-Enlightenment tradition, a sizeable body of literature exists on the German counter-Enlightenment tradition that culminated in Nietzsche's writings. Yet Giddens does not take seriously the efforts to establish cultural studies by Lazarus, Steinthal, Wundt, Simmel, or other followers of *Völkerpsychologie*. This neglect or theoretical amnesia on Giddens's part distorts the true origins of the social sciences; obfuscates the main themes that were imported into the twentieth century by Boas, Freud, Jung, Simmel and others who were concerned with culture; and undercuts Giddens's modernist focus on the skilled and knowledgeable agent who is constrained as well as enabled by social structure. This is because culture, as opposed to structure, is more than constraining and enabling. Culture is the emotional side of life that completes cognitive life. Above all, culture simply *is*. Whether or not one likes the fact that even contemporary, allegedly emancipated, post-traditional human agents engage in habits of the heart in many aspects of their lives, the fact is that they simply do. Thus, contemporary human agents still engage in rituals, recycling of the past, repetition of historical trends, celebrations of tradition, and other non-rational behaviors that are neither constraining nor enabling vis-à-vis human action. To be sure, contemporary emotional actions are not exactly the same as traditional forms of ritual, celebration, and collective effervescence. Giddens (1994) glosses over this important point with a quick reference to post-traditional societies. Giddens is right up to a point that contemporary humans do possess more insight and skill than their ancestors did. For this reason, I have developed a post-emotional theory of society which holds that contemporary humans refract tradition, emotion, and history through modernist filters (see Meštrović 1996, 1997). Nevertheless, modernists are not free from the past, culture, or emotion due to heightened cognition and skill. There is a certain amount of intellectual conceit on the part of Giddens in positing so much human emancipation.

These are the main lines of criticism in relation to Giddens's self-acknowledged vital concerns that will be followed in the remainder of this book. In the remainder of this chapter, I will touch on Giddens's attitude toward contemporary social theory and finish with a brief overview of his critics.

GIDDENS AND POSTMODERNISM

Giddens's treatment of the intellectual trajectory from nineteenth-century social theory to his theory of structuration is no less curious than his treatment of postmodernity, which is the most important rival to structuration theory. As illustration, consider Giddens's extended review of three books on postmodernity, published in *The Times Higher Education Supplement* (17 January 1992: 21).[8] Giddens seems to be aware of what is at stake, as when he paraphrases Zygmunt Bauman's claim in *Intimations of Postmodernity* (1992) that "it is not just Communism that has gone, but with it the dream of a world brought under rational human control" (ibid.). Giddens even admits that he has "a good deal of sympathy with the views which Bauman develops," but adds quickly:

> I don't think that post-modernity exists in the way in which he portrays it. In my view, we need a more thorough-going analysis than he provides of the past development of modernity if sense is to be made of the changes now transforming social life. . . . For if we have indeed entered a post-modern social universe, that universe by definition is not open to systematic study.
>
> (ibid.)

It is not immediately apparent that postmodernism is by definition closed to systematic study, nor what systematic study of postmodernism or anything else could mean. Giddens deflects any serious grappling with the issues of what constitutes postmodernity and whether it exists by his pedantic quip on how to study it. (Nor is this line unrepresentative of Giddens's overall thought, for he makes a similar claim in *The Consequences of Modernity* [1990], which I will take up later.) The grounds for Giddens's dismissal of Bauman's postmodernity thesis is reminiscent of the stereotypical way in which most journal articles nowadays end, with the admonition that further study is needed. It is an evasive conclusion that closes inquiry and discussion.

One should note also that both Bauman and Giddens seem to have concluded prematurely that Communism is a thing of the past. As of this writing, Communism seems to be staging a counter-revolution in Serbia and Russia, as I have predicted that it would (Meštrović 1993b, 1993c, 1996). This does not mean that Communism might return in the same form that it ruled the Soviet Union and its satellites for most of the present century, but, like some sort of cultural perennial, it might reappear as a new form of totalitarianism and authoritarianism. Despite Boris Yeltsin's narrow re-election as President of Russia in July 1996, there is no good reason, yet, to conclude that democracy has taken root in Russia or many other formerly Communist nations.

Perhaps Giddens's claim can be substantiated, but, crucially, he does not substantiate it in this article or in his books. This line is typical of his writing: he opens and closes whole areas of discourse seemingly by decree. He then closes with a familiar summary of his stand on these issues,[9] found in all his recent books:

> Rather than speaking of post-modernity, let us say instead that certain key traits of modernity are becoming radicalized and global-ized: these processes expose to view some of the basic tensions or contradictions of modern institutions. We do not live in a world of centrifugal pluralism, but one in which pluralism meshes uneasily with trends towards a much more developed global unity than ever existed before.
>
> (ibid.)

Again, one might be able to substantiate Giddens's well-known assertion concerning globalism by pointing to the quest for a united Europe, the unification of Germany, the role of the United Nations, the spread of Disneyland to France and Japan, various federations, even international trade. But he does not substantiate his claim, and one could also argue against it. For example, Bosnia-Herzegovina broke away from the federation that used to be Yugoslavia and came to symbolize the many other "Bosnias" in the 1990s, from Chechnya to Rwanda and Burundi. Over twenty nations have emerged following the dissolution of the Soviet Empire. Nor is this centripetal process confined to the Balkans and the former Soviet Union. California recently defeated a referendum by Northern California to secede from the rest of the state; New Orleans wants to secede from Louisiana; factions in Hawaii are preparing to secede from the USA; and in the after-math of the race riots in Los Angeles in April 1992, there is talk again of creating a separate black nation within the USA. These and other examples constitute more than an uneasy mesh with pluralism and globalization. They can be construed as serious ruptures in the modernist project and serious eruptions of nationalism that threaten the existence of the modernist nation-state.

It could be that modernity has expired or is about to expire, and the world is, indeed, entering a phase in which centripetal processes will domi-nate, and "rational control" (whatever that is) is obsolete. This horrifying scenario was foreshadowed long before the postmodernists by Arnold Toynbee (1978), Oswald Spengler ([1926] 1961), and Pitirim Sorokin (1957), among others. What is needed is a thorough theoretical analysis of these and other issues that Giddens touches, but does not treat with suffi-cient depth.

My position on postmodernity is only superficially similar to that of Giddens. Like him, I do not believe that the world has entered a postmodern phase, a decisive break with modernity. On the contrary, I have argued on several occasions that what is called postmodernity actually shares many affinities with modernity (see Meštrović 1991, 1992, 1993a). These affinities include a disdain for the notion of culture as rooted in what Tocqueville called the habits of the heart; the reduction of the world to a cognitive text as opposed to a cognitive–emotional whole; and a Kantian focus on representations as abstractions uprooted from emotions. I have made similar criticisms of Giddens's theory. Indeed, Giddens's theory of structuration is very similar in its assumptions to what Pauline Rosenau (1992) calls affirmative postmodernism (as opposed to the more nihilistic version of postmodernism represented by Baudrillard). The overly felicitous view of the postmodern world as one of tolerance and globalization is remarkably close to Giddens's own hyper-optimistic brand of modernism. To phrase the matter differently, Giddens as well as the affirmative postmodernists exhibit what Herbert Marcuse ([1964] 1991) referred to in *One-Dimensional Man* as the "happy consciousness."

But Giddens and I differ vis-à-vis postmodernism in that I take seriously the pessimistic *rhetoric* of rupture, endings, and apocalyptic themes found in the postmodern discourse even though I do not accept completely the theoretical premises or scaffolding of postmodernism. And against both postmodern social theory as well as Giddens's theory of structuration, I offer postemotional theory as a way of explaining the seemingly sudden intrusion of traditions, emotions, and history in contemporary modernist societies (Meštrović 1997).

AN OVERVIEW OF GIDDENS'S MAJOR CRITICS

There is a refreshing personal quality in Ian Craib's book, *Anthony Giddens* (1992). Craib confesses in his preface, "I have found this a very difficult book to write. I do not think in the same way as Anthony Giddens, and have had to spend much time thinking against myself." Craib notes that Giddens is a major grand theorist and that "he is *the* main interpreter of modern social theory" (ibid.: 1). Craib's rhetoric concerning Giddens's writing style is also worth noting: Giddens is described as "foxlike, a 'honey-bee' flitting from theory to theory, and 'quintessentially post-modernist'; reading his work is like 'trying to catch quicksilver'" (ibid.: 4). Readers cannot decide if Giddens's work is "systematic, eclectic or simply syncretic" (ibid.). Craib writes that Giddens's approach is "not bound together through a logical or rational system," that he is "non-partisan in his partisanship," and that his position is "drawing all positions together" (ibid.: 5). Yet Craib does not pay attention to some important positions that Giddens does *not* draw together (specifically, aspects of social theories and criticisms put forth by Riesman, Simmel, Veblen, and Baudrillard, among others). Craib confesses that after reading Giddens's precise and acute analyses, "at the end, I do not quite know where I am" (ibid.). Finally, he describes Giddens's theory as sensitizing in function: "it is not a theory aimed at telling us what happens in the world, or explaining what happens" (ibid.: 6).

I agree with Craib that Giddens's writing style is postmodern, but I would add that his message is nonetheless quintessentially modernist. As Chris Rojek (1995) points out, an emphasis on constant change and flux is shared by many modernists as well as postmodernists. But the distinctively modernist tendency in Giddens's theory is that it is as imperialist as Parsons's theory: both thinkers try to develop a single theory to encompass all other attempts at social theory, and both thinkers stay on the rational Enlightenment-based trajectory of cognition and rationality as the unifying element. Craib seems to sense this imperialist tendency in Giddens's work, despite describing it as tolerant: "I do not think it is possible to develop one all-embracing theory of the social world; that world is made up of many different phenomena which do not fit together even into a 'contradictory whole'" (ibid.: 7). Giddens's theory is totalizing despite its postmodern gloss.

I also agree with Craib that Giddens is not really writing in the tradition of critical theory – even though Giddens claims to embrace critical theory in his seemingly pluralistic theoretical blend – because he ignores the role of human suffering (ibid.: 11). A similar point is made by Fred R. Dallmayr in a critique incorporated in Giddens's book, *Profiles and Critiques in Social Theory* (1982a: 18–27). Dallmayr claims that although Giddens relies on Heidegger's philosophy as part of the theoretical scaffolding for structuration theory, Giddens ignores Heidegger's emphases on suffering and caring. In his typical style of closing whole arenas of discussion, Giddens replies: "Although I am strongly influenced by certain aspects of Heidegger's philosophy, I am not at all satisfied with his interpretation of human caring" (ibid.: 27). Giddens does not elaborate. In his rejoinder, Dallmayr writes, "I think it is rather careless of Giddens to say that he does not care about Heidegger's caring!" (ibid.). This is a very important point, because Giddens fails to specify how humans are bound to each other and to social structure if not on the basis of *caritas*.

Craib also uses the interesting metaphor of a "theoretical omelette" to capture the diverse "ingredients" in Giddens's theory: linguistic philosophy, phenomenological sociology and ethnomethodology, Goffman, psychoanalysis, hermeneutics, structuralism, and post-structuralism, Marxism, Heidegger, Wittgenstein, and time-geography (among others). But again, Craib does not delve into the modernist order that Giddens injects into this seemingly chaotic mix, nor to the ingredients that Giddens omits. For example, Giddens's reading of Wittgenstein is really second-hand, through the works of Peter Winch, and Giddens omits Alan Janik and Stephen Toulmin's reading of Wittgenstein in *Wittgenstein's Vienna* (1973). Janik and Toulmin argue that Wittgenstein, although he has been misread as a positivist of sorts, was actually an anti-positivist Schopenhauerian intellectual. Most readers of Giddens will not fault him for omitting Schopenhauer, yet Schopenhauer is important because he was, arguably, the strongest proponent of the other, emotional Enlightenment that contemporary social theorists, including Giddens, omit. Similarly, elements of the anti-rational Enlightenment spirit of the previous *fin de siècle* – which are inimical to Giddens's project as a whole – find their way into some of his ingredients, especially psychoanalysis (see Meštrović 1993a). So if Giddens does offer us an omelette, one should add that his ingredients are not healthy-fare or natural, but are pre-processed. Perhaps Craib would agree with me, for he notes that in Giddens's omelette, "what is rejected when he processes his ingredients is of considerable importance. He peels his mushrooms when the peel is the most nutritional part" (1992: 31). But I disagree with Craib when he writes that Giddens "moves around from topic to topic, point to point, thinker to thinker, and I find myself struggling to find the 'point'" (ibid.). Giddens is slippery, but his fundamental point is ubiquitous and never changes: that the human agent is skilled and knowledgeable and uses structure in an enabling fashion.

After reviewing elements of structuration theory along the lines reviewed above, Craib concludes on a positive note regarding Giddens's work:

> My criticism of structuration theory was that it was as much a symptom as an understanding or critique of modernity. The dominant trends in modern intellectual life are away from synthesis, towards an acceptance of fragmentation, relativism, over-simplicity, an abandonment of morality. All of these things are apparent in structuration theory even if some of them are denied by the theory. At the same time, it goes against the tendency of modern thought in its attempt to see the whole. . . . It is difficult indeed to see how English-speaking sociology could have maintained any coherence at all without Giddens raising these issues, and I find it difficult to conceive of any social theory that would not find something in his work on which to build. For the time being, at any rate, structuration theory will be the food at the center of the plate.
>
> (ibid.: 196)

The food metaphor is worth pursuing. I contend that after "eating" structuration theory, one is left still hungry. It is like eating a frozen, processed dinner as opposed to a traditional meal made from scratch with natural ingredients. (And it is drunk with Coca-Cola, that modernist concoction, not wine, the symbol of Dionysus and emotions.) During the course of the many years that Giddens has dominated social theory, sociology's dismal state of internal fragmentation as well as irrelevance as perceived by outsiders to the field has not improved. On the contrary, as of this writing, sociology is more fragmented than ever and its perceived irrelevance has increased.

Also there is a need to address Craib's apparent contradiction in describing Giddens's work as typically modernist in leading to fragmentation as well as coherence. Chris Rojek (1995) resolves this apparent contradiction well by distinguishing between Modernity 1 as the force of disorder and Modernity 2 as the force of order. Modernity is Janus-faced: it promotes both fission and order. Thus, Giddens is quintessentially modernist in pursuing both order and fragmentation simultaneously. But these two aspects of modernity can never be reconciled into an integrated whole, and it is best to finally admit this fact. Real cohesion and integration will be achieved when the *non-modernist* aspects of social life are finally brought to the dinner table, namely, culture, habits, emotions.

The criticisms of Giddens found in *Social Theory of Modern Societies: Anthony Giddens and His Critics* (1989), edited by David Held and John B. Thompson, are still more reverential in tone. The contributors to this volume include Richard J. Bernstein, Zygmunt Bauman, Erik Olin Wright, Bob Jessop, Martin Shaw, Linda Murgatroyd, Derek Gregory, Peter Saunders, and Nicky Gregson. Giddens offers a "reply to my critics." Held and Thompson use a very positive rhetoric in assessing Giddens's work: "renewal," "major significance," "highly original," "powerful analysis": "Anthony Giddens stands out as a figure of major significance" (ibid.: 1). Yet they do little more than summarize his positions. According to Bernstein, Giddens offers a "rethinking of the modern sociological tradition, Parsons and Habermas" and "has written incisively and provocatively about Marx, Weber, and Durkheim" (ibid.: 19). I maintain that Giddens writes in the same synthetic, pro-Enlightenment trajectory as Parsons and Habermas, and that his writings on the founders of the social science are far from incisive or provocative precisely because he tries to force them into that trajectory. Giddens's use of structure is very similar to Parsons's and Habermas's use of the idea of system. At his most critical, Bernstein calls on Giddens to clarify some aspects of his theory, but does not challenge it.

The usually incisive Zygmunt Bauman is no less reverential toward Giddens, in whose work he sees "a critical reassessment of theoretical lore" and a powerful synthesis (ibid.: 34). Bauman does note – I think correctly – that both Parsons and Giddens share a "concern with very much the same dilemma" of human agency versus structure (ibid.: 36). Bauman also notes parallels between Giddens's structuration theory and Norbert Elias's figuration theory, but that is hardly surprising given that neither thinker is interested in the non-civilizing aspects of Western civilization, although it suggests, again, that Giddens may not be as original a thinker as some of his followers assume. Like most of the other authors in this collection, or Giddens's critics in general, Bauman mainly summarizes and restates Giddens's position.

Bob Jessop accuses Giddens of misunderstanding many tenets of Marxism. Nicky Gregson contends that structuration theory is as irrelevant for empirical work as Parsonian theory. Linda Murgatroyd's feminist critique of Giddens is devastating. These three chapters sound the two most discordant notes in this collection and qualify as serious critiques of Giddens. In the concluding chapter, Giddens replies to these critics, and basically restates his positions. Regarding Gregson's claim, Giddens replies that "there is necessarily a gap between theory and empirical research" (ibid.: 253). That seems to be, for Giddens, a typically evasive and not very helpful reply. In reply to Bauman, Giddens writes:

> As Bauman rightly points out, one of my concerns in social theory has been to provide an account of human agency which recognizes that human beings are purposive actors, *who virtually all the time know what they are doing (under some description) and why.*
>
> (ibid.: 253)

Let me state very precisely why neither Bauman's criticism nor Giddens's "reply" (actually, a restatement) is incisive. Contemporary human agents are bombarded with so much cognitive information in contrast to their ancestors that they develop a blasé attitude (uncovered by Georg Simmel about a century ago) and most of the time function as if they were on auto-pilot: they do *not* know what they are doing or why most of the time because the contemporary social world is simply too complex for them to be able to know these things. Georg Simmel's account of human agency is much more convincing (and the reader should note that Giddens, like Parsons, neglects Simmel relative to the other founders of the social sciences). Simmel writes:

> It is a paradox that all higher cultures of our type are structured so that the more they evolve the more we are forced, in order to reach our goals, to proceed along increasingly long and difficult paths, filled with stops and curves. . . . The will of animals and of uncultured humans reaches its goal, if that will is successful, in, so to speak, a straight line, that is, by simply reaching out or by using a small number of simple devices: the order of means and ends is easily observable. This simple triad of desire–means–end is excluded by the increasing multiplicity and complexity of higher life. . . . Thus, our consciousness is bound up with the means, whereas the final goals which import sense and meaning into the intermediate steps are pushed toward our inner horizon and finally beyond it.
>
> ([1907] 1986: 3)

Giddens completely neglects the desire component in Simmel's triad and reduces it to Parsons's dyad of ends and means. Even in this reductionistic account of human agency, both Giddens and Parsons fail to see that contemporary individuals struggle with the question of the meaning of life precisely because the connection between ends and means is elusive in that this connection is veiled, obscured, or sometimes lost entirely. Bureaucracy and technology, non-stop information, competing interpretations, a required sensitivity to contrary points of view, the endless steps to achieving culturally prescribed goals – these are the realities of contemporary life. In *The Lonely Crowd* (1950), David Riesman arrived at a conclusion similar to Simmel's when he traced the progress from tradition-directedness to other-directedness relative to goals and means. For the inner-directed type, the goals are immediately accessible to the means; the inner-directed type sets his or her goals on a *distant* "star" though the relationship is still maintained (ibid.: 115). But for the other-directed individual, the relationship between goals and means has been severed, replaced by the "Milky Way" and its attendant "uncertainty of life" (ibid.: 137).

One may not agree with Simmel or Riesman, but they offer a serious challenge to Giddens's project vis-à-vis both classical and contemporary social theory. The important point is that, as a rule, one does not find such incisive criticisms of Giddens in the literature. Bob Jessop's criticism of Giddens regarding Marxism and nation-states is an exception, for it is incisive. But Giddens's reply is again weak and out of touch with contemporary reality:

> Virtually *all states* in the contemporary world, to repeat what I said in the preceding section, are democratic in the sense that they proclaim values of participation, and accord a range of citizenship rights to their members. The universal appeal of mass democracy today is truly extraordinary if we consider that no state in the world was democratic in this sense prior to the late eighteenth century. It is the "price" ruling groups pay for the compliance they seek to secure from those subject to their administrative dominance.
>
> (in Held and Thompson 1989: 274)

Giddens sounds like a typical Western politician here, and his message invites the typical cynical reaction of many Western citizens: the ruling class tells its citizens that they work for them under a democratic system but the perceived reality by many if not most citizens is that the ruling class is looking out for its own interests and does not care for the common person, and especially not for certain minority groups. Giddens seems oblivious to the widespread cynicism, disenchantment with political life, and even exasperation with government as a social institution that can be found in many if not most Western democracies today. For example, regarding the USA, the Oklahoma City bombing in 1995 is the tip of an iceberg that represents widespread hatred of the US government.

In *Structuration Theory: Anthony Giddens and the Constitution of Social Life* (1989), Ira J. Cohen begins by noting "Giddens's disorganized style" (ibid.: 6), which seems to irritate many readers. Cohen observes that "Giddens has not launched structuration theory through a critical encounter with positivistic principles" (ibid.: 13), but then, Giddens evades such encounters with all the other principles he takes up. Cohen does not challenge Giddens's misunderstanding of Comte or Durkheim (ibid.: 47). Cohen's focus in analyzing Giddens's work is through the perspective of praxis, and in this regard, he often finds it wanting. For example, I agree with Cohen that Giddens fails to provide "a robust ontological account of how subjective wants and desires are formed in his theory of the acting subject" (ibid.: 226). I also agree that a serious problem with structuration theory is that "to date Giddens has proposed no account of the nature or development of motives above and beyond the need for ontological security" (ibid.: 227).

Despite these and other seemingly trenchant criticisms, Cohen is surprisingly gracious toward Giddens in his conclusions. He claims, for example, that Giddens's theory is not yet complete (ibid.: 279). Like many other critics of Giddens, Cohen notes that Giddens's theory does not lend itself easily to empirical research, but contends that this could be solved fairly easily if Giddens were to write "a book devoted exclusively to their [researchers'] concerns" (ibid.: 283). This is a strangely timid criticism given Cohen's emphasis on praxis, for what is research except the practice of inserting theory into the real world? In the second to the last sentence of his book, Cohen claims that Giddens's "writings on structuration theory, in effect, reinvigorate Durkheim's classical ambition, while simultaneously providing a new point of departure" (ibid.: 288). I contend that Giddens viscerates Durkheim's ambition, and that Durkheim needs to be understood in his cultural context before a meaningful point of departure in the modernist cultural context can be achieved.

There is a fair amount of consistency in the existing critiques of Giddens's theory of structuration so that it is not necessary to offer an exhaustive review. Arthur Stinchombe (1986) accuses Giddens of obscurity and empirical abstractness. Smith and Turner (1986) characterize Giddens's work as "influential without being significant." Alex Callinicos (1985) buttresses Jessop by castigating Giddens's mistaken account of Marxism. McLennan (1984) complains, like so many other readers, that Giddens is confused and confusing. While I agree with the gist of these critiques, I intend to show that there is a method to Giddens's apparent confusion.

SUMMARY, AND THE PARAMETERS OF THE PRESENT CRITIQUE

In the remainder of this chapter, let me summarize the basis of my critique of Giddens as representative of modern sociology, and set the parameters of this study. I shall not address the differences and more general relations between Giddens's structuration theory and his theory of modernity, although such an analysis would constitute an interesting study in its own right. Structuration theory is modernist in the sense that it relies on abstraction, champions the individual and his or her agency, and draws on the same modernist assumptions, contradiction, and ambiguities that inform the rest of Giddens's work. It is true that at times, and especially in his *The Constitution of Society* (1984), *The Nation-State and Violence* (1987), and *The Consequences of Modernity* (1990), Giddens provides a rather stark critique of modernity. Specifically, he presents modernity as a juggernaut, addresses the crisis of ontological insecurity brought on by the rise of reflexivity, exposes the rise of surveillance, and analyzes other modern phenomena. Yet I intend to show that despite this apparent gloss of criticism, Giddens is a modernist.

Giddens's modernism is most apparent in his neglect of the concept of culture and in his neglect of the most important cultural theorist from the previous *fin de siècle*, Georg Simmel. To repeat, Giddens mirrors Parsons's neglect of Simmel in this regard. Neither Parsons nor Giddens could incorporate Simmel seriously into their abstract theories because Simmel ([1907] 1986) was self-consciously concerned with "life" (as a mean between Schopenhauer's "will to life" and Nietzsche's "will to power") as it works through culture. I agree with David Frisby (1986, 1992) that Simmel was the first and best theorist when it comes to exploring the dialectic of culture and subjectivity, which is transformed into the dialectic of structure and agency in Giddens's work. In many ways, Giddens's theory is a viscerated Simmelian sociology, with a dash of this and that added for apparent sophistication. But he cannot match Simmel's depth as a thinker because Simmel was concerned with emotions, fate, pessimism, and other topics that do not fit into Giddens's program of the emancipated human agent who lives ambivalently in a modernist nation-state under more surveillance than previous generations could even imagine. Yet I choose Durkheim over Simmel to serve as the foil for Giddens's thought. This is due mainly to the fact that Giddens addresses Durkheim explicitly and frequently in his works whereas he tends to neglect Simmel, so that a comparison and contrast of Giddens and Durkheim is possible, whereas a comparison and contrast of Giddens and Simmel would be mostly implicit. Nevertheless, it is important to note that important similarities exist between Simmel and Durkheim, as I have demonstrated elsewhere (Meštrović 1991).

Furthermore, it would take a number of volumes to show Giddens's relations to each of the thinkers he incorporates into his work (as well as the important ones whom he neglects). Regarding classical social theory, it would be interesting and important to compare and contrast Giddens with Marx, Weber, Simmel, Veblen, and Durkheim, for example. Such a task is clearly beyond the scope of the present study. My strategy is to juxtapose the "real" Durkheim (read in the context of the previous *fin de siècle*) with Giddens's Durkheim to show how Giddens twists Durkheim's concepts to his advantage and also to use Durkheim to criticize Giddens. It may be worthwhile in the future to attempt similar analyses vis-à-vis Giddens and Simmel, as well as the other classical social theorists.

My critique leads to the search for a third way between modernism and post-modernism, namely, the engagement of the passions to overcome the bias toward cognition found in both modernist and postmodernist theories. For this reason, I use Arthur Schopenhauer's anti-rational philosophy, especially in chapters 3, 4 and 5, to expose Giddens's neglect of passions, emotions, and culture. But in the present volume, I do not specify my theoretical alternative to Giddens's modernism or Baudrillard's postmodernism. A separate volume would be required for such a task. The present volume is clearly intended to serve as a critique of Giddens as the "high priest" of modern sociology.

My critique is not "balanced." It is more like Douglas Kellner's trenchant critique of Baudrillard, David Riesman's polemic against Veblen, and other polemics I have cited in the introduction. To be sure, there are many aspects of Giddens's thought which I find commendable: his critique of positivism, his focus on the value of agency, even his sense of hope for the future. While a balanced approach to Giddens might endear me to those who admire his work, I choose to focus on Giddens's weaknesses as a theorist for the following reasons: (1) "balanced" critiques of Giddens abound in the litera-ture; (2) most of these balanced critiques turn out to be overly reverential toward Giddens, so that a somewhat trenchant critique of Giddens is needed for overall balance in the literature; (3) a balanced critique is itself modernist, and my fundamental premises in this and other analyses are anti-modernist; (4) a tally of Giddens's strengths and weaknesses would not offset my guiding conviction that Giddens's work leads to an ominous program of social engineering vis-à-vis human emotions, what he calls the post-tradi-tional construction of synthetic traditions. It would be intellectually dishonest for me to put a modernist gloss on my sense of alarm at this fundamental aspect of Giddens's work. As I argue in *Postemotional Society* (1997), the modernist manipulation of emotions holds the potential for a new form of totalitarianism.

While I use Craib's metaphor of the omelette as a starting point for analyzing Giddens, eventually I will mix metaphors by invoking Keith Tester's (1992) and Zygmunt Bauman's (1987) metaphor of the gardener. As I have already made clear, Giddens does not just throw in a dash of this and that into a theoretical omelette. He only appears to do so. At bottom, Giddens is a modernist thinker, and this is most apparent by considering the theorists he does *not* use in his omelette. But in this regard as well, there are page constraints as to how many thinkers I can invoke to make my points. Thus, I focus on Giddens's neglect of David Riesman's thought, but do not analyze Giddens's neglect of Gramsci, for example. To do so would necessitate a serious grappling of Marx to the extent that he inspired both Giddens and Gramsci. Specifically, both Gramsci and Giddens take their cue from Marx's famous line that "men make history, but not in circumstances of their own choosing." Whereas Gramsci went on to develop a cultural strain of Marxism, Giddens went on to extinguish culture as an analytic concept and replace it with his own constructs. While I agree with Bob Jessop that this is an aspect of Giddens's visceration of Marx, it would be impossible to incorporate Marx into the constraints of the present volume. To repeat, I use Durkheim as the central foil for analyzing Giddens. Nevertheless, the general point remains that it is important to consider the thinkers and concepts that Giddens neglects or omits in his thought.

Finally, as I have noted in the introduction, some readers might object that Jürgen Habermas is really the last modernist and that Giddens is the second to last. It is true that there exist many similarities between Giddens and Habermas, and, again, it is beyond the scope of this volume to explore them. But Giddens uses Parsons, not Habermas, as the straw man for his arguments. Giddens's treatment of Habermas is superficial and dismissive at best. More importantly, Habermas perceives himself (and is perceived by others) as the heir to critical theory, whose popularity is on a steady decline, and whose legacy Giddens seeks to supersede. For these and other reasons already specified in the introduction, I regard Giddens, not Habermas, as the last modernist.

This should serve as an overview of the goals and parameters of the present study. My focus is on Giddens's neglect of culture, his visceration of classical social theorists, his hidden modernist agenda, and his neglect of theorists and concepts that do not fit into his modernist program. There are limits as to how many thinkers and concepts I can invoke for the purposes of the present analysis, but the direction of future analyses has been made clear.

3

THE NEW VERSUS THE OLD RULES OF SOCIOLOGICAL METHOD

> The purpose of any science is to make discoveries.
> – Émile Durkheim ([1895] 1982: 31)

The very title of Giddens's *New Rules of Sociological Method*, first published in 1976 and reissued in 1993, bespeaks the modernist attitude: out with the old, in with the new. The old is assumed to be deficient and obsolete while the new is assumed to be superior and progressive. Durkheim wrote the "old" rules of sociological method, and Giddens gives us the new rules. This move by Giddens is popular, and characteristic of his dismissive attitude toward the non-modern, as when he confesses in *The Constitution of Society* that "this book is written with a definite sociological bias, in the sense that I tend to concentrate upon material particularly relevant to modern societies" (1984: xvii). Or consider a similar comment by Giddens in *The Nation-State and Violence*: "It is *the* task of sociology, as I would formulate the role of that discipline at any rate, to seek to analyze the nature of the novel world which, in the late twentieth century, we now find ourselves" (1987: 33). Elsewhere in this book, Giddens adds: "Social science, in other words, has from its early origins in the modern period been a constitutive aspect of that vast expansion of the reflexive monitoring of social reproduction that is an integral feature of the state" (ibid.: 181). And of course, these and other sentiments expressed by Giddens are in line with his remarks in the Ahmed and Shore (1995) volume, discussed in chapter 2.

Presumably, for Giddens, sociology has little to offer in the way of illuminating the past, the non-modern, or the traditional. Islam, Russia, Africa, the traditional cultures in Eastern Europe – none of these figure in Giddens's analyses. Quite apart from Giddens, these and other non-Western cultures are neglected and misunderstood by others. Yet, arguably, these are among the "hot spots" in the contemporary world. *New Rules of Sociological Method* is the one book by Giddens that is invoked the least by his critics as well as his sympathetic readers, but is, I contend, the most important of his works. It is a transitional book between his earlier work as an exegisist (of sorts) of classical social theory and his later work as the promulgator of structuration theory and the synthetic construction of traditions. In it, Giddens really displays the fundamental "nuts and bolts" of his thought regarding all three of his vital, career-long concerns: the nineteenth-century origins of the social sciences, the themes that were imported into the twentieth century, and his attitude toward contemporary social theory. In the preface to this book, Giddens again betrays a modernist mind-set, as when he discloses that the themes of his study "are that social theory must incorporate a treatment of action as rationalized conduct ordered reflexively by human agents, and must grasp the significance of language as the practical medium whereby this is made possible" (1993: viii).

As we have seen in chapter 2, statements such as these by Giddens are loaded with unsubstantiated inferences, among them: that classical social theorists failed to achieve Giddens's goals, that Parsons and other modern sociologists also failed, and that the desirability of Giddens's goals is self-evident. Nowhere in this study does Giddens mention Wilhelm Wundt, who was an important precursor to his concerns and also to similar concerns by the author of the old *Rules of Sociological Method* ([1895] 1938), Émile Durkheim. Giddens is certainly not the first to note the importance of language for socio-logical theory. Wundt's *Völkerpsychologie* rests on the premise that language is the most important element in the interplay between "individual will" and "social will," terms which foreshadowed in some rough measure Giddens's agency versus structure. This is an important oversight in addition to the reasons already cited in chapter 2. First, Giddens claims that vital to his project as a whole is the concern "to trace out some of the main themes in nineteenth-century social thought which became built into theories of the formation of the advanced societies" (1993: vii). But it seems, rather, that Giddens is extremely selective in his choice of theorists and themes. Second, Wundt's influence on anthropology, sociology, and psychology is so well documented and extensive that overlooking him constitutes a serious flaw, given Giddens's overall aims. Third, Wundt provides a German cultural context for Durkheim's most controversial concepts, such as the collective consciousness, as well as an ethical base for Durkheim's own concern with a "science of morality." It is ironic that instead of reading Durkheim as a skilled human agent who navigated and made sense of numerous cultural and intel-lectual currents extant in his cultural milieu, Giddens reads him superficially as a disciple of Comte and precursor to Parsons.[1]

To phrase the matter differently: Giddens is inconsistent in his high regard for human agency by treating Durkheim as if he were a cultural dupe. Durkheim, in addition to everything else that he was, including a man of heart and soul who paid careful attention to emotional matters in his theorizing, was a capable academic politician. He was promoting a deprecated field, and was able to do so *despite* the disrepute which Comte brought to sociology (see Alpert [1939] 1961).

41

Bringing up the German context for apprehending Durkheim (as well as the many other founders of the social sciences who were German, including Tönnies, Weber, Marx, Simmel, and Freud) is important because of the well-known historical fact that German philosophy followed a counter-Enlightenment trajectory. One should raise the possibility of an implicit ethnocentrism in Giddens's treatment of the origins of the social sciences. This is because Giddens's context for reading Durkheim is the familiar French and British one based on the legacy of the Enlightenment. Similarly, when Giddens does bring up Durkheim, Marx, or Weber, he reads them almost as if they were American, British, or French. For example, regarding Durkheim, Giddens claims:

> As we know them today, the social sciences were shaped by the spectacular advances of natural science and technology in the late eighteenth and the nineteenth century. . . . Comte's influence is fundamental since, *as projected through* Durkheim's writings, his conception of sociological method can readily be traced through to some of the basic themes of "academic sociology" and anthropology in the twentieth century.
>
> (1993: 16; emphasis added)

Such claims are refracted in slightly different forms but restated practically *ad nauseam* in Giddens's other books. For example, in *The Constitution of Society*, he writes that "social science by and large shares the same logical framework as natural science" (1984: xiv). But these claims are only partly true. The model of the natural sciences as rational and modern has become a stereotype, and, like all other stereotypes, contains a kernel of truth that is easily distorted. It is true that Durkheim sought to model the social sciences after the natural sciences, a move that runs contrary to Giddens's aim to liberate the social sciences from the shadow of the natural sciences. But the more important point is that Durkheim's version of science is fundamentally different from Giddens's rendition both of Comte and of natural science methodology, as I will demonstrate later in this chapter. Giddens omits the tremendous influence of philosophy – and especially German philosophy – on the origins of the social sciences, illustrated, for example, by Hegel's impact on Lazarus and Steinthal, who were Wundt's precursors regarding the establishment of *Völkerpsychologie*. In addition, Giddens does not address the intellectual and artistic rebellion against the "spectacular advances of natural science and technology" represented by the spirit of the previous *fin de siècle* even in Britain, France, and the USA (see Meštrović 1991). He does not take into account that leading artists and intellectuals from the previous *fin de siècle* depicted science, technology, and modernity in general in a very negative light. These artists and intellectuals include but are not limited to Fyodor Dostoevsky, Henry Adams, Leo Tolstoy, Sigmund Freud, Ferdinand

Tönnies, T.S. Eliot, and Georg Simmel, all of whom wrote under the general rubric of "civilization and its discontents" (see Meštrović 1992).

Durkheim's writings are no exception to this *fin de siècle* spirit: he portrayed suicide as the "ransom money of civilization" ([1897] 1951: 367); Durkheim warned that "we must not be dazzled by the brilliant development of sciences, the arts and industry of which we are the witnesses; this development is altogether certainly taking place in the midst of a morbid effervescence, the grievous repercussions of which each one of us feels" (ibid.: 368); he criticized Comte severely in addition to paying homage to him for establishing sociology, and, in fact, ascribed even this honor more properly to Henri de Saint-Simon (see Durkheim's *Socialism and Saint-Simon* [1928] 1958); and in general, Durkheim's works can be read as a polemic against Comte and the Enlightenment (as noted by Gouldner 1958).

It is true that Giddens models his work to some extent on Marx and Weber, and uses other German theorists (such as Freud). But he glosses their counter-Enlightenment or other (emotional) Enlightenment strains. Thus, the Marx found in Giddens's (1982b) works is the rational Marx of the economists, not primarily Marx the writer on alienation. The Weber in Giddens's works is the rational Weber of *The Protestant Ethic and the Spirit of Capitalism* ([1904] 1958), not the Weber who coined the term, "iron cage" – or, in Giddens's own words:

> I have often been called a "Weberian" by critics who regard this as some sort of irreparable fault. I do not see the term, as they do, as a slur, but neither do I accept it as accurately applied to my views. If I draw upon Weber, it is from an angle . . . concerned with the multifarious practices and struggles of concretely located actors; with conflict and the clash of sectional interests; and with the territoriality and violence of political formations or states.
>
> (1984: xxxvi)

But this involves reading Weber through the context of the present and of Giddens's aims, not with a sensitivity to Weber's cultural context and connections between his era and ours. As stated previously, Giddens seems to deny the possibility of such connections.

Similarly, instead of taking into account the *fin de siècle* as well as German counter-Enlightenment cultural contexts for apprehending Durkheim's works, Giddens dismisses Durkheim as a French nineteenth-century theorist. Not only is this designation incorrect technically, because Durkheim lived and published in the twentieth century, it is incorrect as a matter of cultural interpretation because the spirit of the previous *fin de siècle* was one of rebellion against the intellectual fruits of the nineteenth century. Despite the misleading title of his book, and its implication that it grapples with Durkheim's legacy, Giddens barely touches on Durkheim and concentrates his discussion instead on selected themes from Mead, Winch, Wittgenstein, Schütz, Garfinkel, Habermas, and others to make his well-known points about agency and structure. But he introduces thinkers and insights seemingly by caprice, and he does not bother to justify or explain his choices versus other possible choices for context. As I mentioned in chapter 2, Giddens's style in this regard leads some readers to regard his blend of theorists and theories as an omelette. (Giddens seems to prefer to call it an "unacceptable eclecticism," 1984: xxii). Yet it is not really chaotic, for Giddens clearly takes from his selected theorists and theories only those elements that support his views and discards the rest. He clearly puts a modernist spin on all his selections, as when he writes, "An end to mystery, and an end to mystification: this is what Comte and Marx alike anticipated and strove for" (Giddens 1993: 17). But such a reading conveniently overlooks Comte's mystic tendencies in seeking to establish positivism as a religion, a move that alienated John Stuart Mill ([1865] 1968) and other followers. It also overlooks the distinctively Hegelian "mysticism" submerged in Marx's thought concerning his certainty about the flow of history, for example.

To be sure, Giddens is a moving target with regard to Comte as well as Durkheim, and his position cannot be pinned down easily. At times he seems to praise and defend both, and at other times is ungraciously dismissive of them. Consider the following passages from Giddens as illustrations:

> [Comte's] influence over Durkheim was considerable, although of course Durkheim distanced himself from some aspects of Comte's views.
>
> (Giddens 1982a: viii)

> Comte's writings, as filtered through those of Durkheim a generation later, connect directly with modern functionalism.
>
> (ibid.: 69)

> Durkheim drew heavily upon Comte's *Cours*, and several of the major emphases in the latter appear in *The Rules of Sociological Method*.
>
> (ibid.: 73)

> The significant influences over Durkheim's mature intellectual position come from within distinctly French intellectual traditions.
>
> (ibid.: 65)

> The term "sociology" was invented by Comte and, until quite recent times, for the most part preserved a strong connection with

the style of thinking of which he was so prominent a representative.
(Giddens 1984: 361)

Giddens's linkage of Parsons and Durkheim is equally problematic. His criticisms of Parsons are apt, but he throws out Durkheim with the bathwater of Parsonian functionalism, as when he writes:

> There are four key respects in which I shall say that functionalism, as represented at least by Durkheim and Parsons, is essentially wanting. One I have already alluded to earlier: the reduction of human agency to the "internalization of values." Second: the concomitant failure to treat social life as *actively constituted* through the doings of its members. Third, the treatment of *power* as a *secondary* phenomenon, with norms of "value" residing in solitary state as the most basic feature of social activity and consequently of social theory. Fourth: the failure to make conceptually central the *negotiated* character of norms, as open to divergent and conflicting "interpretations" in relation to divergent and conflicting *interests* in society. The implications of these failures are so damaging, I think, that they undermine any attempt to remedy any rescue [of] functionalism by reconciling it with other perspectives of a different sort.
>
> (Giddens 1993: 26)

But Durkheim does not write of the "internalization" of norms or values, and writes instead of *homo duplex* vis-à-vis the individual and society. Durkheim writes on the doings of members in relation to collective effervescence produced by rituals, and the effervescence is described by him as spontaneous and as producing the cultural possibility for the equivalent of what Giddens might call human agency (see Durkheim's *Elementary Forms of the Religious Life* [1912] 1965). The careful Durkheim reader will note his frequent use of the terms *sociopsychologie, psychologie sociale, psychologie collective*, and *culture psychologique*. These terms come up so frequently, in fact, that it could be argued that Durkheim (1) invented social psychology as a discipline and (2) was one of the first students of *culture*. In sum, facts do not support Giddens's claim that Durkheim's treatment of the human agent vis-à-vis culture can be equated with the coldly mechanical system of internalizing norms and values found in Parsons's work.

Regarding Giddens's third and fourth points, Durkheim is clearly aware that collective representations are retouched, modified, and changed by individuals, so much so that he regards communication as almost miraculous.[2] Again, this Durkheimian insight exposes a weakness in Giddens's theory, which does not delve into problems that can arise with the use of language by human agents who are using rules in order to enable themselves. No matter how skilled and knowledgeable the agent, miscommunication can arise because of emotional, cultural, and other non-cognitive factors that are part of the process of communicating through language. It is evasive to claim that such possible problems can be solved through "negotiation" and "life politics" (see Giddens 1991a, 1992b) for such problems are also frequently "solved" through violence.

Giddens is amazingly uncritical in explaining the alleged Durkheim–Parsons connection with the line, "Parsons's indebtedness to Durkheim in the formulation of his 'action frame of reference' is explicit and acknowledged" (Giddens 1993: 101). Parsons's acknowledgment is clear, but his "indebtedness" to Durkheim is not. Given his emphasis on hermeneutics, how does Giddens fail to consider Parsons's "indebtedness" as anything other than an interpretation? In fact, Parsons reads Durkheim in a context completely foreign to Durkheim's milieu in order to suit his purposes for establishing his version of functionalism. To complicate matters further, the "fox-like" Giddens is not consistent on this matter, as when he remarks later:

> Although Parsons's interpretation of the drift of Durkheim's thought offered in *The Structure of Social Action* is to my mind definitely a misleading one, the above emphasis undoubtedly ties together the work of Durkheim and Parsons, thereby unifying one dominant tradition in sociology.
>
> (ibid.: 105)

This is a curious, albeit typical, assessment by Giddens, to say the least. Giddens feels that the problems of "order" and "control" were central to both Parsons and Durkheim. But Giddens contradicts himself somewhat in this regard because he writes elsewhere that "Durkheim was *not* primarily concerned with the 'problem of order,' but with the problem of 'the *changing* nature of order'" (Giddens 1971: ix). Actually, Durkheim was primarily concerned – as he states explicitly and repeatedly – with establishing a science of morality. Order and control are typically modernist concerns, and Durkheim was much more concerned with the traditional problems of morality and social solidarity based on compassion, not commonly held norms (see Meštrović 1988, 1991).

Giddens concludes that neither Parsons nor Durkheim offers a real theory of action or social production (see also Giddens 1984). For Giddens, the production of society "is always and everywhere a skilled accomplishment of its members" (1993: 133). True, this formulation is not Durkheimian, but it is of great interest to contrast how Durkheim really felt about agency and structure if for no other reason than to offer an important context for evaluating Giddens. This is especially true with regard to the list of the new rules of sociological method with which Giddens ends *New Rules of Sociological Method*:

1 Sociology is not concerned with a "pre-given" universe of objects, but with one which is constituted or produced by the active doings of subjects.
2 The production and reproduction of society thus has to be treated as a skilled performance on the part of its members.
3 The realm of human agency is bounded. Human beings produce society, but they do so as historically located actors, and not under conditions of their own choosing.
4 Structure must not be conceptualized as simply placing constraints upon human agency, but as enabling.
5 Processes of structuration involve an interplay of meanings, norms, and power.
6 The sociological observer cannot make social life available as a "phenomenon" for observation independently of drawing upon her or his knowledge of it as a resource whereby it is constituted as a "topic for investigation."
7 Immersion in a form of life is the necessary and only means whereby an observer is able to generate such characterizations.
8 Sociological concepts thus obey a double hermeneutic.
9 In sum, the primary tasks of sociological analysis are the following:

   (a) The hermeneutic explication and mediation of divergent forms of life within descriptive metalanguages of social science;
   (b) Explication of the production and reproduction of society as the accomplished outcome of human agency.

(ibid.: 168–70)

Clearly, these are the central elements of Giddens's thought overall as developed in his other works. But it is not clear how some of them flow from the discussion in *New Rules of Sociological Method*, nor that Giddens needed to couch his manifesto in anti-Durkheimian terms. He could have published it without referring to Parsons or Durkheim, to whom he refers in any event rather fleetingly and dismissively. A full analysis of all of his points would require a careful comparison and contrast of the bulk of Durkheim's works, not just *The Rules of Sociological Method*. But these problems stem from Giddens's apparent intention to pursue his aims in the guise of offering an exegesis, and also from Giddens's confusing writing style. As I have stated at the outset of this discussion, Giddens and Parsons share many traits in common as authors: in their pursuit of their respectively modernist manifestos, they pick and choose elements from other thinkers, especially the totemic ones in sociology such as Durkheim, without offering real justification for their moves or interest in the contexts for the objects of their purported studies.

Thus, I see little choice but to concentrate on showing how the "old" rules of sociological method by Durkheim are fundamentally different from both Giddens's and Parsons's misinterpretions. Yet my goal is not to substitute an "authentic" version of Durkheim's *Rules* for Giddens's: I agree with Giddens (and Bauman 1987) that in the twentieth century we are all interpreters so that there is no way to prove conclusively what constitutes a "true" interpretation. My goal is to turn Giddens's strategy on Giddens: to read and criticize Giddens through the counter-Enlightenment Durkheim that Giddens ignores (that is, Durkheim's revenge). Hopefully, this strategy will illuminate problem areas and unsubstantiated assumptions in Giddens's theoretical discussion. To be sure, one could argue that a focus on Durkheim is arbitrary, given Giddens's reliance on Marx and Weber as well. Some readers of Giddens focus on his notion of praxis as refracted from Marx (while others, such as Jessop, argue that Giddens misunderstands the rest of Marx) or of agency as refracted from Weber. Yet Giddens reserves his sharpest barbs for the straw man arguments of Comte, Durkheim, and Parsons, whom he treats as intellectually similar, and he does so consistently in order to emphasize how his thought overcomes their alleged faults vis-à-vis agency and structure. For this reason, an examination of how Giddens reads (or misreads) Durkheim seems to be the more important alternative to an analysis of his interpretations of Weber and Marx. Durkheim is Giddens's most important target.

GROUNDING HERMENEUTICS

One of the problems uncovered in summarizing Giddens's *New Rules of Sociological Method* is that he fails to specify how diverse hermeneutic interpretations of Durkheim or any other theorist or any other phenomenon can be evaluated relative to other hermeneutic interpretations. Which is the "right" one? How can human agents, whether laypersons or scientists or political leaders, find the common ground necessary to communicate with each other as they pursue their interpretations of the world in their roles as skilled human agents? Giddens only touches on this problem with his allusion to the historical and structural boundedness of human agency, but he does not offer a satisfying reply. I have argued elsewhere that the diminution of what Durkheim called the collective consciousness leads to a sort of cultural Balkanization in which atomized individuals orient themselves to competing groups for grounding their views, and that this process is inimical to the process of any sort of durable structure (Meštrović 1994, 1997).

Durkheim's methodological classic is read by Giddens, Parsons, and other leading social theorists from Comtean, positivistic, or other Enlightenment contexts despite the fact that Durkheim criticizes these doctrines. Durkheim also tends to be read as a deductive analyst, with the exception of Giddens, who understands him correctly as advocating induction. I will suggest that for Durkheim, perceptual, inductive knowledge of "things" is superior to conceptual, deductive knowledge; and that the one, well-designed experiment is sufficient for the establishment of scientific laws. This is a fantastic understanding of science on Durkheim's part, one that attempts a fragile *via media* between a historical concern with *events* and a scientific concern with *laws* (see the discussion of this distinction by Park and Burgess 1921). I do not intend to evaluate Durkheim's methodology or vision of science in this discussion. The more important point is that Durkheim's program for a scientific sociology laid out in *Rules of Sociological Method* is not commensurate with Giddens's misreading of Durkheim either as a disciple of Comte or as an ally of Parsons. Additionally, Durkheim's foreign-sounding vision of science can provide an important foil for evaluating Giddens's alternative program laid out in the *New Rules of Sociological Method*.

Unlike Giddens, I will state very precisely my reasons for choosing specific thinkers to provide intellectual and cultural context for analyzing Durkheim, and especially the choice of Arthur Schopenhauer. Schopenhauer is regarded by many intellectuals in diverse fields as the most important philosophical influence in the previous *fin de siècle* (see Meštrović 1991).[3] Schopenhauer, along with Hegel, laid the philosophical groundwork for Wundt's *Völkerpsychologie*. *It was Schopenhauer, not Comte, who ruled the intellectual realm of the previous fin de siècle.* And Schopenhauer is important because he is representative of the German counter-Enlightenment tradition which emphasized the unruly power of the emotions of what Schopenhauer termed the will. By the time Durkheim arrived on the scene in the late 1880s, Comte's philosophy was almost completely passé. Thus, Giddens and I choose two completely different trajectories concerning the origins of the social sciences for establishing a context for interpretation. Comte represents the pro-rational Enlightenment legacy that continues to animate discussions of the Enlightenment "project" of contemporary modernity, whereas Schopenhauer represents the counter-Enlightenment legacy that many contemporary sociologists tend to overlook if not obfuscate. Let me also clarify that by "influence" I do not mean a straight-line sort of influence that Giddens describes vis-à-vis Comte, Durkheim, and Parsons. Rather, I mean that various thinkers and artists in the previous *fin de siècle* refracted Schopenhauer's philosophy in diverse ways, yet the central feature of Schopenhauer's philosophy can be found in their works. That central feature is Schopenhauer's claim that the world is will (passion) *and* representation. For Schopenhauer, the world is not a dualism or a duality (to use Giddens's terminology), but a unity. Thus, human agents do create knowledgeable and meaningful representations of the world in their quest for what might be termed agency, as Giddens maintains, but they are also driven by powerful and often hidden and mysterious passions, something that Giddens never acknowledges and in fact repudiates as the nonsensical notion of an agent within an agent (see Giddens 1984: 42). Nor do I deny the influence of the pro-Enlightenment legacy that Giddens (as well as Habermas) explicates. I point out, instead, that the pro-Enlightenment forces had to cope with an extensive anti-Enlightenment movement, and that this interplay makes the origins of the social sciences complex. Finally, I do not mean that Schopenhauer's philosophy, the German counter-Enlightenment, and the Enlightenment legacies are the only cultural contexts that help to explain the origins of the social sciences in general or Durkheim's sociology in particular. With regard to Durkheim, his Jewish cultural heritage and the fact that he was descended from a veritable rabbinical dynasty cannot be overlooked, as I have argued extensively elsewhere (Meštrović 1988). As a French Jew of German descent, Durkheim struggled to assimilate into French society and its culture of rationalism; to cope with the cultural and scientific superiority of Germany at the previous *fin de siècle*; and to make sense of his Jewish cultural heritage in the face of these cultural forces.

In his book *Revolutionary Jews From Marx to Trotsky*, Robert S. Wistrich quotes Leon Blum regarding the social milieu in which Durkheim lived: "The Jews have made a religion of Justice as the Positivists made a religion of Facts and Renan a religion of Science" (1976: 153). This is an interesting generalization, because it highlights a major concern of Durkheim's that Giddens neglects: morality in general and justice in particular. Even if Durkheim assimilated Comte's worship of facts and Renan's worship of science to some extent, he blended these with his moralism. Thus, Durkheim's *Division of Labor* begins with the claim that he will "treat the facts of moral life according to the methods of the positive sciences" ([1893] 1933: 32) and ends with the admonition that what modern societies need most of all is justice: "Just as ancient peoples needed, above all, a common faith to live by, so we need justice" (ibid.: 388). It is not at all obvious how a "science of morality" can exist, because it seems to defy the commonly accepted fact–value distinction which Giddens attributes to Durkheim and others. Yet it seems that moral concerns nevertheless overrode Durkheim's Comtean and other pro-Enlightenment allegiances. Giddens, along with most contemporary sociologists, really seems to miss the mark by aligning Durkheim so closely with Comte and Parsons because Durkheim's strong sense of moralism is incompatible with the emphasis on value-free science in the works of both. Even Durkheim's methodological manifesto exhibits a strong moral streak, as I will show. Thus, Durkheim's concept of the collective consciousness is a mystical sort of idea, not amenable to the rational Enlightenment project.

Even with regard to the possible influence of Durkheim's Jewish heritage upon his social theorizing, Giddens is superficial. Noting that Durkheim's father was a rabbi, Giddens writes,

> Himself a non-believer, Durkheim nevertheless had good reason to acknowledge the significance of religion in relation to moral conduct. Brought up in an orthodox Jewish milieu, he could hardly fail to feel both the influence of professed belief upon day to day conduct, as well as the coherence of outlook produced by a religious world-view.
>
> (1978: 80)

First, no one knows for certain whether Durkheim was a non-believer. Second, even if he was, the cultural significance of being a non-believer in a Jewish context is entirely different from being a Christian non-believer. Third, Durkheim's childhood did not lead him to focus solely on religion *per se* but on ethics and morality throughout his intellectual career. But Giddens never acknowledges the centrality of Durkheim's moral concerns over his alleged concerns with changing social order. Giddens ascribes far more influence over Durkheim to the Catholic and disreputable Auguste Comte than to Durkheim's own father, the rabbi.

Let me be even more precise in criticizing Giddens's – and, by extension, the popular, contemporary, and superficial – treatment of Comte's influence upon sociology in general and Durkheim in particular. It neglects cross-currents even among those who sought to follow Comte's lead. In France in the previous *fin de siècle*, "scientific positivism" was associated not only with Comte but also with Taine and Renan. But scientific positivism was already challenged within French academe by one of Durkheim's professors, Charles Renouvier, who was preoccupied with Kant, and, specifically, with the Kantian problem of the moral imperative. In addition, Renouvier (1892) was concerned with the origins of Kant's "categories of thought," so that Durkheim clearly extended this concern in his work by hoping to provide a sociological explanation for what Kant accepted as *a priori* categories. Herbert Spencer's writings were also highly influential, with their emphasis on individualistic utilitarianism. But Durkheim's *The Division of Labor in Society* can be read, at least in part, as a polemic with Spencer. Another neglected current is the "biologism" doctrine and the many organicist analogies found in writings in the previous *fin de siècle*. Finally, the centrality of the problem of ethics, especially among German writers, turned the attention of many intellectuals to the quest for establishing morality on a "scientific" basis. (All this and more is covered rather extensively in Robert Park and Everett Burgess's *Introduction to the Science of Sociology* [1921].) Against Giddens's popular focus on the natural sciences as a model, I contend that a focus on a "science of morals" is more central to the establishment of the social sciences.

Regarding sociological methodology *per se*, much has been written about the need for sociological theorizing to become more empirical as a way to overcome contemporary sociology's many crises, including the crisis of relevance. We have seen in chapter 2 that many of Giddens's critics complain that his theory does not lend itself to empirical research. Heightened empiricism is assumed to be a laudable goal in and of itself, without asking the question: "Methodology for what?" Richard J. Bernstein (1986) is right that Giddens leaves open the question of the ends for which social knowledge should be used. (Giddens seems to have corrected some of that oversight with his emphasis on "life politics" in his most recent books.) Durkheim clearly felt that sociological research should be used to make modern societies moral, but most contemporary researchers would reject such an assumption if for no other reason than that little consensus exists on what constitutes morality.

Schopenhauer's ([1818] 1969b) devastating critique of Kant is still relevant in these regards because ethics and morality are central to his philosophy. Schopenhauer attached ethical concerns to epistemological ones by positing the following: scientific investigations must begin either with pre-set conceptions that the human agent who observes phenomena brings to the observation, or with the perceptions of the empirical object before these are elaborated by the human subject into conceptions. In other words, one must choose between a science *from* concepts, which is the Kantian, positivistic, and contemporary version, or a science *in* concepts, which is Schopenhauer's and Durkheim's version. Durkheim ([1893] 1933) extended this line of thought to posit that morals must be studied empirically, as they really exist in social norms, not deductively, on the basis of what moralists believe should be moral. It is interesting that despite the rise of positivism in the twentieth century, Kant's non-empirical and thoroughly transcendental conceptualization of morality continues to dominate studies of morality from Piaget to Kohlberg. Against Kant, Durkheim argued that morality must be rooted in human culture. Against Descartes, Schopenhauer claims that object and subject exist as an antagonistic *unity*, and one cannot have one without the other. (It is worth noting here that Mouzelis [1989] argues that Giddens does not seriously consider the object–subject problem in his structuration theory.) Nevertheless, one must begin an inquiry from concept or perception, subject or object. Thus Schopenhauer ([1818] 1969a:65–70) faults Kant for starting with the human subject's pre-conceived, *a priori* representations of the world, which is suitable for non-empirical, purely deductive sciences such as mathematics but is detrimental for genuinely empirical sciences. According to Schopenhauer, if scientific inquiries begin with pre-conceptions deduced from a theory, then the subsequent observations will be represented in terms of those pre-conceptions, and science will be reduced to a closed game of concepts that can never discover anything new. While Schopenhauer gives Kant suitable credit for his other philosophical achievements, with regard to the issue of finding starting points for scientific inquiry, Schopenhauer's ([1818] 1969a: 415–534) criticisms are severe and leave no room for compromise or a middle ground.

Lalande ([1926] 1980: 280) writes that philosophers generally use the term "empirical" in opposition to rational and in opposition to Kant's transcendental deduction, which attempts to apply *a priori* concepts to experience (ibid.: 205). How, then, can contemporary sociology become genuinely empirical while adhering to rationalist philosophies? Closely related is the question whether ethics can be based exclusively on rationalist principles, as Kant taught, or on non-rational (emotional) factors, as Schopenhauer taught. That is as much a problem today as it was in the previous *fin de siècle*. Comte failed to resolve it every bit as much as Giddens fails. "In formulating structuration theory I wish to escape from the dualism associated with objectivism and subjectivism," Giddens (1984: xxvii) writes, but his escape involves little more than a shift in vocabulary from "dualism" to "duality."

The methodological contributions of Émile Durkheim, in particular, are problematic in light of these philosophical controversies. Durkheim is still apprehended in the context of Comte's ([1855] 1974) and Kant's ([1788] 1956) rationalist philosophies, despite compelling reasons to the contrary. Alvin Gouldner (1958: x) demonstrates in the introduction to Durkheim's *Socialism and Saint-Simon* that in this book Durkheim dethroned Comte as the rightful founder of positivism, sociology, and socialism and was engaged in "a deep-going polemic against Comte." In a clear polemic with Kant, Durkheim and Mauss ([1902] 1963) argue in *Primitive Classification* that society is the empirical origin of Kant's supposedly *a priori* categories. But despite this, Durkheim's critics continue to cling to Comtean, Kantian, and other modernist, pro-Enlightenment interpretations of this and his other works. Durkheim's followers were adamant in pointing out their master's disdain for Kant's *a priorism*, but their works do not inform most contemporary assessments of Durkheim's works.

In particular, Durkheim's *The Rules of Sociological Method* continues to be praised as a methodological classic as well as criticized for being the very opposite, as an ideological manifesto, and for being a bungled attempt to establish sociology on a positivistic basis (see Douglas 1967; Hirst 1975). Lukes, for example, concludes that Durkheim's classic is actually "a sterile prescription for the human sciences" (1982: 15) that is based "upon [Durkheim's] illusory pursuit of objectivity" (ibid.: 18). Parsons (1937) also concluded that Durkheim vacillated between subjectivism and positivism. Most sociologists who comment on Durkheim's *Rules* as it pertains to contemporary methodology follow in the wake of this ambiguous, ambivalent tone for appreciating Durkheim's achievement – including Giddens. Thus, sociologists want to turn to Durkheim as totemic – more precisely, postemotional – support for their various quests and especially for a value-free empiricism, but this aim is thwarted by the reified misconceptions of Durkheim as an exclusive disciple of Comte and Kant.

John Stuart Mill ([1865] 1968) explains that both Comte and Kant share the conviction that the scientist can have no knowledge of anything but phenomena – the very claim that Schopenhauer attempted to transcend – but adds that in the last half of the nineteenth century, neither Comte not Kant had many disciples. This, from a former disciple of Comte's! Mill's (ibid.) observation is commensurate with other analyses that cite positivism's lack of popularity at the time of Durkheim's writings (Bailey 1958; Baillot 1927; Ellenberger 1970), In line with many other writings from 1860 to 1900, Mill's criticisms of Comte and positivism are severe, especially with regard to Comte's mysticism and neglect of inductive logic as a mode of scientific inquiry ([1865] 1968: 55). Historical evidence suggests that Schopenhauer's philosophy filled the void left by positivism from 1860 to 1900 in Europe (see Baillot 1927).

Thus, the most important context for the present analysis of Durkheim's *Rules* shall be Schopenhauer's, not Comte's, philosophy. The signs of Schopenhauer's impact on Durkheim's methodology are Durkheim's penchant for empirical induction versus conceptual deduction; the idea that the central feature of science is that it should *discover* new things rather than prove pre-conceived hypotheses; the preference for the particular rather than the general; the preference for noumenic perception as opposed to phenomenal conception; and, above all, the constant tendency to move away from Kant's *a priorism* in favor of empiricism. The use of Schopenhauer's philosophy in this analysis of Durkheim is not meant to imply that Schopenhauer's many precursors or disciples – especially his disciple Nietzsche, whose importance to the social sciences is analyzed by Bloom (1987) and many other scholars – are unimportant, only that space does not permit their consideration in this chapter. Similarly, there is no intention to trivialize the philosophical problems with induction, particularly the problem of justifying how inferences are drawn. On the contrary, this problem is one of many mysteries left unsolved by Durkheim and other founders of the social sciences from the previous *fin de siècle*.

But of course, the reason for delving into this contextual analysis of Durkheim is to highlight deficiencies in much of contemporary social theory and especially as it is crystallized in Giddens's works. Specifically, it is worth asking: Can Giddens's thought in particular and contemporary sociological theory in general lead to discoveries? (This is *not* similar to the question already posed by his critics and debated frequently: Can Giddens's or any other theory generate hypotheses that lead to social scientific research?) Can Giddens's theory or contemporary sociological theory in general sustain an ethical base for societies? Do Giddens and other advocates of agency induce their claims on human agency from actually observing how humans use knowledge and skill or do they simply deduce these claims from ideology? Finally, are Giddens's theory in particular and sociological theory in general based on *a priorism* to such an extreme extent that they become a closed game of concepts?

SCHOPENHAUER'S CRITIQUE OF KANT

In *The World as Will and Representation* ([1818] 1969a; [1818] 1969b), Schopenhauer attempted to move beyond Kant's ([1788] 1956) distinction of the world into phenomena versus the unknowable noumena or thing-in-itself. Schopenhauer grants that "Kant's greatest merit is the distinction of the phenomenon from the thing-in-itself" ([1818] 1969a: 417). But he adds that "an essential difference between Kant's method and that which I follow is to be found in the fact that he starts from indirect, reflected knowledge, whereas I start from direct and intuitive knowledge" (ibid.: 452). As stated previously, Schopenhauer found a place for the emotions even in enterprises such as science that seemingly concern themselves strictly with unemotional phenomena. Let us note that there is no place for intuition in Giddens's theory nor in contemporary sociological theory in general.

Consistent with his distinctions between the "will" and "representation" (or idea), throughout his writings Schopenhauer aligns phenomenal knowledge with general concepts, *a priori* categories, representations, and other synonyms for the mind. But that is only one side of knowledge, and an inferior one that yields mere intelligence, sagacity, and cleverness, according to Schopenhauer (1899). The other side of knowledge, which includes the will, the thing-in-itself, and the noumenon, incorporates sensual perception, the independence from all categories (including time and space), intuition, and other synonyms for what he calls the heart. This intuitive form leads to understanding, acumen, and requires judgment. Sensual perception generates knowledge whereas Kant's phenomenal apparatus is "nothing but forms . . . it only conceives, but does not generate" (ibid.: 137). Thus Schopenhauer's starting point for scientific inquiry is always the will and its derivatives – intuition, perception, induction – whereas Kant limits science to phenomenal knowledge. This is the essence of the polemic between Kant and Schopenhauer.

Schopenhauer believes that conceptual knowledge is inferior to perceptual knowledge, because concepts can never account for the entry of empirical knowledge into *a priori* categories. In sum, Schopenhauer ([1818] 1969b: 170) believes that "in no knowledge can concepts be the first thing, for they are always drawn from some perception" (see also Schopenhauer [1818] 1969a: 28; [1818] 1969b: 41). Similarly, *I contend that Giddens as well as most contemporary mainstream sociologists begin most of their analyses with concepts, and that such a strategy cannot lead to discoveries.* In the words of the journalist Georgie Anne Geyer (1996), discoveries must begin with "concrete facts," and in this sense, many journalists are better than sociologists at doing inductive sociology.

The most important consequence of Schopenhauer's critique of Kant is that he spurns what has come to be known as repeated empirical verification of hypotheses in favor of what Durkheim later called the one, well-designed experiment. In the first place, a finding can never truly repeat itself, because Schopenhauer believed that one returns to the world as a comparatively different being each time one apprehends it ([1818] 1969b: 138). Claude Bernard ([1865] 1957) and Friedrich Nietzsche (1968: 46) also argued that facts never repeat themselves, because facts are apprehended through arbitrary abstractions and concepts that distort differences and distinctions in the world of things, which, like the human subject, is also forever changing. Moreover, all our representations are in perpetual flux fueled by the restless will. This is no doubt the origin of William James's ([1890] 1950) famous concept of the stream of consciousness. Finally, the repetition of findings traps the scientist at the level of conceptual knowledge and therefore proves nothing that is not already derived from concepts; it is circular, a point that Florian Znaniecki ([1934] 1968) also makes. Schopenhauer notes that with repeated findings the experimenter "does not really have a more accurate and profound insight into what is really essential in all those cases, facts, and casualties," and adds:

> We are sparing of much, we make do with little . . . one case drawn from his own experience teaches more then many a scholar is taught by a thousand cases which he knows, but does not really understand . . . thus this fact is for him the representative of a thousand similar facts.
>
> ([1818] 1969b: 78)

Schopenhauer's distinction between conceptual knowing versus perceptual understanding of experience seems to foreshadow the contemporary concept of reification as a kind of imperfect knowledge (Berger and Luckmann 1967). Thus Schopenhauer concludes that "one case holds good for a thousand" ([1818] 1969a: 396). Obviously, contemporary natural scientists would not agree with such a claim. But as we shall see, Durkheim, Simmel, Freud, and other founders of the social sciences who were emulating a different version of natural science apparently did agree. (It would be interesting to investigate when and how the focus on the one, well-designed experiment changed to the positivistic program of repeated verification.)

In sum, philosophers acknowledge that in the nineteenth century Schopenhauer's epistemology set the stage for a genuinely empirical revolution against Kant's abstract, deductive *a priorism* (Hamlyn 1980; Magee 1983). In the following section Schopenhauer's vision, which guided Durkheim's moves in his *Rules* more than any Enlightenment vision, will be discussed.

SOCIOLOGY AS THE SCIENCE OF DISCOVERIES

In the first preface to his *Rules*, Durkheim claims that "if a science of societies exists," then it must exist in the sense of an empirical science of discoveries, "for the purpose of any science is to make discoveries" ([1895] 1982: 31). This claim, in itself, is noteworthy in its refreshing break with what George Ritzer (1992) calls the contemporary McDonaldization of society such that sociological research in particular and academic research in general have become routinized, bureaucratized, and factory-like. More than a hundred years after Durkheim made this claim, it seems that the purposes of science include securing a comfortable profession and income derived from science, securing large grants, padding one's vita, working on a paradigm established by others, and *verifying* truths discovered by others. C. Wright Mills (1959) foresaw many of these developments in the transition from science as a discovery-making enterprise to science as a bureaucratic enterprise. To be sure, discovery still plays a role in contemporary science, but it does not seem to be the central purpose. Not only should one note how unusual is Durkheim's sentiment toward the purpose of science, but one should also note that Giddens fails to comment on it. Giddens mistakenly aligns Durkheim with the modernist gardener model[4] of the scientist as one who controls, rationalizes, verifies, and is drawn to control and constraint – but not with the natural gardener model of the scientist as an interpreter who *discovers* a new way of looking at Nature. But there can be no mistake about the fact that for Durkheim, science means discovery, and every discovery "more or less disturbs accepted ideas" (Durkheim [1895] 1938: xxxvii).

But how shall one distinguish the empirical from the subjective? According to Durkheim, "a social fact is identifiable through the power of external coercion [or constraint] which it exerts or is capable of exerting upon individuals" ([1895] 1982: 56). Giddens (1993: 114) notes Durkheim's use of constraint, and – like so many other unoriginal analysts of Durkheim – criticizes him for allegedly failing to grasp that social facts are enabling as well as constraining. It is important to note that Giddens makes this criticism of Durkheim's use of constraint in several different books (see Giddens 1971, 1974, 1978, 1984, 1987), and that the criticism is banal. Giddens does not delve into the French usage of *contrainte*, which indicates simply that it is anything that opposes *volonté*, the will (Littré 1963: 1152). Immediately after making the claim that social facts must be treated as "things," Durkheim explains that "a thing is principally recognizable by virtue of not being capable of modification through a mere act of the will" ([1895] 1982: 70).[5] It is not at all clear from this passage that Giddens is justified in accusing Durkheim of writing off human agency and of failing to see humans as skilled agents. (I shall examine other passages in other contexts later in the discussion.) Durkheim seems to be saying no more than that agents cannot create a social world out of their imaginations and through pure hermeneutics – a position that Giddens (1984) might agree with, because of his focus on structuration as a *via media* between agency and structure.

According to Durkheim, to treat social facts as things is to assume a certain mental attitude toward them: to approach their study on the assumption that we are ignorant of their nature; to assume that properties and causes cannot be discovered by introspection; and to approach social reality with the "same frame of mind" as the physicist, chemist, or physiologist "when he probes into a still unexplored region of the scientific domain" ([1895] 1938: xlv). But what is this natural scientific frame of mind? According to Durkheim:

> When he penetrates the social world, he must be aware that he is penetrating the *unknown*; he must feel himself in the presence of facts whose laws are as unsuspected as were those of life before the era of biology; he *must be prepared for discoveries which will surprise and disturb him. Sociology is far from having arrived at this degree of intellectual maturity.*
>
> (ibid.; emphasis added)

Giddens and other analysts of Durkheim are completely unjustified in misrepresenting Durkheim's *logic of discovery* into a logic of constraint, rigidity, and anti-agency. Against this stereotypical and inaccurate portrait of Durkheim, it is clear that Durkheim's system is designed to *enable* the social scientist to make discoveries and to break through social constraints regarding knowledge. And in holding up natural scientists as exemplars for sociologists, Durkheim is merely using his idealistic vision of the natural scientist as discoverer as a vehicle for discussion.

Let us turn the table of criticism on Durkheim's critics. By Durkheim's standards, do modernist methods prepare the sociologist as agent for discoveries that will surprise and disturb him or her? I think the answer is no. Most contemporary discussions in sociology begin with the *a priori* assumption of the skilled and knowledgeable agent, and from this assumption proceed to examine the social world. Modernists, including Giddens, typically do not begin with an inquiry into how agents actually behave in Western as well as non-Western nations, in past historical epochs as well as the present, vis-à-vis the categories of freedom, skill, knowledge, and so on. In summary, modernists fail to treat agency as a social fact. On the contrary, agency has become ideology.

Moreover, Durkheim specifically rejects the charge that he is "explaining social phenomena by constraint" (ibid.: liii) and claims that externality and constraint are not the nature of social phenomena but are only the "external signs" by which they can be recognized (ibid.). Moreover, he adds that his definition of the social fact as characterized by constraint "did *not include all the characteristics of the social fact and consequently was not the only possible definition*" (ibid.; emphasis added). Note again that Giddens misrepresents Durkheim's position by treating the notion of constraint as essential to the idea of the social fact.

Durkheim really should have incorporated footnote number 5 into the main text of his preface to the second edition, because it is an excellent retort to the modernist mischaracterization of his position. Durkheim writes:

> The coercive power that we attribute to it [the social fact] is so far from being the whole of the social fact that it can present the opposite character equally well. Institutions may impose themselves upon us, but we cling to them; they compel us, and we love them; they constrain us, and we find our welfare in our adherence to them and in this very constraint.... There is perhaps no collective behavior which does not exercise this double action upon us, and it is contradictory in appearance only. If we have not previously described social facts in terms of this double functioning ... it is because the objective manifestations are not easily perceptible. The "good" [which is loved] is somewhat more subjective, more intimate, than "duty," and consequently less easily grasped.
>
> (ibid.: liv)

In chapter 1 of the *Rules*, Durkheim attempts to answer the question, "What is a social fact?" If one examines the rhetoric he uses in enumerating possible answers, it sounds like he is offering a definition of *culture*, not anything like the allegedly "hard facts" of contemporary natural scientists. Thus, Durkheim refers to "obligations," "contracts," "duties," "law," "custom," "beliefs and practices," "system of signs," "system of currency," "the practices followed in my profession, etc." ([1895] 1938: 1–2). According to Durkheim, "here, then, are ways of *acting, thinking,* and *feeling* that present the noteworthy property of existing outside the individual consciousness" (ibid.: 2; emphasis added). Note that he refers not only to action and thought, but also to feelings. Notice that the French meanings of *fait* are entirely commensurate with Durkheim's cultural enumeration, because these French meanings imply all sorts of "doing." *Fait* in French does not carry the English connotations of the "hard" scientific fact.

For Durkheim, social facts deal with the "collective aspects" of the "beliefs, tendencies, and practices of the group" (ibid.: 7). Clearly, even the "early" Durkheim is treating social facts as *cultural* phenomena (against the grudging concession that the "late" Durkheim might have done some cultural analysis, but not the "early" positivistic Durkheim).

Durkheim ([1895] 1982: 48) distances himself from Herbert Spencer, Auguste Comte, and John Stuart Mill, because "the great sociologists just cited hardly went beyond generalities" and cursory inquiries concerning social methodology. Giddens does not make note of this fact in his *New Rules of Sociological Method*. On the contrary, as we have seen, he aligns Durkheim with the Comtean project. But Durkheim faults these precursors of sociology for failing to address the issues of how one should observe social facts, the direction research should take, the particular procedures that should be followed, and the rules that should be used for demonstration and proof – "all this remains undetermined" Durkheim (ibid.: 48) writes. Given that Giddens and most other analysts frequently and mistakenly align Durkheim with Comte, one should pause to take note of Durkheim's criticisms of Comte in this section of the *Rules*. Durkheim writes:

> And in truth, up to the present, sociology has dealt more or less exclusively with concepts and not with things. Comte, it is true, declared that social phenomena are natural facts, subject to natural laws. He thereby implicitly recognized their character as things, for in nature there are only things. But when he passes beyond these philosophical generalities and attempts to apply his principle and develop from it the science implied in it, he too, takes ideas for the subject matter of study. It is the course of human progress that forms the chief subject of his sociology. He begins with the idea that there is a continuous evolution of the human species, consisting in an ever more complete perfection of human nature . . . [but] the existence of this assumed evolution can be established only by an already completed science; it cannot, then, constitute the immediate subject of research.
>
> ([1895] 1938: 19)

Let me add that if one substitutes the phrase "human agency" for "human progress" above, much of Durkheim's criticism of Comte's method applies to Giddens's and other contemporary approaches in sociology. This is because Giddens, Comte, and other modernists begin with the idea of human agency and then proceed to "prove" its existence as a universal trait.

Durkheim claims that in his day, "instead of a science which deals with realities [perceptions], we carry out no more than an ideological analysis" ([1895] 1982: 60). I hasten to add that Durkheim's charge seems to still hold more than a hundred years later. The ideology in question seems to be simplistic rationalism as a component of what Habermas calls the Enlightenment project and what Giddens calls reflexivity. As an important aside, let me highlight Durkheim's criticisms of René Descartes made in *Moral Education*, which still seems to hold in the 1990s:

> The fact is that there is a turn of mind which is an extremely serious obstacle in the formation of the feeling of solidarity and which scientific teaching is particularly adapted to combat: it is something we might call oversimplified rationalism. This state of mind is characterized by the fundamental tendency to consider as real in

this world only that which is perfectly simple and so poor and denuded in qualities and properties that reason can grasp it at a glance and conceive of it in a luminous representation, analogous to that which we have in grasping mathematical matters. . . . In modern times, Descartes has been the most illustrious and distinguished exponent of this attitude. Indeed, we know that for Descartes there is nothing real unless it can be clearly conceptualized, made transparent to the mind; and that for him nothing can fulfill this function if it cannot be reduced to mathematical simplicity. If that turn of mind were peculiar to the circle of scholars and philosophers there would be no reason to speak of it here. But for various reasons, *this oversimplification has become an integral element of the French mind.* Although this manner of conceiving things is in principle a theoretical matter, it has had tremendous repercussions in practice – particularly regarding moral practices. Society is indeed an enormously complex whole. *If we apply to it the principle of oversimplified rationalism, we must say that this complexity is nothing in itself, that it has no reality, that the only thing real in society is that which is simple, clear, and easily grasped. Now, the only thing that satisfied all these conditions is the individual. The individual would then be the only real thing in society. Which is to say that society is nothing in itself, that it does not constitute a reality sui generis.* . . . Now, it might be said that in general a Frenchman is to some degree a conscious or unconscious Cartesian. . . . Our language seeks the simple. . . . Everything is under the floodlight of consciousness. Everything is blindingly clear. . . . However, rationalism does not imply the radical oversimplification we have just described.

(Durkheim [1925] 1961: 249–54; emphasis added)

Oversimplified rationalism still seems to characterize the social characters of both contemporary social sciences and contemporary societies. The entire twentieth-century ethos can be summarized as one of trying to break the world down conceptually into its simplest elements, of making everything blindingly clear, and of eliminating all mysteries. Yet, despite these efforts, the world seems to be growing in complexity, human agents often feel confused by information overload, and even faith in the Enlightenment project seems to take on the properties of a blind religious faith. I will be leading to the conclusion that Giddens's and other modernist social theories do not escape these Durkheimian criticisms.

Returning to Durkheim's *Rules*, we note that he claims that the natural as well as the social sciences extant in his day had "dealt more or less exclusively not with things but with concepts" while they should have been developing a "sufficiently strong perception of the details to feel the reality behind them" ([1895] 1982: 63). Clearly, Durkheim was aware of the role of hermeneutics in both the natural and social sciences, but unlike Giddens, who posits the double-hermeneutic as a way out of the impasse, Durkheim seems to hold fast to a position that bears some semblance to Schopenhauer's philosophy of transcendental idealism. By "double-hermeneutic," Giddens means

> The intersection of two frames of meaning as a logically necessary part of social science[:] the meaningful social world as constituted by lay actors and the metalanguages invented by social scientists; there is a constant "slippage" from one to the other involved in the practices of the social sciences.
>
> (1984: 374)

Giddens's double-hermeneutic does *not* attempt to penetrate through to reality but establishes yet another conceptual layer of distance from reality. In contrast to Giddens, Durkheim's Schopenhauerian modification of Immanuel Kant's philosophy assumes that the thing-in-itself remains out of reach to *concepts* – it cannot be known directly through the power of reason – but it can be approached indirectly via sensual and intuitive *perceptions*.

Herbert Spencer is not immune from Durkheim's criticism, for, according to Durkheim, in Spencer's writings one finds that "a certain conception of social reality is substituted for that reality" ([1895] 1982: 65). Similarly, "neither Locke nor Condillac considered physical phenomena objectively" because "it is not sensation they study, but a certain idea of it" (ibid.: 71). I believe that Durkheim's criticisms of Spencer, Locke, Condillac, and Kant still apply to Giddens's notion of the double-hermeneutic.

A strong echo of Schopenhauer is found in Durkheim's claims that

> All the questions that ethics normally raises relate not to *things* but to *ideas*. . . . Moralists have not yet even grasped the simple truth that, just as our *representations* of things *perceived* by the senses spring from those things themselves and express them more or less accurately, our *representations* of morality spring from observing the rules that function before our very eyes and perceive them systematically.
>
> (ibid.: 266; emphasis added)

It is striking that in this passage Durkheim essentially reproduces Schopenhauer's ([1841] 1965) criticisms of Kant's epistemology in general as well as his derivation of morality from an *a priori* basis. In subsequent writings, Durkheim would go on to develop his own version of an empirical "science of moral facts" – in direct contrast to Kant's ([1788] 1956) claim that morality could not be studied empirically (see Meštrović 1988).

Durkheim insists that "to treat phenomena as things is to treat them as data, and this constitutes the starting point for science" ([1895] 1982: 69).

Nevertheless, he does not succumb to naive realism because he acknowledges that perceptual content is retouched, modified, and changed by the human agent into conceptions. Thus, for Durkheim, conceptual categories should *receive* empirical knowledge but are not the originators of knowledge. He is quite explicit in this regard:

> Since it is through the *senses* that the external nature of things is revealed to us, we may therefore sum up as follows: in order to be objective science must *start from sense-perceptions* and *not* from *concepts* that have been formed independently from it. It is from observable data that it should derive directly the elements for its initial definition . . . [Science nevertheless] needs *concepts* which express things adequately . . . *Concepts* formed outside the sphere of science do not meet this criterion. It must therefore create new concepts and to do so must lay aside common notions and the words used to express them, returning to observations, the *essential basic* material for all concepts. It is from *sense* experience that all general *ideas* arise, whether they be true or false, scientific or unscientific.
>
> ([1895] 1982: 81; emphasis added)

Giddens is clearly aware of this passage by Durkheim, which he interprets as follows: "The concepts of everyday activity, Durkheim says, 'merely express the confused impression of the mob'" (Giddens 1993: 138). Giddens's criticism is part of his overall project to demonstrate that the social world is the skilled accomplishment of active human agents. But does it really follow that Durkheim is denigrating the skill of human agents because he does not assume that their conceptualizations are scientifically valid? I think not. The passage which Giddens dismisses is one in which Durkheim refers to Francis Bacon's notion of idols as *notiones vulgares* (Durkheim [1895] 1938: 16–17). Durkheim's point seems to be simply that the layperson is not able to understand reality "at a glance" because social reality – even more than physical reality – is complex (ibid.: 16). Moreover, Durkheim repeats that sociology, "instead of seeking a comprehension of facts already acquired, undertakes immediately to *discover new ones*" (ibid.; emphasis added). Surely Giddens does not wish to imply that genuine discovery is an easy matter for the skilled and knowledgeable agent. In addition, Giddens seems to be overestimating the conceptualizing powers of laypersons who are subject to manipulation by self and others, as decades of research by the Frankfurt School have demonstrated amply.

Thus, in the opening chapters of the *Rules*, Durkheim sets the tone for establishing sociology as a science of discoveries, not as Kant's closed, circular game of *a priori* concepts. In keeping with the tradition established by Schopenhauer and followed by Wilhelm Wundt, Théodule Ribot, Sigmund Freud, William James, Vilfredo Pareto, and other scholars in his time, Durkheim apparently attempted to maintain some kind of dialectic between the physical state of affairs in the brain of the observer and the concepts used to communicate that experience (see Meštrović 1988). This is especially evident in Durkheim's ([1924] 1974) neglected *Sociology and Philosophy*, wherein he devotes considerable attention to the relationship of electro-chemical firing in the brain to representations. Giddens does not address the physical role of the brain in hermeneutics. In short, for Durkheim, the scholar finds it necessary to locate, discover, or even create a word or concept to represent the experience of observation. Durkheim's analysis makes us aware that after the word or concept is used, the concept may take on the property of the perceived reality – it may become reified – and thereby limit science to a game of concepts. Durkheim's admonition that science must continually struggle against this trap of reification seems no less relevant today than it was in his time. Finally, it seems that Giddens does not deal adequately with the danger of reification in relation to his own program for establishing sociology as a double-hermeneutic.

THE NORMAL VERSUS THE PATHOLOGICAL

The most controversial chapter in Durkheim's *Rules* is the one entitled "Rules for the Distinction of the Normal from the Pathological." Giddens (1976), along with Jack Douglas (1967), Steven Lukes (1985), and others, has criticized Durkheim in this regard essentially along the lines that he violated the value-free basis of science. But it is not so much that Durkheim ([1895] 1982: 85) violates this purported standard of science – itself under much criticism since C. Wright Mills – but that he consciously and deliberately rejects it in favor of a new solution that he apparently hoped would help to launch sociology as the science of morality.

Durkheim writes that what is today called value-free science is "stripped, or nearly, of all practical effectiveness and consequently of any real justification for its existence. For what good is it to strive after a knowledge of reality if the knowledge we acquire cannot serve us in our lives?" (ibid.). Durkheim seems to imply that emotions, not cognitive representations, lead to action. (This is an important component of both Schopenhauer's and Nietzsche's legacies.) I have argued elsewhere that postemotional society is characterized, in part, by a radical disjunction between emotion and knowledge such that twentieth-century persons know more than their ancestors ever could, but are not necessarily more enabled to act, morally or otherwise (Meštrović 1997). Durkheim was clearly aware that passions are necessary for human action, while Giddens (1984) does not deal with the role of emotions in skilled human agency at all.

For Durkheim, the important point seems to be that value-laden judgment enters every step of the process in scientific reasoning, including the translation of sensual perceptions into mental conceptions ([1895] 1982: 86). Additionally, Durkheim makes the seemingly obvious but highly neglected observation that the scientist must rely on the faculty of judgment, which is anything but value-free, to determine the ends of science after discoveries are made. Science can shed light on practical problems only if there is an objective method of distinguishing the healthy from the morbid ([1895] 1938: 49). And the morbid or pathological is something escapable, that which is not essential to the constitution of society (ibid.: 51). Durkheim seeks to approach this problem by some external and perceptible characteristics (ibid.: 55).

But perhaps the most important reason why this chapter is so controversial is that scholars have generally misconstrued that Durkheim intended the term "normal" to refer to the average of consciously held norms in society (Lukes 1985; Parsons 1937). Although Durkheim does not make himself clear enough on this issue in *Rules*, his follower Georges Davy (1927: 59–66) demonstrates convincingly that Durkheim did not intend Lukes's misinterpretation (which carries over into Giddens's interpretation of Durkheim), and Davy points to passages in Durkheim's other works to clarify his apparent intentions. When Durkheim writes of the general or average in relation to social life, he refers to a given stage in its development and in terms of the "general conditions of collective life of the social type considered" (ibid.: 64). The concept "general conditions of collective life" is not even remotely similar to widely shared norms. Durkheim's intent here is clearly to avoid ethnocentrism: "One should completely abandon the still too widespread habit of judging an institution, a practice or a moral standard as if it were good or bad in and by itself" (ibid.: 56). He illustrates this point with the claim, "what is normal for the savage is not always normal for the civilized man, and vice versa" (ibid.: 57).

Let us apply this principle to Giddens's and other modernist work. Do Giddens and the modernists succumb to ethnocentrism by claiming that human agency is normal in Durkheim's true sense of normality, for example that it is a constitutive element of all Western societies (while not even considering non-Western societies)? The answer seems to be in the affirmative, because Giddens and other modernist sociologists reject all evolutionism, and do not bother with the question whether human agency is constitutive of social life in traditional societies. In fact, Giddens (1984) is emphatic in claiming that sociology is the study of modern societies. Of course, even the traditionalist is a knowledgeable and skilled agent to some extent, but it is important to determine the extent to which the traditionalist may behave as an agent in contrast to modern societies. Given Durkheim's convincing accounts of the crushing power in traditional societies relative to the individual agent, it seems reasonable to conclude that human agency, as conceptualized by Giddens, may be normal in some modern societies some of the time, but is not an inherent quality of all social life.

The only phenomenon that Durkheim regards as universally normal is crime. That is, he believes that crime is a constitutive element of all societies, past and present, because all societies must label some actions as criminal and punish them in order to preserve their integration. Durkheim adds immediately:

> Let us make no mistake. To classify crime among the phenomena of normal sociology is not to say merely that it is an inevitable, although regrettable phenomenon, due to the incorrigible wickedness of men; it is to affirm that it is a factor in public health, an integral part of all healthy societies. . . . Crime is normal because a society exempt from it is utterly impossible.
>
> (ibid.: 67)

It is worth noting that in Giddens's terms, the criminal behaves as an agent to some extent, even in traditional societies, because skill and knowledge are required to discern as well as break society's rules and then to try to evade punishment. I contend that even more skill and knowledge than was required in traditional societies is required to carry out modern crimes against humanity illustrated by Stalin, Hitler, and, more recently, Karadžić. But curiously, Giddens never considers the anti-social uses to which human agency can be applied. He treats human agency as an unqualified good, even when he invokes Freud (see Giddens 1984: 53–60).

In addition, and contrary to many misinterpretations of Durkheim that he succumbed to a kind of vulgar utilitarianism, he writes that "it is untrue that everything which is [apparently] useful is normal" ([1895] 1982: 96). This is in keeping with the general anti-Enlightenment sentiment extant in Durkheim's *fin de siècle* that utilitarian calculation is a purely mental, conceptual process and therefore an inferior basis for judgment, especially moral judgment. In fact, utilitarianism is useful for rationalizing, after the fact, errors in judgment and immoral behavior. In opposition to the utilitarianism, the faculty of judgment involves linking a conception to the original sensual perception that gave rise to it – in other words, linking the ideas arrived at conceptually to the "will" that gave rise to them. (In this sense, the criminal is an excellent rationalist but a poor judge of his or her own character as well as of the social consequences of crime.) Without going into all the details of how Durkheim applies this philosophy methodologically in his other works, it is interesting that he claims that

> having established by observation that the fact is general . . . [the sociologist] will trace back the conditions which determined this general character in the past and then investigate whether these conditions still pertain in the present or, on the contrary, have

changed. In the first case he will be justified in treating the
phenomenon as normal.

(ibid.: 95)

If one reads the above passage and others like it in the context of the anti-
Enlightenment ethos of the previous *fin de siècle*, a different understanding of
Durkheim's methodology emerges compared to contemporary readings.
Durkheim was apparently attempting to link an observable phenomenon to
its noumenic counterpart, a conception to the original perception which
gave rise to it, a "representation" to its underlying, sometimes hidden
"will." His follower, Maurice Halbwachs (1918: 400), argued in this regard
that Durkheim was attempting a kind of "depth sociology" as a counterpart
to "depth psychology."

To contextualize Durkheim's hundred-year-old claim, let us turn again to
the issue of genocide in Bosnia in the 1990s, which was televised and otherwise highly publicized. The average person living in a Western country with
widespread access to the information media may be conceptualized as
Giddens's skilled human agent who knew about this instance of genocide
more than any other instance of genocide in history (see Cushman and
Meštrović 1996). This is an important observation because it shifts the focus
of human agency from the main actors (politicians, generals, diplomats, war
criminals) to the public consumers of information, the war-watchers, and
seemingly postmodern voyeurs. Public opinion in the 1990s certainly made
it seem as if genocide had suddenly become a normal state of affairs, at least
in the Balkans (wherein many Westerners seem to imply that such hatred is
constitutive of Balkan life), and that indifference was a normal societal
response to it (even though the requirement to put a stop to it is enshrined
in the United Nations Charter). Using Durkheim's method for determining
whether Western response was normal or pathological, one would search for
public assessments of genocide in Western history. It is an open question
whether such an analysis would show that genocide has been thought of
historically as the most heinous of human crimes that had to be expiated and
punished once it was realized, or whether indifference is the normal response
to genocide. This would be a very difficult study because one would have to
control for the amount of knowledge that our ancestors had concerning
genocide in contrast to the widespread knowledge of genocide in Bosnia.
One would also have to determine whether state control in pre-modern societies ever approached the level of surveillance and control of modern states
(along the lines of the argument in Giddens 1987). Regardless of the
outcome of such a proposed study, the disturbing fact remains that, contrary
to Giddens's overall assumptions, the contemporary skilled and knowledgeable agent seems to have been relatively helpless to act on the tremendous
amount of knowledge that was presented to him or her regarding genocide
in Bosnia.

Durkheim's intentions to place the accent on sensual perceptions or the noumenon rather than the concept or phenomenon appear more clearly still in his summation of this chapter:

> For sociology to deal with facts as things, the sociologist must feel a need to learn from them. The principal purpose of any science of life, whether individual or social, is in the end to define and explain the normal state and distinguish it from the abnormal. If normality does not inhere in the things themselves, if on the contrary it is a characteristic which we impose upon them externally or, for whatever reason, refuse to do so, this salutary state of dependence on things is lost. The mind . . . is no longer contained by the subject matter to which it applies itself, since in some respects it determines that subject matter.
>
> ([1895] 1982: 104)

Whatever Durkheim's intentions are in this ponderous assessment, it is clear that he is not just mimicking a stereotype of the natural sciences model of methodology. Durkheim seem to imply that if the scientist remained on the level of phenomenal knowledge only – a move that denies any possibility of distinguishing the normal from the pathological – then knowledge would succumb to a kind of intellectual anomie in which the scientist would become lost in an infinity of concepts (see Meštrović 1988: 76–96). For in that case, what rules would guide the scientist from choosing one representation of the thing-in-itself over another representation (Durkheim [1895] 1982: 104)? The contemporary relevance of Durkheim's grounded approach to sociological theory is illustrated by recent criticisms of Giddens, along with Parsons and Habermas, as engaging in overly intellectual abstractions devoid of empirical content. Apparently, this is precisely what Durkheim sought to avoid with his controversial distinction between the normal and the pathological.

THE ONE, WELL-DESIGNED EXPERIMENT

The faculty of judgment is crucial to Durkheim's methodology in at least two important ways. First, the sociologist must abstract the notion of the "general" (which will be used to distinguish the normal) from an "indefinite multiplicity" of types ([1895] 1982: 111) in using the comparative method which he understood to be an indirect experiment. This intellectual move by Durkheim resembles Znaniecki's ([1934] 1968) notion of "analytical induction" as well as Max Weber's method of abstracting the "ideal type." Second, the sociologist must abstract the notion of cause and effect from these abstract forms of general social types (discussed in chapters 4 and 6 of the

Rules) out of a multiplicity of possible cause and effect relationships. Yet Durkheim insisted that "a given effect has always a single corresponding cause" so that, for example, "if suicide depends on more than one cause, it is because, in reality, there are several kinds of suicide" ([1895] 1938: 128). In both cases, the sociologist does not and cannot observe all the possible types that exist. Even if this were tried and this supposed aim of positivistic observation were achieved, one would "no more than summarize research already carried out" (Durkheim [1895] 1982: 111). Judgment must be rendered on the phenomenal observation, as Durkheim asserts (ibid.):

> Thus once a classification has been established according to this principle, in order to know whether a fact is general throughout a particular species, it will be unnecessary to have observed all societies belonging to this species – the study of a few will suffice. In many cases even one observation well conducted will be enough, just as often an experiment efficiently carried out [*une experience bien conduite*] is sufficient to establish a law.
> ([in French] [1895] 1983: 80; emphasis added)

Durkheim adds that "Indeed, what has often discredited the reasoning of sociologists is that ... they have been more intent on accumulating documents than on criticizing and selecting from them" ([1895] 1982: 153). In contradistinction to this discredited method, Durkheim asserts that for his method "to yield results a few facts suffice" (ibid.). Clearly, Durkheim depicts the social scientist as a skilled human agent who makes value-laden judgments in every step of scientific procedure, and, again, this is an issue that Giddens fails to address. Giddens (1984) rejects positivistic generalizations in favor of making theoretically informed illuminations, but he has been criticized with justification for failing to specify the empirical consequences of such a claim.

Because this aspect of Durkheim's thought – his reliance on the one, well-designed "experiment" – contradicts positivistic methodologies so thoroughly, further investigation is warranted. Durkheim elaborated on this claim in a rarely cited debate, that "If I know A is the cause of B, I know A will always be the cause of B. The link that joins them exists as a reality independently of time and space" (1908: 233). Note that Durkheim focuses on the issue of knowing causes as opposed to the reality of causes. It is fascinating that Durkheim's remark concerning the independence from the Kantian categories of time and space is one of Schopenhauer's (1899) major arguments against Kant (discussed in Magee 1983: 28–48).

Durkheim's followers were apparently as adamant as their master regarding the one, well-designed experiment being sufficient for establishing scientific laws. Znaniecki's ([1934] 1968: 236) version of this continental preoccupation with induction from a few cases is also worth noting, especially because he uses the concept of analytic induction to link thinkers as diverse as Plato, Aristotle, Galileo, Durkheim, Le Play, and W.I. Thomas! Znaniecki alerts one to the possibility that the current interest within sociology in emulating the deductive methodologies of the natural sciences may be mistaken. It may be that both the natural and social sciences are most productive in terms of generating discoveries when they follow essentially inductive methodologies, which presuppose judgment and skill on the part of the analyst. Finally, Znaniecki (ibid.) points to an interesting affinity between the Chicago and Durkheim's Schools with regard to inductive methodologies.

Durkheim disagrees with John Stuart Mill that a given effect can have more than one cause: "If it consists of a relationship which results from the *nature of things*, the same effect can only sustain this relationship with one single cause, for it can express only one single nature" (Durkheim [1895] 1982: 149; emphasis added). It is difficult to think of a philosophy save Schopenhauer's which can explain this intellectual move by Durkheim, because Durkheim seems to be conjoining the noumenal "nature of things" to its phenomenal appearance.

One could argue that Durkheim's assignment of a particular cause to its supposedly unique effect can *seem to be* somewhat arbitrary. To repeat, I have no intention of justifying or defending Durkheim's methodology, only showing that it is not the straw man positivistic methodology that Giddens sets up. In any event, the analyst's judgment is often unspoken in scientific analyses and rarely disclosed in the public presentation of scientific findings, which use the rhetoric of positivistic methodology even if such methodology was not necessarily followed in all ways in the actual scientific work, for reasons already discussed. Durkheim does not specify the criteria by which this phenomenal connection between a unique cause and its effect shall be made. However, it may be too much to expect for any thinker to specify rationally the emotional and value-laden judgments that are implicit in scientific work. It seems that Durkheim was implying that when the noumenal aspect of apprehending the world (such as intuition and perception) is conjoined with the phenomenal knowledge of causes, somehow a unique and skilled interpretation will be given. Perhaps the specific method Durkheim implies in this regard can be gleaned from a careful analysis of the exact process he and his followers used to arrive at their unique cause and effect explanations. More importantly, perhaps, empirical research into how scientists (in the natural as well as the social sciences) actually make discoveries would be fruitful. Such projects are beyond the scope of the present discussion.

In addition, it seems that for Durkheim the scientific laws cannot be falsified just because they are not always verified. This important claim was also made by Claude Bernard ([1865] 1957: 24, 70–2), and it is important to note that Durkheim knew of Bernard's work. Consistent with his contemporaries, Durkheim wrote:

> Constant concomitance is therefore by itself a law, regardless of the state of the phenomena left out of the comparison. Thus to invalidate the method it is not sufficient to show that it is inoperative in a few particular applications. . . . When two phenomena vary regularly together, this relationship must be maintained even when, in certain cases, one of these phenomena appears without the other.
>
> ([1895] 1982: 151)

While Durkheim's justification concerning the criteria by which causes shall be determined is woefully inadequate when judged by contemporary positivistic criteria, it seems clear that his efforts are more in line with the inductive approaches of Schopenhauer and Bernard than the more deductive approaches of Comte and Kant. Clearly, Durkheim's rules for sociological method are more than an exercise in applying mechanized principles to the social scientific realm. He leaves a lot of room for hermeneutics and for judgments to be made by skilled scientific agents.

CONCLUSIONS

Giddens as well as other modernist social theorists seem to *begin* with the thesis that Durkheim was a bad or inconsistent positivist and Comtean, and then use this straw man version of Durkheim to justify their hermeneutic approaches. One point I have tried to make is that Durkheim was a bad Comtean because he was not one, while he seems to have been a fairly consistent Schopenhauerian, including his focus on representations as opposed to the will. This shift in choosing the starting points for analysis holds important consequences for comprehending the origins of modern sociology and for assessing Giddens's work as a whole to the extent that he relies on a straw man argument of Comte's influence for building his social theory.

The implications of reading Durkheim's methodological treatise in this new context are of more than historical interest, although it is important to establish Durkheim's intellectual relationship to his contemporaries more accurately than is the case at present. The epistemological problems that Durkheim addressed are still with us, only they have been renamed as the problems of justifying inductive inferences, reification, and the object–subject distinction. Contemporary sociology continues to struggle with the issues of how to become genuinely empirical and how to emulate the natural sciences even as many postmodernists declare such interests obsolete. The emphasis on hermeneutics and the double-hermeneutics in the present *fin de siècle* have led many social scientists to conclude that the social sciences deal with fictions, not reality (see Ahmed and Shore 1995). Giddens's effort to free the social sciences from the oppressive yoke of the "hard sciences" is admirable, yet his effort is flawed in several respects:

(1) some nineteenth-century natural science methodology was inductive, and entirely compatible with Durkheim's approach; (2) in throwing out Durkheim with the bathwater of Comte and Parsons, Giddens misrepresents an important strand in the origins of the social sciences; (3) Giddens fails to demonstrate that his method is anything but old-fashioned, Kantian *a priorism* that is incapable of promoting discoveries. If the "old" rules by Durkheim were meant to yield sociological discoveries, and the "new" rules by Giddens fail to do so, what, exactly, is the value of Giddens's new rules of sociological method? Giddens's new rules amount to little more than an ideological manifesto concerning human agency and freedom which uses Durkheim as a scapegoat even though his sociology did not oppress human agency in the first place.

In addition, this chapter has exposed the following problems and issues that need to be addressed: Should scientific concepts be used to receive perceptions, as Durkheim and a host of other thinkers from the previous *fin de siècle* advocated, or should concepts serve as the starting point for scientific inquiry? If sociologists continue to take the option of starting with conceptualizations, then how will they reply to Durkheim's criticism that such a starting point can never lead to genuine empiricism and that it leads, instead, to a circular game of concepts? If they take Durkheim seriously and opt for induction, how will they understand or justify the judgments that are involved in analytic induction? In other words, regarding the second option, is hermeneutics fated to stay on the level of phenomena only, or can it ever connect with the "nature of things," the noumenon? Giddens's program for sociology as a double-hermeneutic is not a real solution because it evades these questions. He fails to ground hermeneutics in any sort of system that would suggest that it can interpret reality, not weave concepts out of thin air.

A scholarly and objective response to these contemporary epistemological problems should begin with a reassessment of sociology's origins at the turn of the nineteenth century. Both Giddens (1993) and Parsons (1937) – despite Giddens's dismissive tone toward Parsons – posit something like a straight line from the rationalist philosophies of Comte, Kant, and the utilitarians to current sociology, without noting *fin de siècle* criticisms of these philosophies. Most textbooks, secondary sources, and treatises follow Parsons's and Giddens's mistaken leads, not acknowledging the long intellectual detour from Comte to our era through the *fin de siècle* spirit exemplified by Schopenhauer's philosophy (Ellenberger 1970), although other anti-Enlightenment intellectual and artistic movements were also involved. Schopenhauer's philosophy and other irrationalist movements had supplanted Comte's positivism in *fin de siècle* France (Baillot 1927; Magee 1983; Weber 1986), or, as Nietzsche put the matter, "the cult of feeling was erected in place of the cult of reason" (1968: 84). According to Janik and Toulmin (1973), even Ludwig Wittgenstein's controversial version of positivism was actually influenced by Schopenhauer, not Comte or Kant. This is another contextual factor that Giddens fails to investigate in his reliance on Wittgenstein as part of the theoretical scaffolding in structuration theory.

Thus, this segment of the discussion points to the need to study further the intellectual affinities between Durkheim and several of his contemporaries in the context of Schopenhauer's philosophy, especially Wundt, Ribot, Freud, Veblen, James, Weber, Simmel, Pareto, and various members of the Chicago School. For example, Durkheim's discussion of how a conceptual type should be generated from a diversity of empirical observations resembles Max Weber's notion of the ideal type. Simmel's complex critiques of naive positivism in the context of his Schopenhauerian dualism of life versus forms (Simmel 1971) also resonate with Durkheim's intellectual moves in *Rules*. Florian Znaniecki ([1934] 1968), an important member of the Chicago School, cited Durkheim's method as an example of a methodology he called analytic induction. Park and Burgess (1921) were ambivalent about the historical analysis of *events* versus the analysis of laws by natural sciences. What are the affinities between the methodologies of Durkheim's School and the Chicago Schools, and how did these affinities become obscured into contemporary assessments that posit a hiatus between Durkheim and the symbolic interactionists and ethno-methodologists?

Horowitz (1987) correctly depicts the polemic between quantifiers and qualifiers in contemporary sociology, but a proposed solution is not yet to be found. Yet a reading of Durkheim's methodological classic in the context of Schopenhauer's philosophy at least points to several bridges between these two opposing methodologies. Thus, Durkheim's analysis sensitizes one to the idea that quantitative facts are still representations, mental constructs subject to change and human construction, not the positivistic hard facts they are often purported to be. The mere quantification of data does not qualify it as a social fact, and Claude Bernard ([1865] 1957) was also suspicious of quantification as a ground for empiricism. In this regard, one must guard against reification with regard to both quantitative and qualitative facts. Although quantitative methodologies purport to attempt to replicate previous findings, Durkheim's *Rules* makes one question whether such replication is possible, desirable, or even necessary. Each time a fact is apprehended, object and subject have changed, and reality cannot repeat itself (Bernard [1865] 1957; Nietzsche 1968).

In summary, Giddens (1984, 1993) posits a double-hermeneutic in the social sciences as opposed to the single-hermeneutic in the natural sciences because he believes that social "reality" is fundamentally different from natural "reality." Durkheim treats both methodologies (in the natural as well as the social sciences) as hermeneutical but also as seeking to discover "the nature of things." True, contemporary philosophers of science have abandoned the possibility of making contact with the nature of things, but then what purpose does hermeneutics serve?

Quantitatively oriented sociologists generally cite *Suicide* as the best illustration of Durkheim's proposed methodology in his *Rules*, thereby giving the impression that it is an essentially quantitative methodology. But Durkheim's followers pointed to his *Division of Labor* ([1893] 1933), *The Elementary Forms of the Religious Life* ([1912] 1965) and *Socialism and Saint-Simon* ([1928] 1958) as the best exemplars of his method, works that are completely non-statistical. How does the sociologist treat concepts like the division of labor, religion, and socialism as social facts without quantifying them? That is still a problem worth pursuing.

For example, consider Durkheim's opening lines in his neglected *Socialism and Saint-Simon* in light of the preceding discussion, wherein he writes:

> The truth is that the facts and observations assembled by theoreticians anxious to document their affirmations are hardly there except to give form to the arguments. The research studies they made were undertaken to establish a doctrine that they had previously conceived, rather than the doctrine being a result of the research. . . . If this is so, then to study socialism as a system of abstract propositions, as a body of scientific theories and to discuss it formally, is to see and show a side of it which is of minor interest.
>
> ([1928] 1958: 7)

In contrast to the deductive approach that he criticizes, Durkheim proposes to study socialism as a social fact that represents "the profound uneasiness of which the particular theories are merely the symptoms and episodic superficialities" (ibid.: 10). He adds that socialism "must not be considered in the abstract" (ibid.) and asks in general:

> what does the development of sociology signify? How does it happen that we experience the need to reflect on social matters, if not because our social state is abnormal, because the unsettled collective organization no longer functions with the authority of instinct?
>
> (ibid.: 239)

Durkheim seems to be implying that an important impetus for the establishment of both sociology and socialism was a dimly *perceived*, albeit not clearly conceptualized or articulated, sense of crisis in society.

Throughout this chapter Durkheim's inductive approach to both theory construction and methodology has been emphasized. This is not intended to convey the impression that Durkheim ignored the role of deduction or conceptualization in the scientific process, nor that induction is non-problematic.

Rather, the most important point for Durkheim seems to have been that deduction or conceptualization should not serve as the starting point for empirical investigations. Clearly, this raises the issue as to whether concepts drawn from perceptions might be used subsequently as starting points for further study, an issue treated by Herbert Blumer (1969: 153–70) with regard to symbolic interactionism and by others in different contexts (see Wallace 1971).

It is beyond the scope of this discussion to evaluate Durkheim's extreme emphasis on induction, as the aim has been to uncover it. Nevertheless, an excellent illustration of the refreshing uniqueness of Durkheim's view of science is his treatment of the concept of anomie. Contrary to Giddens and other theorists who deduce an understanding of anomie from pre-conceived theoretical premises – whether it is the problem of human agency or the problem of social order – Durkheim's starting point for anomie seems to have been a perception of the sorrow, unhappiness, malaise, and related psychological symptomatology he found in turn-of-the-century European societies. Anomie is the induced concept he used to receive and express these perceptions of malaise, not a pre-conceived notion he dreamed up to test against reality. Giddens abandons the concept of anomie completely from the sociological vocabulary, because he believes that it is wrapped in the Parsonian problem of social order that he seeks to transcend. But Giddens's social theory needs to address the question: Have modern societies really overcome anomie? Are free and knowledgeable agents incapable of experiencing anomie? I contend that contemporary modern societies may be characterized by more, not less, malaise and unhappiness of various sorts than were present in Durkheim's time. And these phenomena might still represent anomie, only at present these go by the names stress, drug addiction, sleeping disorders, and other representations of collective and private malaise (Meštrović 1994). A purely conceptual theory of society such as Giddens's may make it difficult to perceive the anomie that already exists, yet remains formally unacknowledged even if it is imperfectly perceived.

Finally, this new reading of Durkheim's methodological classic calls into question the reified vision of deductive scientific theory construction that seems to dominate current sociology. Giddens seems to rebel against such reification, but, ironically, his system of double-hermeneutics seems to be an exercise in rhetoric that masks *a priorism* and that is incapable of promoting discovery. As indicated previously, Durkheim was not alone in questioning whether deduction can lead to scientific discoveries. In fact, a close examination of the methodologies of most of the other precursors of the social sciences at the turn of the century would indicate that they regarded deduction as being of secondary importance compared to induction, and that in this regard they perceived themselves in line with Claude Bernard ([1865] 1957) and other natural scientists. James, Freud, Wundt, Ribot, Simmel, Weber, Veblen, Pareto, Mill, and others in that era definitely saw their contributions to science as being empirical but were also definitely more inductive than deductive in their approaches. How and why was this turn-of-the-century focus on induction changed back to deduction in more recent times? How is a genuinely empirical social science going to be achieved? Is an empirical sociology from concepts possible? These are among the issues exposed by this rereading of Durkheim's *Rules* against the grain of Giddens's reading in the *New Rules*.

4

THE ROLE OF DESIRE IN AGENCY AND STRUCTURE

This Enlightenment we must now advance further – unconcerned with the fact that there has been a "great revolution"
against it, and then a "great reaction" again; indeed that both
still exist; all this is mere play of the waves compared to that
truly great tide in which *we* drift and want to drift.
– Friedrich Nietzsche (1968: 85)

If we were to conduct the most hardened and callous optimist
through hospitals, infirmaries, operating theaters, through
prisons, torture-chambers, and slave-hovels, over battlefields
and to places of execution; if we were to open to him all the
dark abodes of misery, where it shuns the gaze of cold
curiosity, and finally were to allow him to glance into the
dungeon of Ugolino where prisoners starved to death, he too
would certainly see in the end what kind of a world is this
meilleur des mondes possibles. For whence did Dante get the
material for his hell, if not from this actual world of ours?"
– Arthur Schopenhauer ([1818] 1969a: 325)

In this chapter I will elaborate upon a central observation made in chapter 3,
and then apply it to the concept of agency: in most treatises, secondary
sources, and textbooks, including those written by Anthony Giddens, sociologists seem to posit something like a straight line from the optimistic,
rationalist philosophies that informed the works of Comte and other
Enlightenment philosophers to current sociology. No acknowledgment is
usually made of the long intellectual detour from that optimistic era to ours
through what Henri Ellenberger (1970) calls the *fin de siècle* spirit exemplified by Schopenhauer's philosophy, by the Romantic and pre-Romantic
forces that led up to it, and by his many disciples, especially Nietzsche.
Following Parsons (1937) as well as Giddens (1993), most social theorists
seem to have assumed (not proved) that rationalist philosophies informed
the orientations of turn of the century social theorists. To borrow

Schopenhauer's distinction between the "heart" and the "mind," one might say that contemporary sociology has placed the accent on the "mind" and has repressed turn of the century sociology's emphasis on the "heart" and its derivatives: the unconscious, feelings, culture, and irrational metaphysics. Giddens is no exception to this generalization.

With regard to the concept of agency – which is central to Giddens's entire system of thought – the consequences of this one-sidedness in theoretical scaffolding are far-reaching. Despite his apparent sense of triumph over Parsons and others whom he accuses of not appreciating the skill and knowledge of the human agent, Giddens ends up offering a carica-ture of the human agent. Giddens's agent is all mind and no heart. Nowhere is this more apparent than in his discussion of agency vis-à-vis Sigmund Freud's theories: Giddens simply amputates Freud's notions of the id and the unconscious and then substitutes his own rationalist equivalents. The result is a portrait of the agent based on oversimplified wishful thinking, a carica-ture based on modernist ideology in which the agent is reflexive, able to monitor his/her actions, skilled, and knowledgeable at all times. And of course, in line with his modernist revisionism of nearly all the classical social theorists, Giddens makes Freud out to be a thinker who is concerned exclu-sively with the modern:

> Radicalizing Freud means showing that what he took to be charac-teristics of civilization in general *are really specific to the modern order*. That order is presented as much more monolithic, and resistant to change, than it really is.
>
> (Giddens 1992b: 170; emphasis added)

But in this chapter, as in this entire book, I shall remind the reader that I see Giddens's move in this regard as fairly typical of modernist social theo-ries in general. Twentieth-century sociology has been "heartless" in ways similar to the aims of Giddens. For example, Marxism became popular primarily because most intellectuals thought of Marx as a rationalist. Some, notably the economists, even thought of his work as scientific. Marx thought that a rationalist explanation of history based on class struggle did not need to take into account that most irrational of phenomenons, nation-alism. He even thought that nationalism would disappear. (I shall return to nationalism vis-à-vis Giddens in later chapters.) Marx has been seen more often as an economist than a philosopher or sociologist, and economists in general think of themselves as rationalists. In this regard, sociology seems much less heartless than most economics, where one finds rationalism at its most extravagant. Nevertheless, Marx the humanist was undeveloped, even within sociology.

Freud met a similar fate in psychology. Freud's assimilation into contem-porary social theory is predicated on the dubious assumption that he was a doctor of the mind who offered mechanistic ways to cure neurosis. Giddens falls into this modernist, erroneous mode of interpreting Freud's importance, as illustrated by his comment in *The Transformation of Intimacy*: "Psychoanalysis has its origins in the medical treatment of behavior pathologies, and was seen by Freud as a method of combating neurosis" (1992b: 31). I invite the reader to read Freud's own accounts of the origins and purpose of psychoanalysis, which I have analyzed in my *Barbarian Temperament* (Meštrović 1993a): Freud was shunned by the medical profession; saw himself as a student of culture; was more inspired by Plato and Schopenhauer in establishing psychoanalysis than by medicine; and did not think neuroses could ever be "cured." On the contrary, he thought that neurosis was everyone's fate, only some people had more insight into their neuroses than others. This is not the place to contrast Freud and Giddens point by point, only to suggest that Giddens misreads Freud because he refuses to read him on his own terms or on the terms of Freud's cultural milieu.

Similarly, modern psychologists value Freud for debunking religion, but do not take seriously his notion of civilization and its discontents. Contrary to Giddens, I interpret Freud's writings on civilization as applicable to eras and societies other than modern. For Giddens, as for other modernists, Freud's rationalism is emphasized more than his pessimism. Similarly, Watson's and B.F. Skinner's versions of behaviorism tried to neutralize the emotional aspects of human motivation into a cognitive model. Contemporary psychology is best known for its contributions to "cognitive science" and cognitive functioning, not for knowledge concerning the emotions or emotional functioning. In general, Freud is depicted by modernists as a "doctor of the mind," not as a pessimistic cultural analyst.

In general, that portion of twentieth-century social science that is thought of by its members and its opponents as mainstream is concerned with being scientific; with being hostile to magic, metaphysics, religion; and with using some parts of economics as its model. Yet the vision of the Enlightenment that has guided this twentieth-century worship of the "mind" at the expense of the "heart" is illusory. Habermas's term the "Enlightenment project" obfuscates the fact that the original Enlightenment philosophers had to keep under cover, so to speak, or flatter political leaders, or keep their views secret because some of their views were viewed as threatening to the established order (Tester 1992). Even during the Enlightenment and immediately afterwards, there was plenty of skepticism concerning its main tenets, but this fact tends to be forgotten in contemporary renditions of the period. Thus, Rousseau and Jonathan Swift expressed a radical distrust of science. Vico was highly critical of some aspects of the Enlightenment. David Hume and Adam Smith were mindful of the power of human sentiments over rationality. The perfunctory references to the Enlightenment project found in most contemporary texts are really a postemotional distortion of the Enlightenment, an artificial, synthesized creation – post-traditional, in Giddens's vocabulary – that is out of touch with historical as well as contemporary reality. For after the critical theorists, it seems more accurate to claim that the modern world is dominated, not by mind, as the Enlightenment *philosophes* had hoped; rather, by a kind of indolent mindlessness.

Giddens repudiates many positivistic tenets of the Enlightenment project while he simultaneously exhibits characteristics of a synthetic, postemotional devotee to it. For example, his writings on the human agent focus on cognitive knowledge, not intuitive knowledge or emotion. As noted previously, there is no place in his theory for suffering, caring, or desire. To the extent that these non-rational phenomena intrude upon the agent, as depicted in his *The Transformation of Intimacy* (1992b), they are dealt with in accordance with the mechanical logic of self-help manuals. By Giddens's own admission,

> One resource upon which I have drawn extensively perhaps needs some comment here: the literature of self-help. Scorned by many, to me it offers insights unavailable elsewhere and I deliberately stay as close to the *genre* as possible in developing my own arguments.
>
> (ibid.: i)

Giddens's knowledgeable human agent is ultimately a rationalist, a modernist caricature of what it means to be human. Overall, Giddens's social theory – despite the loud rhetoric of an alleged break with previous social theory – actually stays on the heartless trajectory of twentieth-century social theory.

DENATURING THE HUMAN AGENT

An excellent illustration of my observations concerning Giddens is to be found in his use of Freud in *The Constitution of Society* (1984). Given my exposition in chapter 3 of Giddens's misunderstanding of Durkheim, it will not come as a surprise that Giddens is not a sensitive reader of Freud. I can summarize my objections to Giddens's reading of Freud vis-à-vis the concept of agency by way of analogy. To read Freud through the eyes of Giddens is like reading Victor Hugo's depiction of Quasimodo through Disney's film *The Hunchback of Notre Dame*. Very little of the pathos and emotion of the original survives in either case. To phrase the matter in a different way: Giddens Disneyfies Freud. It is beyond the scope of the present volume to retrieve fully a contextual understanding of Freud (the interested reader might consult Meštrović 1993a), but it is important to lay out some of that cultural context, albeit in a few sentences, in order to expose the shallowness of Giddens's analysis. In particular, one should note that Freud's writings exhibit the Schopenhauerian flavor of the previous *fin de siècle*. For example, Freud's conceptualizations of the id, the unconscious, and of unruly emotions can and have been read as refractions of Schopenhauer's concept of the will (see Ellenberger 1970). Now, let us consider what happens when Giddens encounters Freud vis-à-vis the concept of human agency. Giddens writes:

> Freud divides the psychic organization of the individual into three divisions represented in English by the unfortunate terms "id," "ego" and "super-ego." I do not believe these terms are particularly useful and shall instead substitute the threefold division suggested in the stratification model: basic security system, practical and discursive *consciousness*. I do not mean these to parallel the Freudian notions directly. The intersecting planes of the interpretative schemes and norms which actors utilize in the constitution of their conduct are embedded in all three dimensions of personality. . . . Freud, of course, regarded the individual as an agent but also often spoke of the id, ego and super-ego as agencies within the individual. . . . How can Freud then say such things as that the ego "decides on the repudiation of the incompatible idea?" Is the ego's deciding some sort of process in miniature of the agent's deciding? *This, surely, does not make much sense.*
>
> (1984: 41–2; emphasis added)

Giddens claims, correctly, that each of Freud's components of the person-ality (id, ego, super-ego) "is a miniature agent within the agent as such" (ibid.: 43). Only it is not obvious that this does not make much sense, as Giddens asserts. It does not make sense in relation to the modernist trajec-tory and context that informs Giddens's work, but it *does* make sense in relation to the cultural context in which Freud lived and worked. And it might still make *some* sense in our *fin de siècle* if points of contact were established between our cultural milieu and Freud's.

Regarding the first point, I mean that the idea of the id or unconscious behaving as an agent within the human agent is a refraction of Schopenhauer's insight that the will acts out its desires beneath and behind the façade of rational consciousness. As Ellenberger observes in *The Discovery of the Unconscious* (1970), this disturbing claim is the foundation for Freud's discovery that the human person is not master of his/her own house (self). This Schopenhauerian assessment of human agency does not make more or less sense than the modernist assessment of human agency as one in which rational consciousness controls the will. Rather, these are two different assessments that lead one to ponder where the truth of the matter might lie. Regarding the second point, it certainly seems that even in our *fin de siècle*, many human agents feel *as if* a second agent were driving them against their will when one considers the widespread social problems at the end of the twentieth century with addictions of various sorts, phobias, obsessions, uncontrollable consumption, and other apparent disorders of an insatiable will.

But Giddens is clearly not interested in such open-ended discussions. Instead, he forces Freud's anti-Enlightenment schemes into his modernist forms. Thus, according to Giddens (1984: 44), "'Unconscious' here means something different from its orthodox Freudian usage," without specifying that usage, namely, that for Freud the unconscious meant, among other things, the repository of sexual and violent urges pertaining to the id (see Laplanche and Pontalis 1973). But for Giddens, "unconscious" is analyzed in relation to states of being "conscious," *not* in relation to the unruly will. Thus, Freud's terminology of the id, ego, and super-ego is replaced by Giddens's terminology of unconscious motives/cognition, practical consciousness, and discursive consciousness respectively (1984: 7). It is fascinating that in making these substitutions and in analyzing Freud, Giddens does *not* rely on Laplanche, Pontalis, Ellenberger, or other well-known analysts of Freud. It is clear that Giddens is not a sensitive reader of other major social theorists.

In any event, Giddens's substitutions eradicate the Schopenhauerian element in Freud's vocabulary. Thus, for Giddens, "discursive consciousness means being able to put things into words" (ibid.: 45) – so much for the super-ego. Practical consciousness is the realm of what is routinized (ibid.: 7) – Freud's very complex depiction of the ego as involving the id to some extent has been jettisoned. Regarding Freud's use of the unconscious, transformed into the issue of unconscious *motives*, Giddens offers no definition, only a polemic with Freud's insistence that all acts have a motive:

> For Freud all human activities are motivated, including (for example) apparent triviata or "errors" such as slips of the tongue. Freud was often concerned precisely to demonstrate that phenomena which might be supposed to be "accidental" do, in fact, have their origin in (unconscious) motives. There is no particular reason to question the illuminating quality of Freud's insights in such matters. But it makes no more sense to claim that every act or gesture is motivated – meaning that a definite "motive" can be attached to it – than it does to treat action as involving a string of intentions or reasons. . . . Criticizing Freud's terminology of agency and self carries with it several implications. The "I" is an essential feature of the reflexive monitoring of action but should be identified neither with the agent nor with the self. By the "agent" or "actor" I mean the overall human subject located within the corporeal time-space of the living organism. The "I" has no image, as the

self does. The self, however, is not some kind of mini-agency within the agent. It is the sum of those forms of recall whereby the agent reflexively characterizes "what" is at the origin of his or her action. The self is the agent as characterized by the agent.

(ibid.: 49–51)

First, it is not self-evident that by "unconscious motivation" Freud meant anything like Giddens's characterization that every act must be attached to a specific motive. In line with readings of Freud by Laplanche and Pontalis (1973) and Ellenberger (1970), it could be that Freud meant simply that the "will" exerts a constant pressure on consciousness and is never asleep or "turned off." Second, note that through the use of various rhetorical devices, Giddens has succeeded in stripping Freud's concept of the unconscious of its most provocative and important elements, namely, its id-like qualities. Third, Giddens's alternative to Freud is completely vague and amounts to a cognitive, rationalist caricature of the agent. What could it possibly mean that the agent is the "overall human subject"? And if such a location includes the body, why does Giddens fail to address the many *passionate* demands made by the body (recalling that for Schopenhauer the body is the seat of the will)? Giddens has not defined, located, or even described human agency in a palpable way. The notion of agency remains, in his work, an ideological catch-all, an idealized vision of human empowerment minus the limitations to that empowerment captured by competing concepts from the previous *fin de siècle*.

Giddens is not more sensitive to Freud's disciples. Thus, in taking up Erik Erikson's work, Giddens reinterprets it in relation to Giddens's modernist vision of the world. For example, according to Giddens, "research into child development suggests rather strongly that the formation of capabilities for autonomous action meshes closely with understanding others to be agents" (1984: 58). Of course, this gets us no closer to understanding what agency means, nor appreciating how children might construe agency differently from adults. Furthermore, much like Giddens rereads and rewrites Durkheim and Freud through his own lenses, he reinterprets Erikson's famous stage of trust as follows:

A sense of trust in the continuity of the object-world and in the fabric of social activity, I shall suggest, depends upon certain specifiable connections between the individual agent and the social contexts through which that agent moves in the course of day-to-day life.

(ibid.: 60)

It is not clear what Giddens means, but it is clear that he has jettisoned the idea found in Erikson that trust is a fundamental *emotion* necessary for healthy psychic functioning, and that it is established in *infants* long before they begin to act like Giddens's agents. This is a very important point: long before the infant can put his or her feelings into words or monitor his/her desires or act as a skilled or knowledgeable agent in general, the infant either exhibits a happy and naive trust in the people around him/her or has already withdrawn into an unhealthy suspiciousness, hesitancy, and fundamental distrust of the world.

FAITH AND TRUST

Giddens's critics have noted that, ironically, he overemphasizes dependency and notions of security in his thought even though he seems to advocate agency. But I would elaborate further upon this criticism: Giddens's notion of trust is strangely mechanical and devoid of emotional connotations when he takes it up in *Modernity and Self-Identity* (1991a), *The Transformation of Intimacy* (1992b), and elsewhere in his writings. Giddens's notion of trust is not equivalent to "innocence" as described by David Riesman (1950) nor to the emotion of "happy confidence" represented by faith in Émile Durkheim's *The Elementary Forms of the Religious Life* ([1912] 1965). For Giddens, trust seems to be a synthetic, watered-down imitation of faith and innocence, a hyper-conscious, pro-agency version of innocence that is no longer innocent. Giddens tries to promote trust as part of the life politics he advocates, whereas I contend that cynical modernists are searching for the faith of traditional religions and for the lost innocence of childhood and the by-gone era of inner-directedness (Meštrović 1997). Giddens believes that "faith almost by definition rests on trust" (1991a: 196), but I contend that trust is derived from faith. Trust presupposes some degree of reflexivity, but faith is emotional and largely non-reflexive. Faith is required not only in the traditional domain of religion, but in science, politics, education, and most other modern institutions. Consider how the normal functioning of these and other societal institutions presupposes that most agents innocently have faith in the scientist's pronouncements, the politician's promises, the teacher's lectures, and so on. If one were routinely to question and doubt each of these social agents, the modern world as we know it could not function. Moreover, if one merely "trusts" scientists, politicians, teachers, and other important social agents, one has still kept a reserve of intellectual doubt and capacity for cynical questioning that is not the same as faith. Giddens seems to be aware of this fact in his own, ambiguous and jargon-filled way: "Abstract systems depend on trust, yet they provide none of the moral rewards which can be obtained from personalized trust, or were often available in traditional settings from the moral frameworks within which everyday life was undertaken" (ibid.: 136). Without using the word "faith," Giddens is really saying that faith has disappeared in modern societies and has been replaced by trust. He argues that a certain amount of risk and therefore diminution of trust have to be accepted as part of modernity, which places the notion of trust in a curious predicament in his discussion of life politics. My position is that without the emotional capacity for innocence and faith, the most fundamental commitments to children, spouses, authorities, and so on that are required in social life become problematic.

But the fundamental objection I raise against Giddens's writings on trust is that innocence and faith are acts of non-agency that paradoxically make agency possible. This is especially clear in children, who are universally regarded as innocent: children are powerless in relation to adults who take care of them, yet seem to place their faith in adults almost instinctively. This faith, in turn, *enables* them to take risks, build self-confidence, and develop a healthy self-concept. While adult commitments will never be that trusting and innocent, nevertheless, a certain amount of "letting go" – a deliberate decision to suspend agency – is a prerequisite for genuine, non-cynical faith in relationships and commitments that range from the most intimate to public faith in the pronouncements of scientists, teachers, and others, previously discussed. But Giddens's understanding of trust in relationship is never that trusting. Consider this passage from Giddens's *The Transformation of Intimacy* as illustration:

> In the pure relationship, trust has no external supports, and has to be developed on the basis of intimacy. Trust is a vesting of confidence in the other and also in the capability of the mutual bond to withstand future traumas. This is more than a matter of good faith only, problematic as that may be in itself. To trust the other is also to gamble upon the capability of the individual actually to be able to act with integrity.
>
> (1992b: 138)

The human agent who enters a relationship with such a calculating, cautious, and gaming attitude toward trust is paradoxically not an agent in the fullest sense of the term, because he or she is holding back in commitment. If one is weighing the capability of the bond to withstand future traumas as an index of how much to invest in the relationship, one is not really committed to the relationship. No amount of rhetorical skills by Giddens can obfuscate this straightforward truth.

SEARCHING FOR THE HEART OF SOCIOLOGY

It may be that the pessimistic and irrationalist orientation of Schopenhauer and the previous *fin de siècle* (see Meštrović 1991) have been so little reflected in twentieth-century social theory because so many social theorists have been "progressive." If not actually Marxists (in the rationalist sense, noted above), these progressive, mainstream types are scornful about contemporary, merely bourgeois society, or mass society, and all the other appellations that pertain to the unreflective tendencies in humans. Using Giddens's vocabulary, they cannot admit that human agents are simultaneously non-agents. Anthony Giddens fits into this progressive mold as he proclaims that human agents are almost always knowledgeable and skillful. His message is well received by the so-called mainstream of social theory. But what could this claim really mean? I am referring to statements by Giddens such as the following:

> Human agents or actors – I use these terms interchangeably – have, as an inherent aspect of what they do, the capacity to understand what they do while they do it.
>
> (1984: xxii)

> To be a human being is to be an agent – although not all agents are human beings – and to be an agent is to have power. "Power" in this highly generalized sense means "transformative capacity," the capability to intervene in a given set of events so as in some way to alter them.
>
> (1987: 7)

Is it not high time to restore some balance to social theory by questioning this blithe, progressive assumption? Are humans really that free and rational all or even most of the time? The human capacity and need for faith is part of an innocence that all children are born with, but that few modern cultures can sustain any longer. It is not sufficient for Giddens (1991a: 196) to dismiss the need for faith as a traditionalist throwback found in fundamentalism and authoritarianism. Faith addresses an important, non-rational and fundamentally emotional part of being human that Giddens and other mainstream theorists fail to address. Can contemporary social theorists still learn something about the limits of progress from the previous *fin de siècle?*

For example, Schopenhauer's most famous disciple, Friedrich Nietzsche, wrote with regard to the turn of the century that "the whole great tendency of the Germans ran counter to the Enlightenment, and to the revolution of society which, by a crude misunderstanding, was considered its consequence. . . . The cult of feeling was erected in place of the cult of reason" (1968: 84). Nietzsche claims that in their emphasis on emotions, the Germans produced "new and stronger geniuses of that very Enlightenment against which they were conjured up," and, to repeat the opening epigraph to this chapter:

86

This Enlightenment we must now advance further – unconcerned with the fact that there has been "a great revolution" against it, and then a "great reaction" again; indeed that both still exist; all this is mere play of the waves compared to that truly great tide in which *we* drift and want to drift.

(ibid.: 85)

Giddens does not delve into the revolution against the Enlightenment that occurred in the previous *fin de siècle*, and is only dimly aware of the roots of the great positivistic reaction to the *fin de siècle*. He never mentions the "other" Enlightenment to which Nietzsche alludes. Thus, his criticisms of positivism are incomplete. Because he fails to account for the vicissitudes of the Enlightenment project through the "cult of feeling" in the previous *fin de siècle*, he not only distorts the origins of the social sciences, he also fails to account for the need to reconcile the modernist worship of rationality with the emotions in almost every topic that he takes up. As a result, Giddens is *still* adrift in the sense that Nietzsche wrote over a hundred years ago.

Nietzsche makes an important and easily verifiable point about the German counter-Enlightenment. In addition to the progressive movement in the twentieth century, why was it generally ignored, not only by Giddens, but by other contemporary social theorists? Schopenhauer is not even mentioned by Giddens or other well-known theorists writing about Durkheim in general, nor by scholars writing about Durkheim's sociology of religion. The "climate of opinion" in which Durkheim wrote, a "climate" that emphasized irrationalism and pessimism, is similarly dismissed by Parsons (1937: 14) as being "irrelevant." Following Parsons, Giddens refuses to consider the role of irrational forces in his structuration theory. For example, he never delves into the issue of what the skilled, knowledgeable human agent might be repressing or otherwise might not know about his or her self.[1] He is not concerned with the passionate origins of human action prior to its crystallization into rational means for attaining a goal in relation to social structure. Similarly, he does not express concern with delusions, deliriums, or other irrationalities on the societal level, including the need for the human agent to have faith in his or her societal institutions.

This glaring oversight in Giddens's overly felicitous and hyper-rational vision of modern societies *disables* (in contrast to his emphasis on enablement) the sociologist from making sense of the origins of the social sciences and also from finding a place for irrationalities in modern societies. For example, Georg Simmel captured the sociological significance of Schopenhauer's philosophy for the previous *fin de siècle* when he wrote that:

With some few exceptions, which amount really to a *quantité négligeable*, all philosophers prior to Schopenhauer conceived of man as a rational being. . . . During the past several dozen years, the absolute preponderance of suffering over happiness in life is the definitive portrait of life's value that gave Schopenhauer's philosophy its general significance and signature, with respect to the culture of emotion. Schopenhauer made suffering into the absolute substance of emotionally experienced existence and did so against a manifold of pessimistic interpretations which declared the world to be a vale of tears, life not to be worth living, and happiness a passing dream: he made suffering into an *a priori* definition that grows out of the central roots of our existence, and made sure that none of its fruits could be of a different essence.

([1907] 1986: 53)

The theme of suffering, practically absent in Giddens's work (a fact noted also by Ian Craib [1992] and Fred Dallmayr [1982]), is of more than historical interest. Schopenhauer wrote about the importance of suffering over a hundred years ago, yet modern societies have enshrined suffering as an important contemporary social fact: consider all the talk and writing on victimhood, the suffering of minorities – current as well as historical – and the frequent disclosure of suffering on television news programs, talk shows, and other programs. Thus, there is no need or desire to be dogmatic about the choice of Schopenhauer's philosophy for the purposes of this analysis. Schopenhauer's thought is still relevant in the current *fin de siècle*. In fact, it should be of great sociological interest that in the present era strong social currents of pessimism, cynicism, and suffering co-exist with the faith in progress, optimism toward the future, and other modernist currents. Ironically, to live in what Giddens (1990) calls high modernity is to live with chronic risk, but this means that the human agent must necessarily be a pessimist. For example, when one takes out insurance on one's home, automobile, or spouse, one is admitting unconsciously the most pessimistic scenario for losing any of these objects of desire. But Giddens manages to derive optimism from risk culture:

> Low-probability high-consequence risks will not disappear in the modern world, although in an optimal scenario they could be minimized. . . . The risks involved are necessarily "unreal," because we could only have clear demonstration of them if events occurred that are too terrible to contemplate. Relatively small-scale events, such as the dropping of atomic bombs on Hiroshima and Nagasaki or the accidents at Three Mile Island or Chernobyl, give us some sense of what could happen. But these do not in any way bear upon the necessarily counterfactual character of other, more cataclysmic

happenings – the main basis of their "unreality" and the narcoticizing effects produced by the repeated listing of risks.

(ibid.: 134)

As an aside, I should say that I regard the dropping of atomic bombs on Hiroshima and Nagasaki not as relatively "small-scale" events, but as instances of genocide. Giddens lists some adaptive reactions to risk which he dismisses: pragmatic acceptance, sustained optimism, and cynical pessimism. He seems to settle for

what I shall call *radical engagement*, by which I mean an attitude of practical contestation towards perceived sources of danger. Those taking a stance of radical engagement hold that, although we are beset by major problems, we can and should mobilize either to reduce their impact or to transcend them. This is an optimistic outlook, but one bound up with contestatory action rather than a faith in rational analysis and discussion. Its prime vehicle is the social movement.

(ibid.: 137)

This version of optimism is commensurate with Giddens's stand on human agency: agents should protest and try to minimize perceived risks. No one would seriously disagree with such an admonition. Yet, beyond rhetoric, it offers little substance. My point is that even the leaders of social movements who protest risks and dangers to the public must necessarily betray an unconscious pessimism by taking out insurance or by taking other precautions, not only against the risks and dangers they seek to minimize, but against the risk of lawsuits and danger to their professions and reputations that stem from other social movements and leaders who oppose them. The other, underlying risk is that even such protests serve more cynical purposes.

Thus, in the USA, it is widely believed that President George Bush exploited the fear of crime in the Willie Horton advertisements in the presidential campaign against Michael Dukakis. (Horton was a convicted murderer who killed a twelve-year-old boy while on furlough.) Similarly, in the 1996 presidential campaign, the Clinton Administration exploited the very real dangers of smoking by running television advertisements that portrayed his opponent, Senator Robert Dole, as being soft on the risks of smoking, especially for children. Even if these marketing strategies were and are effective, they are clearly thought up by advertising agency with the aim of manipulating emotions. Such insight can only promote cynicism, not real agency. Thus, in modern societies, there is a risk even in mobilizing social movements to take actions against perceived risks. One's motives will be suspect.

But I do not wish to stay on Giddens's level of discussing risks. Instead, I would point out that there is something callous in Giddens's reduction of human suffering to risk. The quotation from Schopenhauer that serves as one of the epigraphs for this chapter still captures the unspeakable suffering for many people living today: slavery, torture, unlawful imprisonment, execution, incurable disease, genocidal wars and other sites of suffering still thrive in the current *fin de siècle*. Nietzsche may still have a point that optimism is a nihilistic response to such suffering, and Schopenhauer seems compelling to claim that pessimism is a moral and compassionate response.

HOW GIDDENS ATTEMPTS TO ACCOUNT FOR EMOTION IN HUMAN HISTORY

In this section, I will analyze Giddens's attempt to account for the emotional lacunae in modernism as illustrated in his *The Transformation of Intimacy* (1992b). In summary, rather than invoking any sort of complex reading of the philosophical origins of sociology or the traditional antecedents of modernity – which, as Tocqueville claimed, enshrined emotionally laden habits of the heart as the centerpiece of culture – Giddens engages in what comes across as crude male chauvinism: he equates rationality with men and emotion with women, and then concludes, in his typically ambiguous manner, with a discussion of the transformation of this highly debatable polarity into a "reflexive" phenomenon. But again, it is more important to note that Giddens follows Parsons's lead in this as in other regards: Parsons attributed instrumental roles to males and expressive roles to females. A generation of sociologists accepted this crude dualism without much protest. In face, this simplistic dualism can be traced as far back as Auguste Comte's writings, and further. (Of course, it should be obvious that women can hold instrumental roles and men can be expressive.) In any event, Giddens begins this aspect of the discussion as follows:

> There is *no room for passion* in the routinized settings which provide us with security in modern social life. Yet *who can live without passion*, if we see it as the motive-power of conviction? Emotion and motivation are inherently connected. *Today we think of motivation as "rational"* – the driving pursuit of profit on the part of the entrepreneur, for example – but if emotion is wholly resistant to rational assessment and ethical judgement, motives can never be appraised except as means to ends, or in terms of their consequences. This is what Weber saw in interpreting the motives of the early industrialists as energized by religious conviction. However, in so doing Weber took for granted, and even elevated to the status of an epistemology, what is distinctively problematic about modernity: *the impossibility of evaluating emotion.* Seen as a life-political

issue, *the problem of the emotions is not one of retrieving passion, but of developing ethical guidelines for the appraisal or justification of conviction.* The therapist says, "Get in touch with your feelings." Yet in this regard therapy connives with modernity.

(ibid.: 201; emphasis added)

Given that we have established thus far that Giddens has no real room for emotions in his thought, he hardly has any alternative – in order to be logically consistent – than to dismiss the importance of emotionalism on its own terms, and to reinterpret emotions as a "problem" such that emotions are transformed into rational "conviction" in modern times. I simply do not agree with him that there is no room for passion in contemporary social life. On the contrary, I have argued that our *fin de siècle* is one of exuberant passion, from explosive indignation to the cult of being "nice" (Meštrović 1997). But the closest that Giddens can come to recognizing emotionalism in contemporary life is to admit that "emotion becomes a life-political issue in numerous ways with the latter-day development of modernity" (1992b: 202). By the time emotion becomes an "issue," it is has been so thoroughly rationalized and processed through cognitive filters that it is hardly recognizable as emotion. Given that throughout his work he is not interested in the traditional antecedents to issues that involve emotions, his historical explanation for the state of affairs in which emotions are transformed into life-political "issues" is curious, and seemingly sexist:

> With the development of modern societies, control of the social and natural worlds, *the male domain*, became focused through *"reason."* Just as reason, guided by disciplined investigation, was set off from tradition and dogma, so it was also with emotion. As I have said, this presumed not so much a massive psychological process of repression as an institutional division between reason and *emotion*, a division *that closely followed gender lines. The identifying of women with unreason, whether in serious vein (madness) or in seemingly less consequential fashion (women as the creatures of caprice), turned them into the emotional underlaborers of modernity.* Along the way emotion, and forms of social relations inspired by it . . . became seen as refractory to ethical considerations. Reason cuts away at ethics because of the difficulty of finding empirical arguments to justify moral convictions.
>
> (ibid.: 200; emphasis added)

In contradistinction to Giddens, I have argued in *Durkheim and Postmodern Culture* (1992) that masculine and feminine are two arbitrary cultural labels for forms of expression that apply equally to males and females. Even if rationality has been associated with males in some – but not all – traditional stereotypes, and emotionalism with females, the obvious truth is that males have recourse to a "feminine" (emotional) voice in this regard, and females have recourse to a "masculine" (rational) voice. These two voices need to be balanced, in the manner suggested by Durkheim, for example, such that, metaphorically speaking, society is simultaneously mother and father.[2] By this he meant that society is held together by emotional sentiment as well as rational duty, but that neither principle is superior to the other nor self-sufficient. But far from deconstructing or criticizing the cruel stereotypes which associate one gender with a particular mode of relating to the world (rational versus emotional), Giddens accepts the stereotype as a historical given and opts implicitly for the rational-male "solution." This is how I interpret his line about the difficulty of finding empirical arguments to justify moral convictions. It is worth noting that Carol Gilligan's (1982) focus on a feminine voice in morality to offset Lawrence Kohlberg's (1981) masculine voice – his guiding assumption that morality is strictly a matter of correct moral *reasoning* – is relevant to discussions of this sort, but is conspicuously absent in Giddens's analysis.

In any event, Giddens claims that "Freud rediscovered emotion – through his interpretations of female psychology – but in his thought it remained tied to the dictates of reason" (1992b: 200). This is another curious revisionism of Freud, because he clearly dealt with emotion vis-à-vis many phenomena other than female psychology, and it is not obvious that his conceptualization of emotion remained rational. But the more important point seems to be that Giddens seems to approve, to some extent, of this modernized re-appreciation of Freud, adding: "A passion is today something admitted to only reluctantly or embarrassedly, even in respect of sexual behavior itself, partly because its place as a 'compelling force' has been usurped by addiction" (ibid.: 201). And addictions, for Giddens, are amenable to rational control:

> In a post-traditional order, the narrative of self has in fact continually to be reworked, and life-style practices brought in line with it. . . . Once institutional reflexivity reaches into virtually all parts of everyday social life, almost any pattern or habit can become an addiction. The idea of addiction makes little sense in a traditional culture, where it is normal to do today what one did yesterday.
>
> (ibid.: 75)

It is not at all self-evident how a modern addiction, in the sense used by Giddens, is different from a traditionalist's doing today what one did yesterday. Don't addicts do today what they did yesterday? Giddens's point seems to be that the modernists have "an obligation to discover themselves in their actions and habits" (ibid.). According to Giddens,

Addictions, then, are a negative index of the degree to which the reflexive project of self moves to center-stage in late modernity. . . . An addiction is an inability to colonize the future and as such transgresses one of the prime concerns with which individuals now reflexively have to cope.

(ibid.: 76)

Thus, Giddens writes, if "romantic love was essentially feminized love" (ibid.: 43) that was "incompatible with lust" (ibid.: 45), then the modern sexual revolution is the freedom of decentered sexuality, unshackled from the needs of reproduction, that can lead to a democratized intimacy. "Who says sexual emancipation, in my view, says sexual democracy" (ibid.: 182). Modernist women emancipate themselves from the constraints of romantic love and from emotionalism in general:

The more sexuality became detached from reproduction, and integrated within an emerging reflexive project of self, the more this institutional system of [sexual] repression came under tension. Women became charged, de facto, with managing the transformation of intimacy which modernity has set in train. The system of institutional repression was from the beginning subject to strain because of the exclusion of women from the public sphere.

(ibid.: 178)

Again, Giddens introduces but does not challenge the stereotypes to which I have alluded earlier: "The fostering of democracy in the public domain was at first largely a male project," whereas the democratization of personal life "is a process in which women have thus far played the prime role" (ibid.: 184). But Giddens seems mostly unaware that in positing the democratization of modern intimacy in this manner, he is implicitly giving privilege to the male model of rationality. First, I do not agree that public democracy was either an exclusively male project or even a wholly beneficial one, for democracy depends upon sentiments and passions every bit as much as it depends upon rationalism. And democracies have had their share of racism, oppression, imperialism, and other social evils. Second, because Giddens's model of the female democratization of power might involve emotions, he relies instead on reflexively derived "convictions." Thus, ironically, he discounts a feminine contribution to democracy. In effect, he is arguing, albeit implicitly and in his typical Giddens-like style, that the girls want to be like the boys.

THE PARADOX OF AGENCY
LEADING TO LESS AGENCY

An important corollary to Schopenhauer's portrait of the mind versus the heart conceived as a dualistic *unity* (neither a dualism nor a duality, using Giddens's vocabulary) is that the heart is stronger than the mind, and the will (passion) is stronger than the representation. If, for the sake of argument, one accepts Giddens's chauvinist dualism between men (rationality) and women (emotion), the Schopenhauerian conclusion would be that emotion is superior to rationality, and women are superior to men. This is an important observation because it exposes the implicit and largely unanalyzed assumption in Giddens's and other modernists' work that rationality is superior to tradition and emotion. In general, Schopenhauer turns upside down the Enlightenment understanding of human nature, in which the mind is ultimately granted a superior position in relation to the heart, while Giddens and other mainstream theorists cling to it. By this summary, I do not mean to enter into a discussion of Schopenhauer's own misogyny and chauvinism, which is of a different sort from Giddens's, only to expose an important presupposition in Giddens's thought.

According to Schopenhauer ([1818] 1969a: 311), the will "is a constant striving without aim and without rest" that is inexorably insatiable. Lasting happiness is impossible in Schopenhauer's scheme because of the insatiability of the will. Moreover – and this is a crucial point for trying to analyze Giddens as a modernist – that insatiability is exacerbated, not appeased, by enlightenment, knowledge, and heightened consciousness:

> Awakened to life out of the night of unconsciousness, the will finds itself as an individual in an endless and boundless world ... its desires are unlimited, its claims inexhaustible, and every satisfied desire gives birth to a new one. No possible satisfaction in the world could suffice to still its craving, set a final goal to its demands, and fill the *bottomless pit* of its heart.
>
> (Schopenhauer [1818] 1969b: 573; emphasis added)

Compare Schopenhauer's intent, even terminology, with Durkheim's famous dictum in *Suicide* that human desires are "unlimited so far as they depend on the individual alone. Irrespective of any external regulatory force, our capacity for feeling is in itself an insatiable and bottomless abyss" ([1897] 1951: 247). But isn't Durkheim's characterization remarkably similar to Freud's original depiction of the id (see Meštrović 1988)? Durkheim aligns anomie with civilization, progress, and the development of the division of labor, in line with Freud's depiction of civilization and its discontents. In contrast to Freud and Durkheim, Giddens is oblivious to any negative consequences of knowledge and skill on the part of the human agent (I will return to this omission in the following chapter). For Giddens, reflexivity and rationality seem to be good in an unqualified sense.

While Giddens is clearly aware that Parsons misrepresented Durkheim's position on anomie, he does not clarify what Durkheim might have meant; sees no commonalities to Freud's writings on the id; ignores the interaction of emotion and rationality in anomie; and he certainly does not seek a place for the concept of anomie or an equivalent in his theory. Again, Giddens is not unique, but a typical modernist theorist in these and other regards. For example, he writes:

> Durkheim's treatment of anomie offers some recognition of interest-conflict in so far as anomic "deregulation" derives from a situation in which actors have definite aspirations which are not "realizable" (an avenue later developed by Merton), rather than from a moral vacuum, an absence of moral norms which are binding upon actions. But this possibility, which could have been linked to the analysis of what Durkheim referred to as the "forced division of labor," and thereby to the analysis of class conflict, remained largely unexplored in Durkheim's writings, and disappears from view in Parsons's theoretical scheme altogether, since Parsons defines anomie as "the polar antithesis of full institutionalization," or "the complete breakdown of normative order."
>
> (1993: 105)

Giddens, like Parsons before him, misses completely Durkheim's anti-Enlightenment spin on anomie as a universal human condition of insatiable passion that is exacerbated by modernity and its rationalist fruits. To put this in the vocabulary of Giddens: the more that modernists act like knowledgeable and skilled agents, the more vulnerable they become to the insatiable will and to anomie. This is a subtle paradox that Giddens's blunt depiction of agency cannot capture. I shall return to it in chapter 7.

Durkheim ([1912] 1965: 354–6) concludes his classic work on religion with the gloomy claim that suffering is the price one must pay for social life to exist. This is because of Schopenhauer's and Durkheim's extreme interpretation of the general Western theme that humans are torn between society's representations and their own lustful, desiring bodies, and that this tension can never be overcome completely. By contrast, Giddens offers a disembodied vision of the human agent as solely a meaning-making organism whose representational capacities are not at war with desires emanating from the body.

DURKHEIM'S DEPICTION OF FAITH IN
RELATION TO EMOTIONAL LIFE

Although I began this chapter with Freud, a discussion of this sort must lead inevitably to Durkheim, and especially to Durkheim's theory of religion. Durkheim was concerned with the sociology of religion for reasons that Giddens seems to shun this topic: religion is a traditional phenomenon concerned with *emotions* that carries over into modern times and refuses to disappear; religion concerns *faith*, not trust; all other social institutions evolve out of religion. In contradistinction to Durkheim, Giddens writes in *The Consequences of Modernity*:

> The declining impact of religion and tradition has been so frequently discussed in the literature of the social sciences that we can deal with this quite briefly. Secularization is no doubt a complex matter and does not seem to result in the complete disappearance of religious thought and activity – probably because of the purchase of religion upon some of the existential questions previously referred to. Yet most of the situations of modern social life are manifestly incompatible with religion as a pervasive influence upon day-to-day life. Religious cosmology is supplanted by reflexively organized knowledge, governed by empirical observation and logical thought, and focused upon material technology and socially applied codes. Religion and tradition were always closely linked, and the latter is even more thoroughly undermined than the former by the reflexivity of modern social life, which stands in direct opposition to it.
>
> (1990: 109)

Giddens, like most other contemporary social theorists, assumes that religion is a matter of self-conscious identification and "activity" pertaining to a church, and, in that sense, religion is indeed declining. But the cornerstone of Durkheim's understanding of religion is that it involves the absolute heterogeneity of the categories sacred and profane ([1912] 1965: 7), and, in that sense, religion never declines – it is merely transformed into new categories of sacred and profane representations. The sacred, for Durkheim, is a mental category that can attach itself synthetically to flags, nations, causes, ideas, institutions, and a host of other phenomena. Thus, the patriot, nationalist, activist, scientist, and other social types can be said to be partaking in religion even if they never set foot in a church and do not subscribe to any church dogma. Durkheim's understanding of religion is much more fruitful than Giddens's and other modernist understandings, and clearly more relevant for understanding the many types of "worship" of "sacred" totems in modern societies, from rock and roll stars to politicians. In sum, Durkheim's

96

writings lay the foundation for apprehending *civil religions*, which have not disappeared in contemporary times. On the contrary, such deification of persons, places, and things seems to have increased in the present *fin de siècle*, when one considers all the new nations, national myths, celebrities, and cults that have appeared.

For Durkheim, an object is sacred because it inspires "a collective sentiment" of respect which removes it from the profane or the pedestrian (ibid.: 307). Various Durkheimian scholars, including Giddens, have objected to the fact that Durkheim imposes only two categories, reasoning logically that there might exist three or more categories, including the category of the mundane. Scholars also tend to read Durkheim's discourse on the sacred and the profane from the vantage point of a sociology of knowledge, as strictly cognitive categories. These and other pedantic responses to Durkheim's sociology of religion seem to miss completely Durkheim's point that the sacred is the site of society's *emotional* effervescence so that the profane is the mundane, the dreary and unemotional. All these picayune objections are passé by now, and are beside the more important point that if Durkheim is correct, then society's collective effervescence is the real source of emotion and postemotionalism. Thus, *an important distinction between Giddens, Parsons, Comte, and other modernists versus Durkheim seems to be that modernists associate women with emotionalism whereas Durkheim associates the category of the sacred with emotionalism.* Of course, Giddens and the modernists make no place for the category of the sacred in his thought.

For the purposes of the present analysis, the most important aspect of Durkheim's characterization of religion is that it applies to nearly all of society and culture to the extent that these involve the category of the sacred. For Durkheim, a religious character is to be found in the notion of private property, science, respect for authority and government, the use of currency, respect for the flag, even traditional taboos associated with women, along with many other phenomena that Giddens and other modernist theorists do not regard as religious and believe to exemplify reflexive agency. Because Durkheim felt that *faith* underlies the authority of rites and rituals found in diverse social phenomena (ibid.: 403), it follows that the diminution of faith caused by general enlightenment afflicts society's ability to function as a whole. This is the devastating inference to be drawn from a contextual, *fin de siècle* reading of Durkheim's classic on religion, and it poses a serious challenge to Giddens's and other modernist efforts to patch up the strains caused by modernity with the synthetic, reflexive, and mostly abstract category of trust.

Durkheim also claims that religion must involve "delirious imagination" (ibid.: 107) and that religion and myth are inseparable. This sounds like Nietzsche's central thesis in the *Birth of Tragedy*, even the theme in T.S. Eliot's "The Waste Land," except that Durkheim claims that the *sacred is the real*: religion cannot be built on an illusion even if it does involve delirium (ibid.: 86). According to Durkheim, religion may be *emotionally* a delirium, but it is a well-founded one because it is based on emotional realities created by the group (ibid.: 258). All social thought, like all religious thought, is in a sense delirious, that is, based on socially agreed upon sentiments, feelings, ideas, and values (for example, the flag, postage stamps, blood, emblems, and so on).

Thus, let us examine Durkheim's rhetoric in his long-winded discussion of the clan, totem, and other sacred categories. According to Durkheim, these sites of the sacred involve "collective enthusiasms," "collective passions," "collective sentiments," the "reinforcement of common faith," "energy," "sensations," "respect," "passionate energies," "effervescence," "transports of enthusiasm," "social life," and "religious life" (ibid.: 220–52 *passim*). The sacred involves the "enthusiastic," the "emotional," the "concentrated," and "ceremonies," while the profane involves the "uniform," the "languishing," and the "dull" (ibid.: 246). In fact, according to Durkheim, all social life involves the social periodicity of sacred transports of enthusiasm with ordinary, profane, routine. This is why societies establish holy calendars, feast days, holidays, and all sorts of celebrations. One can hardly resist the generalization that the sacred is the site of the emotional.

When the aborigines or other traditionalists engage in totemism, they are really participating *emotionally* in collective representations, or, more accurately, representations of the collectivity. One must keep in mind that the representation is not only a cognitive category for Durkheim, but involves passion and idea as a Schopenhauerian unity, as I have demonstrated in *The Barbarian Temperament* (1993a) and elsewhere. Thus, totems are engraved on woodwork and walls, totem poles, even on bodies, but in all cases, the totem as name or emblem is also a sacred thing. Sanctuaries are established; totems are kept in sacred places; there are collective treasuries, sacred oak trees, and so on. The totem is treated with the emotions of devotion, respect, and awe. By extension, the totemic believer is also sacred: he or she bears the totemic mark and thereby partakes in the sacredness of the totemic mark.

Totemic mythology and other mythologies weave genealogical connections between humans and Nature. Traditional religions teach a "mystic sympathy" (ibid.: 174) between humans and things. But Durkheim felt that modern societies must achieve these same episodes of collective effervescence and emotional transport in order to exist. Robert N. Bellah (1967) captured some of this Durkheimian intent with his controversial notion of "civil religion." There can be no doubt that both Durkheim and Bellah are correct: contemporary societies still attempt at least to *imitate* the collective emotional excitement of traditional societies by bestowing a contagious sanctity to money, emblems, celebrities, dates, battles, places, and ideas. Rationality alone is not sufficient to bind individuals together in a society. Had Giddens taken up this aspect of Durkheim's thought or Bellah's, he probably would concur, because in his latter writings (Giddens 1994) he writes of the need to establish *synthetic* traditions. But modern types are cynical: they have lost the capacity for faith as well as spontaneous emotion, and one should question whether an artificially concocted notion of trust can act as a substitute for faith, or whether a synthetically created civil religion can substitute for civil religions created through spontaneous collective effervescence. Referring back to Riesman's (1950) metaphor of the Milky Way of choices that confronts the other-directed type, one can rephrase this as follows: there are too many alternatives, choices, and interpretations in the modernist sky – all of which can be debunked, deconstructed, and de-differentiated – to allow the modernist type to feel faith in his or her decisions to act. This is a key point for Durkheim: *faith is before all else an impetus to action* ([1912] 1965: 479). Without faith and its derivatives – the emotion of happy confidence, reliance on others, shared sentiments, and so on – one *cannot* act as Giddens's enabled, reflexive, and emancipated agent. More than knowledge and use of structure for enablement are required for agency. One senses a collective loss of faith in contemporary phenomena that range from the inability of many persons to choose a person to marry to the inability of the West to choose a course of action to stop the slaughter in Bosnia.

Durkheim concluded that despite individual differences in interpreting events, collective representations present guarantees of objectivity precisely because they are collective, hence generalized and persistent. This faith in the objectivity of the collectivity was the basis of his infamous concept of "social facts." Interestingly, this is one of the most vilified concepts in sociology, as we have seen in chapter 3. American sociologists, especially, but Giddens as well, object to the apparent anti-individualism that accompanies this concept: "The point here is that 'social facts' have properties that confront each single individual as 'objective' features which limit that individual's scope of action" (Giddens 1984: 172). Yet without this guarantee of some sort of objectivity, individuals are left in a Tower of Babel of private meanings, are unable to produce states of collective effervescence, and are unable to experience faith in societal institutions of diverse sorts.

Oblivious to the Schopenhauerian flavor in Durkheim's approach to faith and society, Giddens refers to Durkheim's epistemology as "sociological Kantianism" (1978: 84). To Durkheim's claim that society is the origin of conceptual categories, Giddens replies:

> A Kantian could simply reply that the recognition of social time or social space already presupposes the discrimination which it purports to explain; one could not grasp concepts of time and space without possessing the faculty of organizing one's experience in these terms.
>
> (ibid.: 105)

A Schopenhauerian retort to Giddens's Kantian reply would be that mental categories are not sufficient for knowledge or action. The human agent must *believe* that the social categories (whether they originate *a priori* or for Durkheim, culturally) are accurate in order to act. But this presupposes faith, and belief is a matter of the will or passion, not cognition.

The rest of Durkheim's discussion of the drawbacks to Kantianism ([1912] 1965: 488–96) involves a critique of Kant in the context of Schopenhauer's philosophy, as depicted above. Durkheim begins by arguing that Kant fails to account for the empirical, perceptual origins of the *a priori* categories of time, space, and force (ibid.: 488) – a move anticipated by Schopenhauer. Durkheim even adds a new category that subsumes all the others, the category of "all" or "totality," whose empirical origin is society:

> This idea of *all*, which is at the basis of the classifications which we have just cited, could not have come from the individual himself. . . . And yet there is perhaps no other category of greater importance; for as the role of the categories is to envelop all the other concepts, the category *par excellence* would seem to be this very concept of *totality*. The theorists of knowledge ordinarily postulate it as if it came of itself, while it really surpasses the contents of each individual consciousness taken alone to an infinite degree.
>
> (ibid.: 489)

Thus, the concept of "totality" does not originate *a priori*, but originates in a vague, obscure, even unconscious *perception* or feeling or intuition of society. The closest parallel in Giddens's thought might be the concept of structure, but Giddens does not explore how structure comes to be known or intuited. Furthermore, and in line with Durkheim's critique of Kant, Giddens fails to account for the origins of the perception of structure. Giddens really does treat structure as a mental category that is self-begotten. This problem must be confronted: how does the human agent come to perceive structure? Durkheim adds in a footnote that "at bottom, the concept of totality, that of society and that of divinity are very probably only different aspects of the same notion" (ibid.: 490). It must also be noted that Durkheim does not regard society as purely conceptual. On the contrary, he writes that society "has its own personal physiognomy" (ibid.: 493), that it is "the most powerful combination of physical and moral forces" (ibid.: 495), that it expresses itself in various perceived rhythms (ibid.: 490), sensation (ibid.: 13–16), and so on. It is clear that Durkheim argued that society is somehow *felt* by individuals in addition to being known cognitively. It is important to highlight this aspect of Durkheim's conceptualization of society in order to demonstrate that Giddens and other modernists are wrong to accuse Durkheim of presenting society as static or mechanical, and to note that modernist conceptualizations of society do not mention rhythms or other living properties.

Consider the introduction to the *Elementary Forms*. Like Schopenhauer, Durkheim attacks the notion of *a priorism* on the grounds that it leads to an empty game of concepts devoid of empirical content: "Thus in so far as they [*a priori* concepts] aid us in thinking of the physical or biological world, they have only the value of artificial symbols, useful practically perhaps, but having no connection with reality" ([1912] 1965: 31). Durkheim elaborates:

> It is said that an [*a priori*] idea is necessary when it imposes itself upon the mind by some sort of virtue of its own, without being accompanied by any proof. It contains within it something which constrains the intelligence and which leads to its acceptance without preliminary examination. The apriorist postulates this singular quality but does not account for it: for saying that the categories are necessary because they are indispensable to the functioning of the intellect is simply repeating that they are necessary.
>
> (ibid.: 29–30)

In a self-consciously but obviously problematic, non-Kantian (ibid.: 23) and non-Cartesian (ibid.: 16) manner, Durkheim argues that religion should not be studied as a "logical concept, a pure possibility, constructed simply by force or thought," but rather "what we must find is a concrete reality" (ibid.). Like Schopenhauer, whose philosophy attempts to lift the veil of phenomenal appearances to get to the reality of things (namely, the will that objectifies itself in phenomena), Durkheim argues that in the study of religion "one must know how to go underneath the symbol to the reality which it represents and which gives it its meaning" (ibid.: 14). We have seen in chapter 3 that this search for "reality" is the basis of a fundamental difference in Durkheim's old versus Giddens's new rules of sociological method. One can add at this point that for Durkheim, "reality" seems to be primarily something emotional and social.

Durkheim attacks both *a priorism* and a naive empiricism on grounds similar to Schopenhauer's, claiming that "the rationalism which is immanent in the sociological theory of knowledge is thus midway between the classical empiricism and apriorism" ([1912] 1965: 31). He also argues that society is the perceptual, sensual origin of Kant's categories, that "the categories are . . . essentially collective representations" dependent on society's "morphology, upon its religious, moral and economic institutions, etc." (ibid.: 28). For Durkheim, society is "natural," "objective," and expressive of the "nature of things" (ibid.: 31–2), not an *a priori* concept. Indeed, later in the book he concludes: "It is unquestionable that a society has all that is necessary to arouse the *sensation* of the divine in minds" (ibid.: 236), and that "society also gives us the *sensation* of a perpetual dependence" (ibid.: 237), and so on (emphasis added). In other words, society is not just another Kantian category, but the perceptual origin of these categories.

Schopenhauer's philosophy seems to explain Durkheim's many claims in *Elementary Forms* that science and religion were born from the same "spirit" (ibid.: 87); that science is not essentially different from primitive cosmologies (ibid.: 270); that "between the logic of religious thought and that of scientific thought there is no abyss" (ibid.: 271); and that "scientific thought is only a more perfect form of religious thought" (ibid.: 477). These assertions run contrary to Comte's belief that metaphysics and theology would eventually be supplanted by science, and they seem to reflect the Schopenhauerian view that both religion and science are merely systems of representations used to account for raw, empirical perceptions. Durkheim's view on the religious aspects of science – even in modern societies – also contradicts Giddens's (1993) claims that Durkheim enshrined value-free natural science as the model for the social sciences. On the contrary, Durkheim seems to put science "in its place," and it is a low place as judged from Comte's perspective. Note also that contrary to Giddens's claims, Durkheim strongly disagrees with Comte in this very important regard concerning the relationship of religion to science.

The most important conclusion that Durkheim draws from this linkage between science and religion is that the modern institution of science requires *faith* every bit as much as traditional religion. Durkheim is explicit:

> At bottom, the confidence inspired by scientific concepts is due to the fact that they can be methodically controlled. But a collective representation is necessarily submitted to a control that is repeated indefinitely; the men who accept it verify it by their own experience. It is true that it may express this by means of imperfect symbols; *but scientific symbols themselves are never more than approximate.* On the other hand, it is not at all true that concepts, even when constructed according to the rules of science, get their authority uniquely from their objective value. *It is not enough that they be true to be believed. If they are not in harmony with the other beliefs and opinions, or in a word, with the mass of the other collective representations, they will be denied; minds will be closed to them; consequently it will be as though they did not exist.* Today it is generally sufficient that they bear the stamp of science to receive a sort of privileged credit, because we have *faith in science. But this faith does not differ essentially from religious faith.*
>
> ([1912] 1965: 486; emphasis added)

For Durkheim, in modern times, science is taking away from religion its speculative (cognitive) function. Science will even supersede religion in this cognitive arena (ibid.: 478). But religion will not disappear. While religion must reckon with the authority of science (ibid.: 479), the irony is that scientific authority is religious in nature. Science cannot extend its domain over many fields in modern times without assuming that modernists will have faith in scientific findings and exhibit respect for scientific authority. I believe that Durkheim's insight in this regard is still applicable, and is devastating for Giddens's and other modernist projects: Giddens assumes that scientific reflexivity can undo some of the negative "consequences of modernity," but he fails to investigate the emotional base for science and reflexivity.

THE EMOTIONAL COMPONENTS OF
SOCIAL STRUCTURE

There is no overt emotional component to social structure in Giddens's work: structuration, for him, is purely abstract. As we have seen, Giddens touches on emotion fleetingly here and there, as in his discussions of Freud, women, and nationalism, but emotion is not an integral part of his work as a whole. In this section, I intend to contrast Durkheim's treatment of women and emotionalism in general in order to expose further the limitations of Giddens's thought.

More pages in *Elementary Forms* are devoted to the ideas of mana, force, blood, and other variations of the sacred than to any other theme. Durkheim's obsession with these derivatives of the will is made more comprehensible when we review his essay "Incest: The Nature and Origin of the Taboo," the first essay published in the first issue of the journal he founded in 1897, *L'Année sociologique* (reprinted in Durkheim [1897] 1963). Schopenhauer makes the interesting remark that "the will objectifies itself most immediately in the *blood* as that which originally creates and forms the organism" ([1818] 1969b: 255). Similarly, in the *Elementary Forms* Durkheim writes that "the blood is in itself a sacred liquid" ([1912] 1965: 148). In general, "there is no religious ceremony where blood does not have some part to play" (ibid.: 60). "Man also has something sacred about him," namely "the blood and the hair" (ibid.: 159). In his 1897 essay, Durkheim argues that the totem is perceived as the original ancestor of the group since its "life force" resides in blood. Because of this, "all blood is terrible and all sorts of taboos are instituted to prevent contact with it" ([1897] 1963: 83). In other words, blood is sacred, and one reacts to it by separating it from the vulgar, the pedestrian, and the profane. Thus, according to Durkheim, "the taboo is none other than this abstention, organized and elevated to the height of an institution" (ibid.: 96).

According to Durkheim,

> the blood is taboo in a general way, and it taboos all that enters into contact with it. . . . Thus the woman, in a rather chronic manner, is the theater of these bloody demonstrations.

> (ibid.: 85)

Women are associated with blood during the burst of puberty, menstruation, the sexual act, and childbirth. Thus, during these phases in a female's life, women were taboo in traditional societies: they were often removed from contact with social life, often cruelly and irrationally. Clearly, Giddens is wrong to claim that Durkheim was unaware of the role of power in the vicissitudes of agency and structure. Durkheim is poignantly aware of power as a social category. Yet Durkheim argues that the abstention associated with women and blood is an extension of the general taboo associated with blood as the life-force of the group:

> The religious respect that blood inspires proscribes any idea of contact, and, since the woman, so to speak, passes a part of her life in blood, this same feeling involves her, marks her with its imprint, and isolates her.

> (ibid.: 90)

Durkheim goes as far as to suggest that psychological distinction between the sexes is something like religion:

> The two sexes must avoid each other with the same care as the profane flees from the sacred, and the sacred from the profane; and any infraction of this rule invokes a feeling of horror which does not differ in its nature from that which confronts the person who violates a taboo.

> (ibid.: 72)

One should note that Durkheim regards women, not men, as sacred.

Let me list several aspects of Durkheim's assessment that are relevant to the present discussion. Concerning Giddens's neat and tidy dismissal of anthropology as the study of the past or the traditional while sociology studies the modern, Durkheim is clearly able to find connections between modern and traditional concerns. Nor are his thoughts irrelevant to modern times because blood still evokes the emotions that Durkheim describes. In fact, it is interesting that in his discussion of women Giddens does *not* delve into puberty, menstruation, and childbirth, all of which involve blood, and which simply cannot be dealt with by a masculine sort of reflexivity alone. Moreover, Durkheim's assessment is verified by many anthropological studies: it is true that in traditional societies especially, women are taboo at precisely the junctures he specifies. Finally, Durkheim subsumes the traditional emotional reactions to women, sociologically speaking (for the taboo is part of the category of the sacred), under the general category of the sacred. In other words, women are not associated with emotion on the basis of some crude chauvinism, but because they are associated with the sacred, and the sacred is emotional. Again, there is plenty of anthropological and historical evidence to suggest that female deities preceded male deities precisely because the traditional mind associated them with the mysteries of life and blood. This is not to suggest that such deification of women was not cruel or oppressive – on the contrary. But as Henry Adams ([1901] 1983) and others have observed, femininity was perceived to be a power and a force stronger than rationality for many centuries prior to the previous *fin de siècle*.

Some scholars are fond of pointing out that Durkheim's distinction between the sacred and the profane cannot be "empirically verified" by more contemporary ethnographers studying the aborigines or other traditional peoples. In the context of Durkheim's complicated epistemology, these authors seem to expect a Kantian category to jump out of the Australian bush. Their criticism entirely misses Durkheim's point: namely, that the *conceptual* distinction between the sacred and profane is all around us at all times; only it is hidden as if behind a veil, and it owes its *perceptual* basis to the notion of blood as the primal symbol for the will to life. For "empirical verification," Durkheim points to the so-called war between the sexes, present among the aborigines as well as so-called civilized peoples:

> In all probability, one must say that, if in our schools, in our daily meetings, a sort of barrier exists between the sexes: if each of them has a determined form of clothing imposed by habit or even by law; if the male has functions which are forbidden to the female, even though she might be well suited to fulfill them, and if the reciprocal is true; if, in our daily relationships with women, the men have adopted a special language, special mannerisms, etc., this is in part due to the fact that, some thousands of years ago, our fathers structured the reality of blood in general, and menstrual blood in particular, in the manner that we have suggested.
>
> ([1897] 1963: 113)

This is a fantastic explanation, to be sure. Schopenhauer argues that the will exists independently of the Kantian categories, including time and space. Hence, it is possible in Schopenhauer's philosophy for a perception that is thousands of years old still to operate today. Both Freud and Durkheim seem to have accepted this argument to some extent. Giddens's theory denies or does not concern itself with the question whether historical taboos can still operate in contemporary, modern societies. In support of Giddens, one might argue that modern women are surely freed from these terribly repressive constraints vis-à-vis blood. Is not one consequence of the women's movement that the barriers between men and women which Durkheim likens to an irrational religion have been finally overcome? This seems to be one of Giddens's implicit arguments in *The Transformation of Intimacy*.

In support of Durkheim's claims, however, one might point to the continued existence of women's colleges in many Western countries, one of whose functions is to maintain a moratorium from the male world prior to the entry of their graduates into the male-dominated work world. It is also true that toy as well as clothing manufacturers still maintain all sorts of barriers and distinctions between boys' and girls' toys: the color blue, trucks, and a preoccupation with violence regarding boys; and the color pink, dolls, and an emphasis on being "nice" for girls. Even birthing rooms in many hospitals in the USA are still color-coded pink for girls and blue for boys, as is the entire post-birth process (for example, the color of socks and caps for newborns). Similarly, it is well known that the Internet is dominated by males and by stereotypically masculine imagery and interests. Girls were self-consciously lured to the computer through the sale of Barbie software. All this is still occurring despite decades of feminist consciousness raising. And that brings up the important point: perhaps consciousness, cognition, and reflexivity are not sufficient for overcoming these sexist barriers between men and women because the barriers are based on irrational factors about which most agents are unaware.

How does Giddens's skilled and knowledgeable agent deal with these powerful *emotional* constraints in modern society? Herein lies another gap in Giddens's theory concerning human agency. Even if a determined, non-sexist parent chooses to fight these constraints by trying to force his or her daughter, for example, not to succumb to commercial culture's overemphasis on the color pink, the parent is likely to encounter resistance from the child. As stated from the outset, the child's levels of cognition and skill are "undeveloped" vis-à-vis the world of adults: what the adult perceives as commercial exploitation the child perceives as other-directed constraint (from Riesman) to do what "the other kids do." Victory for the parent might have been possible in previous, inner-directed eras, but is likely to result in a serious feeling of being ostracized by the child's peer group in today's other-directed Western cultures.

Giddens might disagree, for he believes that the general democratization of all of society, public and domestic, based on reflexivity, applies to the relationship between children and adults. Thus, he writes in *The Transformation of Intimacy*:

Can a relationship between a parent and young child be democratic? It can, and should be in exactly the same sense as is true of a democratic political order. It is a right of the child, in other words, to be treated as a putative equal of the adult. Actions which cannot be negotiated directly with a child, because he or she is too young to grasp what is entailed, should be capable of counterfactual justification.

(Giddens 1992b: 191)

Let us suppose, for the sake of argument, that Giddens is correct. Giddens's assessment still begs the question of how an adult who wishes his or her child to be free of sexual stereotypes can impose his or her will on the child, even through negotiation, without causing emotional damage to the child. Those modernists who believe that culture is to blame for the stereotyping overlook the fact that children self-select from modern culture's myriad symbols and images those which seem to fit gender preferences. Giddens seems to assume that the child is a reflexive reflection of the adult whereas I contend that children, because their rational abilities are not as developed as those of adults, react to culture on a more emotional basis. For this reason, they reproduce many of the traditional divisions between boys and girls that Giddens assumes have disappeared from modern times.

Of course, one can argue endlessly, and without resolution, whether more consciousness raising will finally free modern societies of these seemingly traditional constraints. On the other hand, there is the possibility that some of these barriers between the sexes, especially in children, will continue to resist such cognitive manipulation. Freud was right that at specific ages boys and girls seem to abhor each other's company, and prefer the company of like-gendered friends. It is true that, against Freud, modern societies are co-educational even in day care and kindergarten, but it is also true that society's influence does not always penetrate into the friendship circles formed by children.

In any event, Durkheim's explanation for these observations is fantastic. The original event that gave rise to this perception of blood is something like Freud's primal killing of the father, and in this regard Freud's *Totem and Taboo* ([1913] 1950) and Durkheim's discussions of the totemic meal in *Elementary Forms* ([1912] 1965) are strikingly similar (discussed in Meštrović 1988: 97–116). The important point is that all of the characteristics, symbols, and rituals Durkheim tendentiously reviews in relation to totemism and religions are eventually reduced by him to the perceptual origins of the idea of force. Similarly, for Schopenhauer the "will to life" is the primal force beneath all phenomenal appearances (discussed in Magee 1983).

Durkheim concludes his tedious discussion of totemism with the claim that "the real totemic cult is addressed neither to certain determined animals nor to certain vegetables nor even to an animal or vegetable species, but to a vague power spread through these things" ([1912] 1965: 228).

Regardless of what is adored or feared phenomenally, it is due "to the fact that they are thought to participate in this force which alone is able to have things a sacred character" (ibid.: 229). And the category of the sacred involves the *emotions* of awe, respect, exuberance, as opposed to the category of the profane, which is described by Durkheim as "dull," "languishing," and ordinary. Clearly, the idea of force is more than a cognitive conceptualization: it also involves intuition and dimly perceived irrational feelings. These play no role whatsoever in Giddens's theory.

Durkheim's next move is to suggest that totemism is the first form of the scientific idea of force (ibid.: 232). For example, he argues:

> In fact, the *wakan* plays the same role in the world, as the Sioux conceives it, as the one played by the forces with which science explains the diverse phenomena of nature. This, however, does not mean that it is thought of as an exclusively physical energy; on the contrary. . . . But this very compositeness of its nature enables it to be utilized as a universal principle of explanation. It is from it that all life comes, "all life is *wakan*"; and by this word life, we must understand everything that acts and reacts, that moves and is moved, in both the mineral and biological kingdoms.
>
> (ibid.: 232–3)

"So the idea of force is of religious origin," Durkheim writes (ibid.: 234). He notes that this has already been foreseen by Comte, "but [Comte] concluded from this that the idea of force is destined to disappear from science," since it is a metaphysical notion. Durkheim *disagrees with Comte – again –* however, and asserts that he is "going to show that, on the contrary, religious forces are real, howsoever imperfect the symbols may be, by the aid of which they are thought of." Obviously, Durkheim intended to maintain some version of metaphysics in scientific explanations. Durkheim devotes many pages (ibid.: 393–413) to the argument that the scientific notion of "cause" is derived from the religious idea of "force," which in turn "was the *mana, wakan, orenda*, the totemic principle or any of the various names given to collective force objectified and projected into things" (ibid.: 406).

Schopenhauer criticizes Kant's understanding of causality as an *a priori* category because Kant fails to explain the perceptual basis for the categories. Durkheim follows Schopenhauer closely, writing in *Elementary Forms*:

> There can be no doubt that by himself, the individual observes the regular succession of phenomena and thus acquires a certain *feeling* of regularity. But this feeling is not the *category* of causality. The former is individual, subjective, incommunicable; we make it ourselves, out of our own personal observations. The second is the work of the group, and is given to us ready-made. It is a framework

in which our empirical ascertainments arrange themselves and which enables us to think of them, that is to say, to see them from a point of view which makes it possible for us to understand one another in regard to them.

(ibid.: 411; emphasis added)

In other words, society supplies the primal perceptual basis for the Kantian category of "cause" through its notion of "force," which then enables us to perceive, conceive, and communicate knowledge of the world. To repeat, "society" is for Durkheim the primeval begetter of all things in the world – but this is metaphysics, not rationalism. I have no intention of defending Durkheim's fantastical explanation, only of demonstrating its reliance on irrationality. And my purpose in exposing Durkheim's reliance on irrationality as an explanatory factor in discussing what Giddens calls agency versus structure is to highlight the poverty of Giddens's account. Giddens fails to explain the miracle by which human agents communicate with each other; he fails to explain how agents come to perceive social structure; and he fails to explain the origins of the agent's *faith* that his or her actions will result in specific consequences. For Giddens, all of these aspects of agency and structure are seemingly self-begotten, which is not an adequate sociological explanation as an emancipatory or an excellent sociological explanation should be.

CONCLUSIONS AND IMPLICATIONS

Like Parsons before him, Giddens stays on the trajectory of "rational social action." The difference between Giddens and Parsons seems to be primarily that Giddens feels that Parsons did not really present a theory of action. My point is that both theorists ignore completely what might be termed "irrational social action" as a component of human agency in general. Thus, Giddens amputates Freud's understanding of id as a cauldron of *passions*. Similarly, Giddens neutralizes Durkheim's concept of anomie as the infinity of *passions* by going along with Parsons's and Merton's misunderstanding of anomie as a state of normlessness. Giddens's theory of human agency overall is incomplete because it is not mindful of emotions and their context, human culture. A more complete conceptualization of agency would focus on the following issues: How is a sense of human agency constructed *culturally as well as by the individual* despite all the irrational forces that work against agency? In other words, given the overwhelming power of human passion or will conceptualized as the id or anomie or some similar term, how does the individual manage some degree of rational control over these forces? How is the idea of structure perceived in the first place? Giddens would have one believe that it is conceived on a strictly rational basis, but surely intuitions and sentiments play a role in perceiving structure. Finally, how do agents transcend their egoisms in order to be able to communicate and form societies? An important aspect of Durkheim's reply is that humans must have an innocent sort of faith in social facts as guarantors of objectivity. Without such emotional faith – not just rational trust – human agents could not believe in the objectivity of human institutions (religion, the family, the state, and so on) sufficiently in order to be able to act on their perceptions and conceptions.

I took up Giddens's analysis of women's roles in intimacy because this topic is one of the few in which he confronts emotion to some extent (the other one is nationalism, to be taken up in the next chapter). But Giddens's analysis is brittle and mechanical. It amounts to little more than the perpetuation of common stereotypes concerning men and women, especially the association of men with rationality and women with emotion. He does not write about feminine and masculine "voices" as shared by men and women equally, but about men and women as different creatures. His implicit theory of women's emancipation is that they must abandon emotionality and take on male rationality.

I contrasted Giddens with Durkheim on the subject of women as well as his many other assumptions, carried over from chapters 2 and 3, among them: that modern societies are radically different from traditional societies, that sociology is the study of the modern, that science is strictly a rational enterprise, and so on. Durkheim's thought emerges as much more complex, and relevant to the present, than Giddens's shallow and stereotypical theorizing. In particular, Durkheim is much more convincing than Giddens to claim that there are continuities between modern and traditional societies, that sociology studies the modern as well as the traditional, and that science involves faith and emotion as well as rationality. With regard to women, Durkheim seems to have a valid point when he writes:

> But who does not sense that everything which can contribute to the weakening of the organic unity of the family and of marriage must necessarily have the effect of eliminating [a] source of feminine grandeur? The respect shown her, a respect that has increased over historical time, has its origin mainly in the religious respect which the hearth inspires. If the family were henceforth considered only as a precarious union of two beings who could at any moment separate if they wished to, and who, as long as the association lasted, each had his or her own circle of interests and preoccupations, it would be difficult for this religion to subsist. And women would thereby be diminished. No doubt, some think that what they would lose on the one hand they would recover on the other in consequence of the more considerable role which they would play in civil life. It is still true that the gain which they would owe to the conquest of the

rights which are claimed on their behalf would be compensated by important losses. This suffices to show that the problem is less simple than one would think, and that is all that we wished to establish.

(Durkheim [1906] 1978: 144)

At this point, that is all that I wish to establish also with regard to Giddens, namely, that his thought regarding human agency, emotions, and women, among other topics, is simplistic.

5

GIDDENS'S POLITICAL SOCIOLOGY

Now senseless delusion, now intriguing politics, incite
[humans] to wars with one another; then the sweat and blood
of the great multitude must flow, to carry through the ideas of
individuals, or to atone for their shortcomings. . . . The
tumult is indescribable. But what is the ultimate aim of it all?
To sustain ephemeral and harassed individuals through a short
span of time.

– Arthur Schopenhauer ([1818] 1969b: 357)

If, as I have suggested in chapter 4, Giddens's efforts to confront emotion
and culture on a private and intimate level – through reading Freud and
taking up feminism with the aim of constructing a modernist conceptualization of reflexive self-identity – seem brittle and frankly chauvinist, his
efforts to confront emotion on a more collective level, through nationalism,
are equally stiff and frankly authoritarian. If he tries to replace traditional
emotion with modernist conviction regarding personal intimacy, he
attempts to replace the concept of nationalism with the modernist notion of
the nation-state. Consistent with his tendencies to amputate history and
tradition from the present, he simply cannot fathom connections between
the sentiments that animate the nation-state and traditional patriotism. And
for all his tedious efforts to present the nation-state as an entity with clearly
demarcated borders and surveillance, in the end, his thought comes across as
obsolete. For example, the information revolution in general and the
Internet in particular have made state borders seem old-fashioned: electroni-
cally mediated information travels across such borders as if they did not
exist. But the underside of the modern nation-state is that old-fashioned
nationalism has grown more, not less, powerful in contemporary times, such
that nationalists around the world – who are better informed than our ancestors could have imagined, precisely because of the information revolution –
no longer hold state borders as sacrosanct. Finally, the general drive toward
national emancipation is constantly at loggerheads with the modernist
desire to enshrine permanent state borders. These are among the tensions

that characterize political life in contemporary times, which Giddens's modernist thought cannot grasp.

Consider, for example, Giddens's pronouncements in his book, *The Nation-State and Violence* (1987):

> The modern state, as nation-state, becomes in many respects the pre-eminent form of power container, as a territorially bounded (although internally highly regionalized) administrative unity.
>
> (ibid.: 13)

> In indicating just how different modern states are from all forms of traditional state, I endeavour to highlight some key elements of the discontinuities of modernity referred to earlier.
>
> (ibid.: 84)

> Both the nation and nationalism are distinctive properties of modern states and in the context of their original emergence as well as elsewhere there is more than a fortuitous connection between them.
>
> (ibid.: 116)

> A "nation," as I use the term here, only exists when a state has a unified administrative reach over the territory over which its sovereignty is claimed.
>
> (ibid.: 119)

> The nation-state, which exists in a complex of other nation-states, is a set of institutional forms of governance maintaining an administrative monopoly over a territory with demarcated boundaries (borders), its rule being sanctioned by law and direct control of the means of internal and external violence.
>
> (ibid.: 121)

I shall analyze the rest of Giddens's argument in *The Nation-State and Violence* later in this chapter, but for now, let me point out some immediate problems with Giddens's assertions. If it were true that the nation-state and nationalism are modern phenomena, they would have to be self-begotten. Furthermore, one would be at a loss to understand previous, traditional forms of nationalism if they were completely unrelated to modern forms of nationalism. If the nation-state framework laid out by Giddens connected with reality, one could not explain how national boundaries in Western Europe were pulverized in two world wars, and how they are again made fictitious by Greater Serbian expansionism made possible by renewed European appeasement. In sum, Giddens's pronouncements on the nation-state come across as extremely problematic.

I shall take up *The Nation-State and Violence* (1987) after analyzing Giddens's treatise, *A Contemporary Critique of Historical Materialism*, first published in 1982, and conclude with an analysis of his 1994 *Beyond Left and Right: The Future of Radical Politics*. This intellectual journey will reveal the connections between his vital theoretical concerns and political views. In the latter book, his interests range from commenting on Francis Fukuyama to Bosnia, life politics, and masculinity. In all three books, he pushes the unconvincing line that democratization is an inevitable and inexorable process in politics (much as he argues in *The Transformation of Intimacy* that intimate relations are being democratized) and that democracy is sufficient for creating the good society. While I do not deny that some variation of democracy seems to be inevitable, I note that democratization occurs in a tension-filled process alongside Balkanization, authoritarianism, and barbarism even in Western countries. And I hold that democracy, alone, is not sufficient for a good society. An independent source of ethics based on *caritas* must complement democracy lest it degenerate into anomic forms.

In these three books, Giddens does not depart from the standard rhetoric in his earlier works, except that his focus is more on Marx than on Durkheim and Weber. Of course, a "processed" Marxism and Anglo-Americanized Hegel emerge in Fukuyama's *End of History and the Last Man* (1992) as well. Ultimately, to travel from 1982 to 1994 via these three books by Giddens is to move from Giddens's views on Marx as a utopian world reformer to Giddens's own program for renewal and social engineering on a cosmopolitan scale that avoids what he calls traditionalist fundamentalism as well as post-modern nihilism. The world has changed dramatically since 1982 as well, from a Cold War setting that invited fantasies on the part of Westerners concerning the global triumph of capitalism over socialism and the inviola-bility of state borders, to a post-Cold War cynicism concerning what this victory has wrought. Despite the post-Cold War eruption of nationalism, prime-time genocide in Bosnia (which occurred alongside all the "Never Again" refrains), palpable hatred of Western governments on the part of much of their citizens, and a tendency toward societal fission, Giddens stays on the pre-Cold War trajectory of thought by writing about globalization, the triumph of democratization, the permanence of the nation-state, and fixing the modernist project through the reinvention of synthetic traditions. Let me repeat that in these and other regards Giddens is merely reflecting dominant modernist prejudices of the current *fin de siècle*.

Giddens's political sociology is marred by seemingly insurmountable contradictions. If the nation-state is defined by clear borders and surveil-lance, how can its existence be reconciled with globalization? For Giddens, "globalization can thus be defined as the intensification of worldwide social relations which link distant localities in such a way that local happenings are shaped by events occurring many miles away and vice versa" (1990: 64). Defined this way, globalization is simply incompatible with the nation-state. If the thrust of Giddens's thought is toward democratization and emancipation, why is he as concerned as he seems to be with the problem of social order, which does not necessarily promote democracy? These are among the many problems with Giddens's political sociology that I seek to uncover in this chapter.

GIDDENS'S CRITIQUE OF MARX

A Contemporary Critique of Historical Materialism (1982b) appears to be an attempt by Giddens to achieve two tasks simultaneously: to offer an exegesis of Marx's historical materialism in relation to the modernist problem of social order and to offer another version of Giddens's effort to construct structuration theory. But the tone as well as substance of Giddens's analysis toward both Marx and Parsons is hostile. Thus, Giddens claims that functionalist theories have lacked adequate accounts of human action because they "discount agents' reasons in favour of society's reasons," and that they must be abandoned (ibid.: 18). As for the exegesis of Marx, Giddens sets out to expose what is "mistaken, ambiguous or inconsistent" in Marx's thought, adding: "In many respects Marx's writings exemplify features of nineteenth-century thought which are plainly defective when looked at from the perspectives of our century" (ibid.: 1). Giddens arrives at the conclusion that "Marx's materialist conception of history should be discarded once and for all" (ibid.: 105).

It seems somewhat strange that Marx is analyzed alongside Parsons and the functionalists. In the 1960s especially, the Marxists and the functionalists represented two completely different programs for societal engineering. Yet Giddens believes that "Marx's analysis can be interpreted, and often has been interpreted, in a functionalist vein," and he believes that a reformulated "problem of order" is a central feature of Marxist and functionalist theory (ibid.: 15). Reformulating Marxism as functionalism is an incredible move. After wading through this same intellectual strategy of attacking a straw man of past social theory (in this case, Marx Parsonized as a functionalist) so as to set up structuration theory, formulated and re-formulated in roughly the same way in Giddens's thought in book after book, one has to confess that it becomes tedious. First, it is unoriginal, for Parsons already tried to force-fit too many diverse thinkers into the paradigm of social order. It is worth repeating that Parsons could not force Simmel and Veblen into this paradigm, and leaves them out of action theory. But Giddens also cannot find a place for Simmel or Veblen in his theory, even though both were concerned with modernity, albeit taking a pessimistic and highly critical stand toward it. Second, Giddens avoids completely the affinities among Simmel, Veblen, and Marx vis-à-vis cultural studies. The Marx that both Giddens and Parsons misappropriate is the non-cultural Marx of the economists. Third, it is a crude and awkward strategy that does not take seriously the distinctive projects that Durkheim, Marx, Parsons, and other leading sociological theorists might have had. Why is it that for Giddens, so many different sociologists must be cut from the same cloth? Fourth, and perhaps most obviously, Giddens's strategy is arbitrary. Why, for example, does he not read Parsons from a Marxist perspective? One possible reply is that because Marx lends himself fairly easily to postmodern discourse, and because Giddens rejects postmodernity, a more conducive strategy for his purposes is to modernize Marx rather than postmodernize Parsons.

"I have no dispute with the assertion that 'the' problem of social theory is 'the problem of order,' " Giddens writes, so long as this problem is phrased in terms of "how social systems bind time and space" (1982b: 30). This is another interesting contradiction in Giddens's thought, for in an article published in *The American Journal of Sociology*, Giddens (1976) had concluded that the problem of social order was a myth. But it is also another illustration of Giddens's consistent strategy of finding an ambiguous middle ground between modernist and postmodernist positions. Thus, forced to choose between modernist order and postmodernist disorder, Giddens chooses order based on binding time and space. In any event, by 1982, rather than formulating this problem in terms of society's functionally related parts, as Parsons had done, Giddens formulates it in terms of "time-space distanciation and the generation of power" (1982b: 92).

Giddens is quite obscure as to what he means by this new vocabulary, and his reliance on a processed Heidegger to make his points only makes matters worse. Giddens (ibid.: 32) quotes Heidegger as to the "openness" that the conjunction of time and space opens up, yet he seeks to force this conjunction into the problem of social order – to bind time and space. There is something sinister sounding in this contradictory interpretation of time and space by Giddens: "binding" time and space does not seem to foster democratization. C. Wright Mills (1959) called Parsons's writing unintelligible, and Giddens deserves the same reprimand when he makes such contradictory claims. (One should add that much like Mills claimed that Parsons's thesis could be summarized in a paragraph, there is no real need for Giddens to have written so many books to make the same, simplistic point.) Nevertheless, if one tries to summarize Giddens's renovation of the problem of order vis-à-vis Marxism, one should say that in capitalism time becomes a commodity, "freely exchangeable with all other time, time distinguished and separated from the substance of Being" (1982b: 134) and that time-space is transformed from community to city to the nation-state. Power is a matter of allocating and transforming time and space. According to Giddens, "capitalist states emerged as nation-states"; "the 'nation-state,' as I use the term, only came to maturity in the nineteenth century"; and "the nation-state replaces the city as the 'power-container' shaping the development of the capitalist societies" (ibid.: 12). There is no discussion by

Giddens of the possible Durkheimian ([1950] 1983) objection that both time and space are rooted in culture, so that they constitute entirely different phenomena in the USA versus, let us say, the Czech Republic, but we have noted from the outset that Giddens's theory is anti-cultural. Moreover, I believe that capitalist states emerged prior to the emergence of nation-states as defined by Giddens and certain cities are still "power-containers" in the 1990s regardless of the nation-state to which they belong (for example, New York, Hong Kong, London, Paris, Washington DC).

The growing contemporary problem of nationalism is invoked by Giddens as illustration. With regard to his other aims, he concludes that the theory of nationalism represents Marx's greatest failure (Giddens 1982b: 179). There may be some truth in this claim, because Marx apparently hoped that nationalistic antagonisms would disappear following the dissolution of capitalism. In this regard, at least, Marx was the quintessential modernist. (But this may not be the whole story, given Marx's writings on reification and alienation, which are suitable for some analyses of nationalism.) But the more interesting irony is that Giddens seems to mimic Marx's failure regarding nationalism:

> What makes the "nation" a necessary element of the "nation-state" in my definition is not the existence of sentiments of nationalism (however strong these may be) but the unification of an administrative apparatus whose power stretches over precisely defined territorial bounds.
>
> (ibid.: 13)[1]

Clearly, Giddens does not take nationalism any more seriously than Marx did. Giddens distinguishes between nationalism (symbols and beliefs) and the nation-state (an administrative apparatus), which he thinks do not have to converge, but sometimes do. He regards nationalism as "an attenuated form of those 'primordial sentiments' " often found in tribal and traditional societies, while he regards the nation-state as a modern "power-container" of time and space (ibid.: 193). He elaborates on this issue as follows:

> Nationalism is a specifically modern phenomenon and as such, I believe, expresses psychological sentiments that feed upon the rootlessness of an everyday life in which what Geertz calls the "primordial sentiments" of social reproduction, grounded in tradition, have become substantially disintegrated. . . . We can explain the "Janus-faced" nature of nationalism, I argue, in terms of the fragility of ontological security in the wasteland of everyday life.
>
> (ibid.)

Giddens's view of nationalism is another manifestation of his modernism, and is most probably mistaken. I believe that Durkheim ([1950] 1983) is much more accurate to link modern nationalism to traditional patriotism, and to argue that the state behaves like an ego to the nation conceived as something like the id (discussed in Meštrović 1993b). For Durkheim, the state needs the consent of the nation in order to rule. Against Giddens, and in line with Durkheim, it seems that since 1991 nationalism has emerged as a powerful social force in modern capitalist as well as formerly Communist countries precisely because various nation-states can no longer count on the consent of some of the nationalisms that comprise them. Thus, if the nation-state of Canada does not need Canadian nationalism in order to exist, one is unable to explain secessionism in Quebec. Similarly, Yugoslav nationalism – the feeling of being Yugoslav as opposed to Croat, Bosnian, Serb, and so on – evaporated and led to the disintegration of Yugoslavia. Something similar happened to the Soviet nation-state and the feeling of Soviet nationalism. Against Giddens's typically modernist interpretation that the nation-state does not depend upon nationalist sentiments, it would seem that the nation-state is extremely dependent upon nationalism.

As for Giddens's assertion that modern nationalism is fundamentally different from traditional "primordial sentiments," consider counterfactuals such as French nationalism in ultra-modern Quebec. The indignation expressed by many citizens in Quebec at the Canadian coat of arms with the inscription "Desiring a Better Country"[2] is not fundamentally different from the Serbian indignation at the Croatian coat of arms that was one of the sparks that ignited the Balkan War in 1991. And one can hardly imagine a more modernist, Western country than Canada. Yet modernists persist in calling Serbs and Croats primordial tribalists while Canadians as well as the denizens of Quebec are considered modernists who should have outgrown the primordial pulls of traditionalism. Why, then, does allegedly primordial traditionalism erupt in modern nation-states such as Canada and threaten their very existence? In tandem with the decline of modernist nationalisms that sustained large federations (a feeling of being Canadian, Soviet, or Yugoslav, for example) and the rise of new nationalisms that felt oppressed in these federations (Croat, Lithuanian, Slovene, and so on), the nation-state is becoming obsolete. The fission of Bosnia-Herzegovina – created from the fission of Yugoslavia – under the watchful eyes of the modern world community has riveted the attention of the West partly because it symbolizes the unconscious fear in many nation-states that Bosnia might symbolize their fate. I will return to this theme later when I discuss Giddens's remarks on Bosnia. But for now let me note that the creation as well as the dissolution of Bosnia vis-à-vis Yugoslavia parallels the creation and *de facto* dissolution of many new nation-states that emerged from the fission of the Soviet Union (Khazanov 1995). This fission led to the emergence of nations in search of states. I shall have more to say on this connection between Yugoslavia and the Soviet Union later in the chapter.

According to Giddens, capitalism needs the nation-state, which is not based on sentiments (while nationalism purportedly is), and the nation-state depends on power structures that promote capitalist aims. Again, one should question how any nation-state could exist without sentiments. Who would pay taxes, salute the flag, or give up one's life for one's nation-state in the armed forces on the basis of purely mental calculation? It seems obvious that the nation-state relies on sentiments every bit as much as nationalism did and does. To be sure, the nationalist sentiments that support or supported large federalist nation-states such as the USA, Great Britain, Canada, the former Yugoslavia, and the former Soviet Union are qualitatively, but not fundamentally, different from the new fractionalized nationalisms that have emerged since the end of the Cold War. The more important point is that, for example, the idea of American nationalism, which used to be taken for granted until recently, is becoming fractionalized into African-American, Hispanic American, Native American, and other American nationalisms. Something similar is happening in many other nation-states throughout the post-Cold War world. A genuine emotional revolution is occurring in the post-Cold War world, and Giddens, like so many other modernists, is oblivious to it.

Giddens also rejects the allegedly Marxist claim that capitalism could not exist without the notion of private property, claiming that private property was widespread in non-capitalist civilizations. I would add, based on Durkheim's ([1950] 1983) analysis of private property, patriotism, and nationalism, that all of these notions involve *emotional* attachment and the category of sacredness. In no meaningful sense have modern nation-states outgrown this allegedly tribal and traditional emotionalism. Robert N. Bellah's (1967) notion of "civil religion" is particularly helpful in explaining how the political symbolism and imagery of the modern nation-state draws its emotional power from the traditional religious category of the sacred. Giddens is immune to arguments of this sort.

Thus, the crux of Giddens's analysis is that Marx's "historical materialism" should be rejected and replaced by an updated version in which time and space, not property, are the criteria for power, and in which it is supposed that capitalist states emerge as nation-states. This move by Giddens is consistent with his other attempts to balance modernity and postmodernity.

Apart from the lack of fit with Balkanizing developments in the contemporary world, it does not seem that Giddens is fair to Marx. It is too facile to contend that Marx never analyzed the concept of property in detail and, to use the overworked phrase, that Marx was "standing Hegel on his feet again" (1982b: 73). Marx did not use the concept of property as just material "stuff" (as Giddens alleges, ibid.: 113), and Hegel was not just an "idealist" whom Marx used to advance his materialism. The concept of alienation is completely missing from Giddens's analysis, as is the fact that Marx

119

treated property as an idea that is the cause, effect, and expression of alienation. So, for example, the idea of private property reduces all the senses to the alienation of the senses, namely, the sense of *having*, even owning and having other persons (this is especially evident in Marx's early writings). Erich Fromm elaborates on this Marxist insight to argue in *The Art of Loving* (1956) and other works (Fromm 1955, 1962) that modernists treat each other as property and call this interpersonal commodification love. In fact, many critical theorists have elaborated in creative ways on Marx's notions of alienation, reification, and private property. Baudrillard's early reliance on Marx as a precursor to his later version of postmodernism should not be overlooked either (Kellner 1989). And whatever Marx did to Hegel philosophically – the debate is tedious – Marx clearly kept Hegel's faith in the advance of reason, which would emancipate and humanize persons. It is interesting that Giddens clearly shares with Marx some of this optimism concerning the Enlightenment project despite the fact that he rejects many of Marx's Enlightenment-based premises. He also shares with Marx the modernist assumption that "the development of çapitalism marks a series of fundamental discontinuities with previous history" (Giddens 1982b :81).

In sum, this sometimes unintelligible book by Giddens is *not* any more sensitive to Marx than his other books are to Durkheim, Weber, Freud, or to other founders of the social sciences. It is *not* a deep work of exegesis, and it keeps sociology trapped within the confines of the problem of social order despite the rhetorical devices that Giddens uses to make it seem as if structuration theory has transcended this problem. One might say, cynically, the problem with contemporary sociology, as well as with Giddens's theory, is that the problem of social order remains a problem: it has become Max Weber's iron cage. Will sociologists ever be able to escape from it? Giddens tries desperately to postmodernize the modernist notion of social order, but it remains the stultifying problem of order. Will there be enough sociological imagination left to guess what might lie outside this cage? I have suggested earlier that the problem of morality vis-à-vis culture and local habits of the heart lies outside the cage imposed by social order. This is because one can imagine living in Giddens's modernist society of high risk, reflexive freedom, agency, a structure devoted to life politics, a political apparatus that controls time, space, and even deviants, yet not achieve what is idealized as universal justice or morality. Because the notions of justice and morality vary across diverse cultures and subcultures, the task facing modern humanity is to reconcile these diverse standards vis-à-vis empathy and some variations of *caritas* (see Meštrović 1993a). Post-Cold War developments make it clear that modernist attempts to impose a single, universal (Western) standard of justice and morality will continue to be met with cultural resistance.

ELABORATING GIDDENS'S POSITION ON
NATIONALISM AND THE NATION-STATE

In *The Nation-State and Violence* (1987), Giddens becomes even more entrenched in his modernism, writing, for example, that

> Treating modern societies as the culmination of a process of progressive expansion of the forces of production fails to disclose how *different* they are from all forms of traditional order. Modern "societies" are nation-states, existing within a nation-state system. Traditional states – or what I call "class-divided societies" – contrast very substantially with these, both in their internal characteristics and in their external relations with one another. Social scientists are accustomed to thinking of "societies" as administrative unities with clearly defined boundaries. Class-divided societies were not like this, and if modern ones are it is not because of anything intrinsic to social association in general, but a result of distinctive forms of social integration associated with the nation-state.
>
> (ibid.: 1)[3]

It is extreme for Giddens to claim that modern nation-states are different from *all forms* of traditional social structures, but he reiterates this claim forcefully: "My main concern is to demonstrate that modern states can be contrasted in a generic way to traditional ones" (ibid.: 83). If this were true, one would be unable to explain the celebrations of civil religion in modern nation-states which clearly call upon traditional forms. For example, the 4th of July celebrations in the USA in the 1990s clearly celebrate America's rebellion against Great Britain that occurred over two hundred years ago. And what do the French celebrate on Bastille Day if not an ancient event? And so on for other Western countries: not one has escaped the pull of collective representations derived from the past. Giddens is also incorrect to claim that all social scientists tend to think of societies as nation-states. Durkheim thought of societies as systems of collective representations that overlap and clash with other collective representations emanating from other societies. Weber also thought of nationhood as a system of ideas that often contradicted established borders. Similarly, Veblen, Simmel, Tocqueville, Riesman, and a host of other social scientists thought of societies in *cultural* terms, in terms of social character or habits of the mind or habits of the heart or other equivalents. Thus, Riesman demonstrates admirably that other-directed social character or "society" can be found in Los Angeles, London, Paris, or a host of other Western cities regardless of administrative borders. In this way, he is able to discuss other-directed societies without the slightest concern for Giddens's emphasis on administration.

Giddens claims that traditional states have frontiers, not borders (1987: 3). But with the advent of the information revolution, one could argue that modern nation-states also have frontiers and that borders are increasingly becoming obsolete. He claims that "the modern world has been shaped through the intersection of capitalism, industrialism and the nation-state system" (ibid.: 5). Again, this is an extreme statement, because there were many other additional factors involved in the shaping of modernity, from the Protestant Ethic (Weber) to inner-directed and other-directed social character (Riesman). According to Giddens, the modern nation-state is based on the control of information, surveillance, and the control of the means of violence. He elaborates:

> In most types of non-modern society, the possibilities of surveillance . . . are relatively limited. Only in cities could direct and regular surveillance be maintained by the central agencies of the state.
>
> (ibid.: 15)

Giddens's claims, above, are counter-intuitive and run against the grain of a vast tradition in sociological theorizing. For example, Durkheim ([1897] 1951) is more believable in claiming that the traditionalist was subject to much more group surveillance than the modernist. Isn't emancipation one of the hallmarks of modernity? Similarly, Simmel (1971) has made a lasting impression on urban sociology with his astute observation that the urban environment allows for *anonymity* in contrast to the strict surveillance of communal life. This is not to deny that modern societies do engage in sophisticated and mostly electronic forms of surveillance, but Giddens overstates his case by the extreme and exclusive way that he formulates his argument.

Regarding the alleged control of violence, it is simply not true, as Giddens claims, that in modern nation-states

> The sanction of the use of violence is quite indirect and attenuated. Moreover, military power on the whole tends to become rather clearly distinct from policing power, the one turned "externally" the other pointed "internally."
>
> (1987:15)

Contrary to Giddens's claims, the end of the twentieth century has witnessed a blurring of military and police powers in Western countries. For example, widespread hatred of the government in the USA is based in large measure on the blurring of military with police power from Ruby Ridge to Waco, Texas, culminating in the revenge bombing at Oklahoma City in 1995. Similarly, United Nations-sponsored "peacekeeping" operations are a hybrid of ineffectual military–police functions that result in neither peace nor military victories. Thus, "peacekeepers" in Bosnia were military soldiers who (1) used the projected threat of violence in foreign, "external" situations, (2) were prohibited from taking sides or engaging in the military defeat of any side in the conflict, and (3) did not keep the peace, and instead became passive spectators of genocidal warfare. President Clinton assured the American people that US military troops went to Bosnia in 1995 in order to make peace, not wage war. More alarming is the fact that, domestically, those who opposed this American "military" involvement wondered out loud why American soldiers were not used in the "war against drugs" and in American cities to preserve "peace." Bosnia is not an exception to the general rule that, increasingly, US soldiers are used in "peacekeeping" operations, as in Haiti, Somalia, and Macedonia.

Furthermore, when Giddens refers to "the withdrawal of the military from direct participation in the internal affairs of the state" (ibid.: 192) in modern times, he overlooks the importance of the military–industrial complex.

According to Giddens, modern societies tend to be peaceable whereas traditional societies are war-like, and he uses Herbert Spencer's social theory as support in this regard: "Whereas pre-industrial societies are pre-eminently warlike, industrial society, according to Spencer, is inherently pacific" (ibid.: 23). But if one extrapolates the notion of "war" to include trade wars, economic sanctions, the piracy of commercial goods, the war against drugs, the war against cancer, and the myriad of other metaphorical "wars" in modern societies, then, clearly, modern nation-states are every bit as war-like as traditional ones were. But the most important example of this veiled war-like tendency of contemporary democracies is the use of economic sanctions against other nations. According to the *New York Times*, "President Clinton and Congress imposed sanctions or passed legislation that threatened to do so 60 times against 35 countries from 1993 to 1996."[4] These sanctions invariably hurt children, the elderly, women, and the poor, not the dictators who are the purported objects of the sanctions. In inner-directed times, sanctions were used during real wars. In today's other-directed era, sanctions are used as a bludgeon by democratic nations against the weak and helpless in Iraq, Cuba, Bosnia, Croatia, Mexico, Colombia, and other countries to demonstrate that the US or other Western democracies do not like some aspects of these countries.

Giddens betrays the irrelevance of his thought for the post-Cold War period with his statement that

> We live in a world dominated by the nation-state form in which a
> fragile equality in weaponry possessed by the two most powerful

nation-states [the USA and the USSR] is the main brake upon global violence within the context of a novel international order.

(ibid.: 23)

But the Cold War is over, and the current *fin de siècle* is confronted with the threat of *international* terrorist groups that clearly do not respect the borders of nation-states. Moreover, the nuclear arsenals of the former USSR are suspected to be leaking to many such international terrorists.

We have seen that Giddens amputates modern notions of nationalism from traditional forms of patriotism. But he goes a step further by reducing nationalism – as a modern phenomenon – to something strictly psychological:

By nationalism I mean a phenomenon that is primarily psychological – the affiliation of individuals to a set of symbols and beliefs emphasizing communality among the members of a political order. . . . By a "nation" I refer to a collectivity existing within a clearly demarcated territory which is subject to a unitary administration, reflexively monitored both by the internal state apparatus and those of other states.

(ibid.: 116)

He illustrates this claim with a dubious account of English nationalism and nationhood:

By the 16th century there can easily be traced a few core components of "being English," associated also with speaking English. Whether it could accurately be described as "nationalism" is highly dubious; the nationalism that emerges in the 19th and 20th centuries is "British" rather than "English," although complicated by both Scottish and Welsh nationalist feelings.

(ibid.: 118)

Presumably, early English nationalism was primarily psychological in that it gave some English individuals a sentimental sense of distinctiveness due to a common language. What Giddens conveniently omits in this quaint account is that many Scots and Welsh in the 1990s still resent how English nationalism, far from just being psychological, took on imperialist dimensions after the death of Mary, Queen of Scots. Great Britain, like Greater Serbia and so many other "greater" nationalisms of various sorts, had to have been *sociological* in that these vast nation-states could be constructed by oppressing the nationalisms of other peoples. Nationalism has a psychological dimension, but cannot be reduced reasonably to a strictly psychological phenomenon.

Giddens claims that "nationalism helps naturalize the recency and the contingency of the nation-state through providing its myth of origin" (ibid.: 221). This is a convenient explanation for Giddens's guiding assumption that both nationalism and the nation-state are modern phenomena. And it may be true to some extent in explaining the nationalism pertaining to federalist nation-states such as Great Britain, the USA, and the Soviet Union. But, clearly, it does not explain the persistent nationalisms that these federations have attempted to eradicate and whose origins can be traced further back than the creation of these nation-states. Thus, Scottish nationalism persists in Great Britain and its function is clearly *not* to naturalize the myth of Great Britain's existence; Southern nationalism in the USA led to civil war, and in the 1990s one still comes across the line "Those damned Yankees" in the South; and the Soviet Union failed completely to suppress the nationalisms of its many constituent peoples. In summary, Giddens refuses to concede that these traditional nationalisms that persist into the present are nationalisms, properly speaking. But beyond the rhetorical success of his argument, Giddens has not solved the riddle of what fuels these nationalisms, nor how secessionist nationalisms survived attempts by federations (such as the Soviet Union, Great Britain, Canada, and so on) to eradicate them.

According to Giddens,

> Nationalism is the cultural sensibility of sovereignty, the concomitant of the co-ordination of administrative power within the bounded nation-state . . . [it] presumes elements of cultural homogeneity . . . a nation-state is a conceptual community in a way in which traditional states were not.
>
> (ibid.: 219)

He is partly right: nationalism is the cultural sensibility of sovereignty, but *not* always in relation to a nation-state. Clearly, the many nationalist movements across the globe in the twentieth century as well as historically suggest that many peoples within a nation-state feel oppressed by the dominant nationality, and seek emancipation *from* the nation-state. This was illustrated recently be the desire of so many latent nations to escape from the shackles of the Soviet Union, which was dominated by Russia, and of Yugoslavia, which was dominated by Serbia. Giddens seems completely unable to grasp the persistence of national identity despite modernist efforts to assimilate various nationalities into a larger nation-state: "Conditions involved in the reflexive monitoring of the modern state, as a surveillance apparatus, are the same as those that help generate nationalism" (ibid.: 220). The failure of the Soviet Union's surveillance apparatus to extinguish the nationalisms of non-Russians should make it clear that Giddens is simply wrong in this assessment.

Finally, Giddens writes of "inherent connections between the nation-state and democracy" (ibid.: 201). Of course, he is forced to this conclusion because, as a modernist, he believes that nationalism, the emergence of the nation-state, capitalism, and democracy are all relatively recent twentieth-century developments that work in tandem. There is nothing original in this claim by Giddens; it merely reflects a dominant prejudice in the current *fin de siècle*. But again – what about the Soviet Union? It was clearly a nation-state, but never a democracy. And even within seemingly *bona fide* democratic nation-states such as the USA, Canada, and the UK, there are nationalist voices that claim they are oppressed and do not have access to democracy: African-Americans and many others in the USA; many citizens of Quebec in Canada; the Scots, Welsh and Irish in the UK, and so on.

Quite apart from these factual misrepresentations of both recent and more distant history, the implicit assumption in Giddens's conceptualization of the nation-state is problematic. Whereas in *A Contemporary Critique of Historical Materialism* (1982b), Giddens displays a not so wholesome obsession with the problem of social order – a concept that calls to mind policemen and other instruments of authoritarianism – in *The Nation-State and Violence* (1987) he betrays a similar authoritarian streak. A neat and tidy nation-state with clear borders, massive surveillance, and control of violence sounds frightening to all those who hold to cultural or national values that the nation-state does not value. It would be one thing if Giddens criticized the authoritarian overtones of the nation-state as thus depicted – but he does not. Instead, he makes the incredible claim that the nation-state and democracy are linked! (He is correct only in the ironic sense: many so-called democracies really are overly authoritarian due to the tremendous power of central governments.) One might be sympathetic to Giddens's vision if he wrote about minority rights and the accommodation of the majority national group in a nation-state with nationalisms within it that hold less power and have less opportunity. But he never tackles such issues.

GIDDENS ON POST-TRADITION

One can sense a long period of gestation from Giddens's 1982 work on Marx and his 1994 work on the contemporary political scene. He now seems at least dimly aware that problems have arisen on a global scale with the nation-state, the idea of democracy, and other modernist ideas that he took for granted in his earlier writings. The nation-state needs some traditions in order to produce social solidarity – reflexivity is not enough. Democracy suffers from apathy and cynicism on the part of citizens – the passions of citizens must be aroused. And globalization has met stiff resistance from local cultures. Nevertheless, Giddens does not feel compelled by these disturbing developments to alter the fundamental assumptions of his theory of modernity or to concede that the postmodernists may be making a valid point. Giddens's *Beyond Left and Right* begins in his usual style, which I have already analyzed:

> We can speak today of the emergence of a *post-traditional social order*. A post-traditional order is not one in which tradition disappears – far from it. It is one in which tradition changes its status. Traditions have to explain themselves, to become open to interrogation and discourse.
>
> (1994: 5)

Note that whereas in *Consequences of Modernity* (1990) Giddens tried to find a middle ground between modernity and postmodernity, in *Beyond Left and Right* (1994) he tries to extend his balancing act to include traditionalism. But not quite. This is because tradition that is open to interrogation and discourse is fundamentally different from traditional traditions, which were not questioned but were accepted on the emotional basis of faith (as argued in chapter 4). According to Giddens, the post-traditional world will be "a world of clever people" who "more or less have to engage with the wider world if they are to survive in it" (ibid.: 7). As usual, Giddens is aware of some problems with his formulations, such that the nation-state "is not well equipped to meet the demands of a reflexive citizenry in a globalizing world" (ibid.: 10). But he does not concede that the world might be Balkanizing, despite the rhetoric of globalization. He is aware, however, that "the combination of capitalism and liberal democracy provides few means of generating social solidarity" (ibid.). Indeed. Solidarity used to depend on tradition. Should humanity retreat into tradition (even if it could) or accept the liberating effects of the end of tradition proclaimed by many postmodernists? Giddens's reaction to such pessimistic second-thoughts about modernity is typical:

> Should we therefore perhaps accept, as some of the postmodernists say, that the Enlightenment has exhausted itself and that we have to more or less take the world as it is, with all its barbarities and limitations? Surely not. Almost the last thing we need now is a sort of new medievalism, a confession of impotence in the face of forces larger than ourselves. We live in a radically damaged world, for which radical remedies are needed.
>
> (ibid.)

I agree with the last sentence in the passage quoted above, but do not consider Giddens's proposed remedies as radical enough. To consider the possibility that the Enlightenment has exhausted itself, finally – a consideration that I take seriously – is not to accept barbarism, impotence, or medievalism. It may involve finally facing up to the Enlightenment's disregard for the emotional side of being human, including the human need for culture, for its disregard for all those who fall outside the purview of the "civil society" of the dominant nationalist group in a nation-state, for its inability to foster *caritas* and accommodation among many nationalities, and remedying this fundamental defect in the West's blueprint for action (Meštrović 1997). To dismiss all of postmodernism as an ideology of impotence is simply unfair to the "affirmative postmodernists," as Pauline Rosenau (1992) calls them, who are clearly doing more than throwing their hands up in despair at some of the problems caused by modernity. As Cushman (1995) demonstrates, for example, rock music fans in the Soviet Union passionately rejected the Soviet version of modernity. They were neither impotent nor despairing. Alas, their innocent faith in America – perceived by them in the manner depicted by Tocqueville, as a beacon of light set high upon a hill – proved ill founded. Contemporary Americans are too cynical about themselves to follow through on the inspiration the traditional image of America still holds for others.

What are Giddens's radical remedies? He lists six of them, using a vague and evasive style that makes summarizing difficult:

1   "There must be a concern to repair *damaged solidarities*, which may sometimes imply the selective preservation, or even perhaps reinvention, of tradition." Note that both "selective" preservation and reinvention of traditions involve modernist social engineering. Giddens puts no stock in the spontaneous proliferation of traditions. Nor does he seek to revive civil societies, but is in favor of "reconciling autonomy and interdependence" (1994: 13).
2   "We should recognize the increasing centrality of what I call *life politics* to both formal and less orthodox domains of the political order" (ibid.: 14).
3   Generative politics must be fostered along with trust.
4   A more radical form of democracy must be fostered. This "dialogic democracy" "advances to the degree to which such relationships are ordered through dialogue rather than through embedded power" (ibid.: 16).
5   "We should be prepared to *rethink the welfare state* in a fundamental way – and in relation to wider issues of global poverty" (ibid.: 17). Giddens endorses "positive welfare" that "places much greater emphasis on the mobilizing of life-political measures, aimed once more at connecting autonomy with personal and collective responsibilities" (ibid.: 18).
6   "A program of radical politics must be prepared to confront the role of *violence* in human affairs" (ibid.). Giddens believes that dialogue is the best way to avoid violence due to individual and cultural differences.

The underlying assumption for Giddens's six-point program of radical renewal is that for the first time in history "we can speak of the emergence of universal values – values shared by almost everyone, and which are in no sense the enemy of cosmopolitanism" (ibid.: 20). These values include the sanctity of human life, universal human rights, the preservation of species, individual and collective responsibility. I would like to note first that faith, justice, and compassion are conspicuously absent from Giddens's discussion of values. Second, it is not remotely self-evident that the values Giddens lists are universal. For example, if the sanctity of human life were truly universal, how would one explain genocide in Cambodia, East Timor, Bosnia, Rwanda, Zaïre, and elsewhere in recent years? Moreover, the general thrust of recent cultural studies is that all social phenomena are retouched, modified, and filtered by local cultures. After so many years of postmodernism, deconstruction, decentering, and poststructuralism, one can hardly believe in the universality of any values. Yet Giddens concludes: "There is no single agent, group or movement that, as Marx's proletariat was supposed to do, can carry the hopes of humanity; but there are many points of political engagement which offer good cause for optimism" (ibid.: 21).

Giddens's program bears some resemblance to Amitai Etzioni's communitarianism in that both theorists seek to willfully and deliberately produce social bonds based on artificial traditions that will be achieved through social engineering. For Giddens, as we have seen, this may even involve "reinventing" traditions. Given that a tradition involves both an external ritual and an internal emotional core, it is not clear how one can reinvent emotions, even though it is possible to reinvent rituals as the outer shell of traditions. Above all – and harking back to the discussion in chapter 4 again – the synthetic re-invention of traditions cannot re-invent faith in traditions. One should keep in mind that the Soviet experiment in reinventing traditions failed miserably with regard to what Soviet citizens actually felt. To repeat, Giddens steers clear of the Soviet failure in modernization, in stark contrast to Zygmunt Bauman's (1992), Keith Tester's (1992), Thomas Cushman's (1995), Anatoly Khazanov's (1995), and other excellent analyses of this colossal failure in societal engineering. In general, neither Giddens nor Etzioni seems to be particularly bothered by the failures of previous grand experiments in social engineering nor the degeneration of some of these experiments into various forms of totalitarianism. Their modernist reaction to these grand failures seems to be "try, try, try again." Nevertheless, the critical reader should keep in mind that Hitler and Stalin reinvented traditions in the name of causes that many people at the time regarded as noble. A more recent example of such postemotionalism and synthetic communitarianism is found in the Serbian revival of the Kosovo Myth dating back to 1389. Western-sponsored dialogue did not stop the final degeneration of this Serbian nationalist myth into genocide committed against Bosnian Muslims over the course of five years, the most publicized and televised instance of genocide in human history. Giddens does not seem to be concerned that his program could unwittingly produce conditions even worse than the ones depicted in Orwell's *Nineteen Eighty-Four*.

Giddens's modernism comes through also in his apparent belief that the traditions which would be synthetically created can be enumerated, much like natural scientists have mapped out DNA or any number of other complex compounds. He writes:

> The evacuation of local contexts of action – the "disembedding" of activities – can be understood as implying processes of intensified detraditionalization. We are the first generation to live in a thoroughly post-traditional society, a term that is in many ways preferable to "postmodern." A post-traditional society is not a national society – we are speaking here of a global cosmopolitan order. Nor is it a society in which traditions cease to exist; in many respects there are impulses, or pressures, towards the sustaining or the recovery of traditions. It is a society, however, in which tradition changes its status. In the context of a globalizing, cosmopolitan order, traditions are constantly brought into contact with one another and forced to "declare themselves."
>
> (1994: 83)

Do all traditions declare themselves or do some slip through undeclared? It is difficult to imagine the complete declaration of each and every tradition. The examples Giddens gives of this "remolding of tradition" and new traditions that are "invented" include nationalism, "renewed forms of religion," and traditions pertaining to gender and the family (ibid.: 84). He distinguishes sharply between his program for engineering traditions and that of the fundamentalists, whom he defines as those who seek "to defend tradition in the traditional way – in circumstances where that defence has become intrinsically problematic" (ibid.). But let us apply Giddens's own definition of fundamentalism to his program: how is Giddens's program any less fundamentalist than the traditional traditionalists he criticizes? In a sense, he is defending the *modernist* tradition in the traditional way of social engineering, and I would argue that his program is just as "intrinsically problematic." Borrowing from Ernest Gellner (1992), one might characterize Giddens as an "Enlightenment fundamentalist." The social engineer, no matter how well intentioned, cannot control the degeneration of nationalism, religion, new forms of gender and family relations, or any other synthetic tradition into new forms of oppression. Any and all traditions, old-fashioned as well as the new synthetic ones, are inherently oppressive unless tempered by cultural standards of justice and mercy (or compassion). Moreover, once traditions meet each other and "declare themselves," the result may well be violence, not dialogue; the splintering of the cosmopolitan consciousness into smaller group-consciences that are hostile to each other; and a furthering of social fission that seems to run contrary to Giddens's goal of social fusion.

It is all too easy to find illustrations of these negative scenarios. When gays and lesbians tried to march in the traditional-traditional (as opposed to the proposed synthetic-traditional) St Patrick's Day Parade in Boston, Massachusetts, both sides declared their traditions openly, but the result was divisiveness and a court battle. The Thanksgiving Holiday in the USA is no longer depicted in the traditional way as a commemoration of cooperation between Pilgrims and Native Americans, but in recent years has become a commemoration of the oppression of Native Americans, of the Pilgrims as invaders, of similarities to other tales of oppression such as slavery, and so on. Again, the result of this clash of synthetic traditions is not social cohesion, but increased social divisiveness. It is hard to imagine how things could be otherwise because these synthetic traditions are *rationally constructed* and nothing leads to disputes, arguments, and divisiveness more than rationalization. Giddens does not seem to be aware that social cohesion is primarily an emotional, not a cognitive, matter.

Giddens's call for a cosmopolitan social renewal based on the post-traditional society corresponds in many ways to what I have called elsewhere the postemotional society (Meštrović 1996, 1997). We both seem to converge on the insight that contemporary Western societies are extending rationalism and mechanization to traditional domains, especially the emotions. George Ritzer's (1992) elaboration of Weber's insight into the "McDonaldization of Society" is fast becoming the McDonaldization of emotions. However, we differ in two key respects. First, I focus on the rationalist manipulation of emotions whereas Giddens does not analyze the emotional component of traditions. Second, whereas Giddens welcomes this extension of the postmodern concern with simulation – for what is a synthetic tradition if not fake? – I regard it as a possible neo-Orwellian tool for oppression. Giddens fails to address the issue of who will be in charge of this project in creating artificial traditions. (The critical theorists suffered from the same arrogant fault in their program for reinventing the Enlightenment. Was Adorno going to be in charge? Is Habermas going to be in charge of this program today?) Should one assume that, whoever is in charge, one should trust that their intentions will be benign? And even if the intentions of the post-traditional *nomenklatura* are benign, is that a guarantee that the outcome will be benign?

GIDDENS'S VERSION OF THE END OF HISTORY

Giddens is clearly aware of and discusses Francis Fukuyama's *The End of History and the Last Man* (1992). Fukuyama's central thesis in this book is simplistic in the extreme: that the collapse of Communism marked the triumph of Western democracy and ushered in the end of history. By "history," Fukuyama refers broadly to all traditional anti-democratic phenomena such as nationalism, irrationalism, tribalism, and Balkanization. As we have seen in the previous chapter, Giddens rejects the notion of endings, so one cannot expect him to endorse Fukuyama's position whole-heartedly. Yet, given Giddens's modernist assumptions and conformity to popular ideologies in the current *fin de siècle*, one can expect him to sympa-thize with Fukuyama overall and to *modify* Fukuyama's position such that the contemporary world is perceived as one of increasing and globalizing democracy whose problems can be resolved through reflexivity and the synthetic reinvention of traditions. This is precisely what Giddens sets out to achieve.

Giddens is no less boosterish and naive than Fukuyama in proclaiming that "Suddenly everyone has discovered democracy!" (1994: 104) and in referring to the "universal enthusiasm for democracy" (ibid.: 105). It is simply not true that, as Giddens claims, "Fascism failed long ago, Communism is no more" (ibid.). Let me repeat that one finds such facile assessments of the current political scene in popular magazines and the information media in general. Yet fascism is alive and well in Serbia in the 1990s; China is still Communist (along with several other countries, such as North Korea and Cuba); and, as of this writing, Communism is degener-ating into new forms of authoritarianism in the former Soviet Union. And it is not a question of traditional Communism *per se*, but of its possible muta-tion into new forms of totalitarianism in the former Soviet Union, and to some, albeit lesser, extent Eastern Europe (Meštrović 1993b). There are many other oppressive regimes in the world, from Hussein in Iraq (the West's former ally against Iran) to Gaddafi in Libya. Finally, the general level of cynicism in purportedly democratic Western nations is so extensive that it seems unrealistic to be cheering for the apparent triumph of democ-racy. Opinion polls in the USA suggest that most Americans distrust the officials they have elected to government office and are disgusted with the two-party system. Moreover, the widespread political corruption uncovered in governments from Italy and France to the USA (especially the Clinton Administration) are bound to take their toll on the alleged enthusiasm for democracy even in so-called democracies.

Giddens writes of the formerly Communist nations as "catching up" with the West. He does not consider the possibility that Russia may not catch up, and, in recent years, has been decidedly hostile to the West. Former East Germany is catching up nicely, albeit at a great cost. More importantly, and as noted by Cushman (1995) and others, Giddens does not consider seriously the fact that Soviet Communism was a *modernist* system that promised eman-cipation but delivered totalitarianism. Many other formerly Communist Eastern European nations have elected former Communists and not demo-cratic reformers to key positions of power. Historically, most social revolutions have degenerated into new forms of oppression, and there is no good reason that the apparent demise of Communism will be an exception. And Bolshevik habits of the heart – like any other habits of the heart – do not dissolve easily. Moreover, Giddens does not consider that with the disintegration of the belief, even a vestigial belief, in socialist orthodoxy has come a dramatic rise of criminality in Russia.

What was amazing about formerly Communist countries is that Communist egalitarianism was not able to keep the more productive parts of the Soviet and Yugoslav nation-states on the same low level as the more productive parts. The Soviet Union had not been able to pull the more Western Baltic republics down to its own level of living despite decades of effort at levelling. Similarly, in the former Yugoslavia, Belgrade was unable to level the amazing productivity of Western-leaning Slovenia and Croatia despite similar efforts. Up to a point, Giddens and Fukuyama are right in their unabashed admiration for Western culture: there is a strong basis for admiring Western free-market and democratic institutions because even in small doses these institutions have worked wonders. But even where Western cultural phenomena were partially successful in the former Communist world, they were modified through the cultural prisms of local habits of the heart. Nor is this different from any other portion of the World. Western free markets and democracy differ in the USA, Canada, Great Britain, France, and Germany. Similarly, the Islamic world has been unable to speak in one voice from Malaysia to Libya.

Nevertheless, Giddens reviews with some approval Fukuyama's linkage of allegedly universalist democracy with capitalism. Giddens asks, "Yet how satisfying to live in will this social universe of triumphant liberal democracy be?" (1994: 107). He notes that, according to Fukuyama, it will be a boring, mediocre existence. He also endorses Fukuyama's view that democratization originates in "a desire for autonomy and respect" (ibid.: 108). He faults Fukuyama for not taking into account capitalism's disregard for ecological concerns; failing to explain "why democratization has accelerated so rapidly in very recent times" (ibid.); and not taking seriously the threat to "social order" posed by nihilistic and bored citizens living in the end of history. My objection to both Giddens and Fukuyama is that in their depictions of an idealized and purportedly universal capitalism they both overlook the fact that no such phenomenon exists. American capitalism is completely different from French capitalism, for example, which is more socialist in its orientation. The "pure capitalism" that is being exported to formerly Communist nations is really pure fiction: it never existed and does not exist in this form anywhere in the world. Not surprisingly, it has caused tremendous human hardship and disillusionment in formerly Communist nations that sought to emulate the West. How quickly Fukuyama and Giddens have forgotten the days of the robber-barons in capitalism's heyday in the West, as well as the new-style robber-barons who rule today's capitalism. Finally, why should the West feel superior to formerly Communist nations with regard to widely available day care services, medical care, and other social services that many Western countries offer only to those who can afford them?

Giddens's alternatives to Fukuyama's perceived deficiencies in explaining the collapse of Communism and the triumph of democracy include the following: the electronic media globalized the Velvet Revolution and contributed to it. (This constitutes one instance of Giddens's few, fleeting, and superficial references to the media in all of his writings.) Communist states collapsed not because they were weak but because wider democratic forces in global society were strong. "Democratization processes today are driven by the expansion of social reflexivity and detraditionalization" (ibid.: 111). Giddens also argues that the essence of democracy does not lie in the participation of the electorate but in dialogue and public discussion of issues. Yet modern democracies such as the USA, Canada, and Great Britain have undergone many scandals in recent years concerning government secrecy and illegal withholding and manipulation of information. For example, President Bill Clinton has been embroiled in such issues concerning Whitewater, the misuse of FBI files, the illegal firing of his travel staff, the misappropriation of campaign finances, and other related scandals. The Pentagon apparently deceived the American people about the alleged accuracy of "smart bombs" and the expensive, technologically advanced weapons that were used in the Gulf War. The FBI was found to be negligent in its crime-fighting activities. The CIA withheld information concerning chemical weapons storage during the Gulf War. And so on. Reflexive processes do not necessarily lead to openness, but can lead to more skillful deception. And such processes are not sufficient for sustaining democracy without the revivification of traditions designed to promote social solidarity. Giddens is careful to note that he is not advocating a return to traditional forms of community or civil society because these were often inimical to human autonomy. Instead, he advocates the careful reconstruction of communities and traditions that will promote reflexivity, autonomy, and dialogue. (Let me repeat that I make a sharp distinction between Durkheim's notion of spontaneous revivification of civil religions and Giddens's program of synthetic reinvention of traditions.)

Although Giddens cites Tocqueville to illustrate the oppressive forms of community that must be avoided, he omits any mention of Tocqueville's most devastating claims vis-à-vis Giddens's optimism concerning democracy: Tocqueville's not so latent doubts about democracy are clear in his reaction to the 1848 revolution in France and also in his overall reaction to the American experiment in democracy. Giddens's and other modernists's unbridled optimism concerning the Velvet Revolution in which Communism collapsed needs to be tempered with Tocqueville's observation in *The Old Regime and the French Revolution* ([1856] 1955) that aristocracy was more entrenched five years following the French Revolution than prior to it. In other words, all revolutions are subject to creeping counter-revolutions. In addition, Tocqueville felt that democracy leads to conformity, not autonomy – in this regard, Tocqueville may be considered a precursor to Riesman's (1950) notion of conformist other-directedness – and he consistently compared and contrasted the benefits and disadvantages of democracy with aristocracy. Consider the following passages from Tocqueville's *Democracy in America* as illustrations of democracy's possible disadvantages:

> The advantage of democracy is not, as has been sometimes asserted, that it protects the interests of all, but simply that it protects those of the majority.
>
> ([1845] 1945:257)

> No sooner do you set foot upon American ground than you are stunned by a kind of tumult; a confused clamor is heard on every side, and a thousand simultaneous voices demand the satisfaction of their social wants.
>
> (ibid.: 259)

> This senseless agitation which democratic government has introduced into the political world influences all social intercourse.
>
> (ibid.: 260)

> In America the same passions are to be met with as in Europe, some originating in human nature, others in the democratic condition of society. Thus, in the United States I found that restlessness of heart. . . . I found there the democratic feeling of envy expressed under a thousand different forms.
>
> (ibid.: 336)

> I believe that the Indian nations of North America are doomed to perish.
>
> (ibid.: 354)

> The legal barrier which separated the two races is falling away, but not that which exists in the manners of the country; slavery recedes, but the prejudices to which it has given birth are immovable.
>
> (ibid.: 373)

> These two races [white and black] are fastened to each other

without intermingling; and they are alike unable to separate
entirely or to combine.

(ibid.: 370)

Tocqueville's gloomy predictions about the state of race and ethnic relations in the USA are slowly but surely coming true. His comments on
American restlessness and open-ended desire for gain remind one of
Durkheim's descriptions of anomie. Opinion polls indicate that most
contemporary Americans still feel that the government serves the interests of
the elite, who have become a "majority" in terms of power even as the
numerically larger "minority" of ordinary people should act as the power
broker. Tocqueville was realistic about democracy's advantages as well as
shortcomings. Again, it is important to note that Giddens's glib misreading
of Tocqueville is typical of other modernists, who misread *Democracy in
America* as an endorsement, not a critique.

It is not clear that Giddens's high modernity version of democracy will be
able to avoid the pitfalls that Tocqueville has already mapped out. Can
dialogical democracy convince ethnic minorities in the USA or other
Western democracies that they are full participants in democracy? The
current, dismal state of ethnic relations in the West suggests that this will
be a difficult task. Will reflexivity curb anomic consumerism in Western
democracies? There are no good reasons to suppose that this is possible. And
American provincialism and ethnocentrism – democracy for us, history for
them – have only increased since Tocqueville's writing, as have similar
phenomena in other Western democracies. (Baudrillard is on target in this
regard – the have-nots must exit.) Western democracies today are characterized by shrill accusations of racism, sexism, power elites, and injustice
coming from all sides, not a generalized feeling of happy confidence in
democracy.

Against Giddens's modernist pronouncements on the inherent desirability of democracy and free markets, it is probably more realistic to claim
that certainly not capitalism and probably not democracy *per se* suffice for a
good society. Capitalism, that is, the market, is efficient and has many uses.
Democracy is preferable to tyranny, but as Herbert Marcuse ([1964] 1991)
and other critical theorists point out, it can and does lead to its own distinct
forms of "totalitarianism." (One should keep in mind that Giddens [1982a]
is dismissive of Marcuse.) If Communism suffered because it became an
empty ideology out of touch with the repressive realities it produced, the
effort to make capitalism and democracy into an ideology seems inevitably
suspect. Such efforts are already being rejected as Western cultural imperialism in many formerly Communist countries.

Finally, Giddens misses Tocqueville's most important cultural point:
every country that adopts democracy will develop it in a unique and idiosyn-
cratic way because democracy must mesh with the "habits of the heart" of a

136

particular people. Had Western analysts taken Tocqueville seriously, they might have attempted to tailor Western standards of democracy and capitalism to suit Russian, Polish, and other habits of the heart in formerly Communist nations. Instead, Western nations attempted to arrogantly impose "pure" capitalism and democracy onto these newly liberated countries, and mostly failed. Similarly, Giddens's high modernity version of democracy is not mindful of local differences in habits of the heart that might not be receptive to his ideas of reflexivity, agency, dialogue, and so on. More importantly, he seems unaware that the meanings of reflexivity, agency, and dialogue vary across cultures. In addition, Giddens seems to assume that habits of the heart can be universalized and even created synthetically. Such modernist assumptions fail to grasp what habits of the heart are all about, namely, rootedness in the local and the particular.

THE MEANINGS OF BOSNIA

Francis Fukuyama (1992) dismisses the 1990s genocide in the former Yugoslavia as a regrettable incident that holds no larger meaning for his theory or for the rest of the world so long as it is "contained" within the borders of the former Yugoslavia. One would expect, by way of contrast, that Giddens's structuration theory should suggest that genocide in Bosnia cannot be "contained" in the traditional, materialist way because of time-space distanciation. Specifically, the information media have disembedded Bosnia from the former Yugoslavia and brought it into the living rooms of Western homes via television. But the perception that there is something special about Bosnia because it has been globalized is not developed explicitly by Giddens. If one were to develop this line of analysis, one would have to challenge other core assumptions of his theory of modernity. For with regard to Bosnia, "clever people" in the modern West "knew" a lot about the horrors that occurred there, but were not able to act as human agents to influence their governments to put a stop to it as mandated by the UN Charter (Cushman and Meštrović 1996). Actually, the whole question of what to do became problematic, because the impetus to stop genocide seems to be an old-fashioned tradition based on what used to be called moral imperatives, and the new, synthetic tradition for dealing with widely publicized genocide through other-directed negotiation seems to be in a nascent state. Nevertheless, from Giddens's comments on Bosnia in relation to the rest of his argument, it is becoming clear what this synthetic tradition is becoming: it is crystallizing into a new ethic of avoidance of taking sides and of stopping genocide through "dialogue."

Not surprisingly, Giddens's program for dealing with violence through dialogue fits the spirit of the times in which we live. Regarding Bosnia, the emphasis on negotiating a peace settlement instead of taking decisive military action against the Serbian perpetrators of the genocide is to be found in the official positions put forth by the UN, the European Community, Jimmy Carter, and, most recently, President Clinton. The negotiated peace settlement brokered by President Clinton in Dayton, Ohio, in November 1995 suggests why Giddens is popular. His theory correctly foreshadowed such an outcome against the many traditional voices who called for old-fashioned military action against the Belgrade regime to stop the genocide. Whether the cause is Riesman's other-directedness or Baudrillard's postmodernism, there no longer exists a distinction between "good guys" and "bad guys." Everyone has a valid point of view – victim as well as victimizer – that must be expressed in dialogue. Yet if Bosnia is a harbinger for a Giddens-like future, it is not self-evident that such a future is benign. The traditionalists may have a point that the current peace plan for Bosnia actually rewards Serbian genocidal aggression and promotes peace without justice (even though there are many cultural standards of justice). As of this writing, most refugees cannot return home and most indicted war criminals are not in custody. Giddens may be right to imply that such traditionalists will eventually be forgotten as the new synthetic tradition of dialogue takes over. If his synthetic, post-traditional world becomes realized, today's inner-directed moralists will soon be forgotten. Yet it is hard to believe that the primordial thirst for justice can be extinguished that quickly.

Giddens's discussion of Bosnia is to be found in a chapter entitled "Political Theory and the Problem of Violence." It follows a discussion of male violence against women, from which Giddens generalizes:

> Men's violence against women, or a great deal of it, can be understood as a generalized refusal of dialogue. Couldn't one see this as a Clausewitzian theory of interpersonal relations? Where dialogue stops, violence begins. Yet such violence is (in principle) as archaic in the personal domain as Clausewitz's theorem in the wider public arena.
>
> (1994: 242)

One can see in this passage an affinity to his earlier claims in *The Transformation of Intimacy* (1992b) that dialogue and rationality can democratize relations between the sexes. He applies the same formula regarding emotions and women to nations, interpersonal as well as international relations: dialogue can stop violence. Let me point out that with regard to domestic violence Giddens does not consider seriously women's violence against men, other women, or children, nor men's violence against men or children. These phenomena get passing reference (ibid.: 122–3).[5] Are all of these the results of blocked dialogue? If they are, Giddens has not proved it. More importantly, he underestimates the cunning of human reason: many "clever" abusers go to therapy, understand their problems, engage in surface dialogue with the objects of their violence, and still continue to be violent. In any event, Giddens leaps from domestic violence to violence in Bosnia and other countries to demonstrate the same principle. According to him:

> As I write these lines, a tenuous dialogue has been established between warring parties in Israel and in Bosnia; the armed conflicts in Somalia, Angola, Afghanistan and elsewhere look set to continue. To move from violence against women back towards such military confrontation might appear as heterodox as the link developed with overall processes of pacification. Yet the connections are there. The war in Bosnia, for example, witnessed the systematic rape of Muslim women as a deliberate way of humiliating them. . . . Confrontations such as those in the former Yugoslavia and other regions might perhaps be a residue of the past – a clearing-up of lines of division and hostility. Alternatively, *and more disturbingly, they may be the shape of things to come.* For the very changes that act to reduce the possibility of wars between states might increase the chances of regional military confrontations – the more so since fundamentalisms of various kinds can act to sharpen pre-existing ethnic or cultural differences.
>
> (1994: 243; emphasis added)

A few factual corrections are in order. Rape in the former Yugoslavia was committed overwhelmingly by Serbs, and involved the rape of Muslim men as well as women (Cigar 1995). In fact, documentation exists that the rape was bestial and often involved sadistic torture and genital mutilation. Far from being a "regional conflict," the so-called Yugoslav conflict involves a war between states. Bosnia-Herzegovina is a duly recognized nation-state that was attacked by the rump Yugoslavia consisting of Serbia and Montenegro. It has been well documented that Serbia's President Milošević continued to arm and supply the so-called Bosnian Serbs up to, during, and following the Dayton peace talks in 1995, so that the appearance of a civil war is just that – a ploy (see Cushman and Meštrović 1996).

How can such conflicts be "inhibited or contained," asks Giddens? He replies that there are three potential remedies:

> The first is the potential influence of dialogic democracy; the second, the countering of fundamentalism; the third, controlling what I shall call degenerate spirals of emotional communication. All relate to, or draw on, ideas discussed in other parts of this volume.
>
> (1994: 223)

Several theoretical aspects of this program for preventing Bosnia-like violence are of interest. In a typically modernist way, Giddens regards emotions as the culprit in such violence. He cannot grasp that genocide is a meticulously planned, rational act. Yet he seems to contradict his overall emphasis on synthetic traditions by failing to consider that the "emotions" which set into motion the war against Bosnia might have been synthetic as well. Why would 1990s Serbs suddenly want to expel or kill all Muslims in the name of a tradition that harks back over six hundred years to the 1389 Battle of Kosovo? If it were spontaneous collective effervescence, one would still have to explain it. But far from being spontaneous, it was apparently orchestrated and organized in a very modernist way by the Milošević regime (Cigar 1995; Cohen 1996). Second, who are the fundamentalists in this picture? Giddens does not name the parties to the conflict – indeed, he does not mention the Serbs by name anywhere in his book. Is one to assume that the Bosnian Muslims are the fundamentalists who must be countered? Or can modernists conceive of Serbian Christian modernist fundamentalists who are not countered precisely because they claim to act in the name of European civilization? The indicted Serbian war criminal, Radovan Karadžić, has stated on numerous occasions that he and his followers are doing Europe a favor by persecuting the Muslims (for documentation, see Meštrović 1996).

In his concluding paragraph to this chapter and discussion, Giddens is no less vague or evasive:

> I would define a degenerate spiral of communication as one where antipathy feeds on antipathy, hate upon hate. And this observation brings us full circle. For how else could one explain the events in Bosnia, and parallel happenings elsewhere? Fundamentalisms, as I have said earlier, are edged with potential violence. Wherever fundamentalism takes hold, whether it be religious, ethnic, nationalist or gender fundamentalism, degenerate spirals of communication threaten. What is originally merely an isolationism, or perhaps only an insistence on the purity of a local tradition, can, if circumstances so conspire, turn into a vicious circle of animosity and venom. Bosnia sits on a historic fault-line dividing Christian Europe from Islamic civilization. Yet one cannot produce a sufficient explanation of the Yugoslavian conflict only by reference to old hostilities. Those hostilities, when refocused in the present, provide a context; once conflict begins, and hate starts to feed on hate, those who were good neighbors can end as the bitterest of enemies.
>
> (1994: 245)

This description is commensurate with the many Western views of the Balkans as a cauldron of ancient as well as contemporary hatreds. Giddens implies that the globalization of dialogic democracy can eventually serve as an antidote to such "fundamentalist" ills. But in fact, the Bosnian tragedy is not the result of some fictitious picture of neighbor turning against neighbor. As Norman Cigar (1995), other authors, and even the information media have documented conclusively, the Belgrade regime planned, organized, and managed the genocide from the very beginning (see also Cushman and Meštrović 1996). In other words, Milošević used modernist techniques – and especially television – to give genocide the appearance of tribal conflict. Moreover, the West's "dialogic democracy" vis-à-vis the "warring parties," which repeatedly brought them to negotiating tables in order to partition Bosnia along ethnic lines, actually served the cause of the Belgrade regime.

Ironically, Baudrillard, whose previous stands on postmodernism might have led him to conclude that there is no meaning to the Bosnian tragedy, takes a definite stand against the Belgrade regime as well as Western Europe in this regard. Baudrillard has published three essays on the Bosnian War in *La Libération*, on 7 January 1993, 3 July 1995, and 17 July 1995.[6] In these essays, he does nothing less than accuse the West of active collaboration in Serbian genocide against Muslims. One would not expect such a reaction from a postmodernist. His essays are worth contrasting with Giddens's comments on Bosnia. This contrast exposes the fact that Giddens's thought is consistently and typically Western and modernist while Baudrillard – despite the many savage criticisms made of him – is a radical thinker.

Baudrillard begins the essay "No Pity for Sarajevo" by justifying the anger expressed at the West by a citizen of Sarajevo who said, "I spit on Europe." According to Baudrillard:

> The fine point of the story is the following: in carrying out ethnic cleansing, the Serbs are Europe's cutting edge. The "real" Europe in the making is a white Europe, a bleached Europe that is morally, economically, and ethnically integrated and cleansed. . . . Some say that if we let this happen in Sarajevo, it will be our due later on. We are, in fact, already there, since all European countries are on the road to ethnic cleansing. This is the true Europe, slowly in the making in the shadows of national parliaments, and spearheaded by Serbia. . . . The miraculous end will be at hand only when the exterminations come to an end, and when the borders of "white" Europe have been drawn. It is as if all European nationalities and policies had acted in concert to take out a contract for murder with the Serbs, who have become the agents of the West's dirty jobs.

Unlike Giddens, Baudrillard captures succinctly the amazing paradox that after five years of dialogue, negotiation, and touting of Western human rights standards, the West essentially let the Serbs keep the spoils of their genocide in Bosnia. It is incumbent upon Giddens to explain how this was possible despite all his lofty theorizing about dialogue, reflexivity, democracy, and globalization.

In the second essay, "The West's Serbianization," Baudrillard notes astutely that the West has finally concluded that "the Serbs are the aggressors," but that this fact will not move the West to stop the Serbs. Indeed, the world's respected fact-gathering organizations had concluded that Serbs were responsible for over 90 percent of the human rights abuses and 100 percent of the genocide in the Bosnian War (see Meštrović 1996). Baudrillard continues: "This rather platonic recognition of the executioners as executioners does not imply that the victims will be recognized as victims." Baudrillard claims that the West did not act to stop the Serbs because

> No one dares, nor wants to step up to the final analysis: to recognize that the Serbs are not only the aggressors (this is a bit like breaking down an open door), but *are our objective allies in this cleansing operation for a future Europe,* freed of its bothersome minorities, and for a future world order, freed from all radical challenges to its own values – based on the democratic dictatorship of human rights and on free markets.
>
> (emphasis added)

Baudrillard captures the darker scenarios to which I alluded earlier in this chapter in my discussion of Giddens's rosy assessment of democracy. Democracy, like all other cultural institutions, can become pathogenic if not restrained by habits of the heart pertaining to justice and compassion. (To repeat, American or other standards of justice and compassion will not be exactly the same as Bosnian standards of these same phenomena, yet there will be some overlap.) But what is amazing is that Baudrillard, often referred to as the "high priest" of postmodernism, is implying something similar. Perhaps it is also true that, as Baudrillard claims, "We suggest our job is done once we have declared the Serbs the 'bad guys', but not the enemy." As in the previous essay, he claims that Europeans "are fighting exactly the same enemies as the Serbs: Islam, the Muslims," from Chechnya to Algeria. The West's many ostentatious efforts at "dialogue" in the Bosnian War may have been a sinister mask for hiding collaboration with Serbia. If this is true, then the Western powers (especially Great Britain and France) who have covertly favored the Serbs and have done their secret best to manipulate the United Nations so as to prevent effective action being taken against the Serbs are guilty not simply of failing to meet their legal obligations to prevent genocide (under the UN Charter), but also of complicity in it. Given all that we have learned from Hegel and Marx concerning the cunning of rationality, this sinister possibility should be taken seriously.

In his concluding paragraph, Baudrillard asserts that imperialism has changed faces:

> What the West wants to impose on the world, from here on out and in the guise of universals, are not completely disjointed values, but its lack of values. . . . We generously distribute the right to be different, while secretly and inexorably working to produce a pale, and undifferentiated world. This terrorism is not the result of fundamentalism, but of an unfounded culture. It is the integrationism of emptiness, whose stakes are beyond any political forms or vicissitudes.

This passage could have been written as a rejoinder to Giddens! Giddens promotes a synthetic universalism that is not rooted in habits of the heart. Giddens cites fundamentalism as an obstacle to the globalization of democracy while he is oblivious to the fundamentalism of his own position.

In the third essay, "When the West Stands in for the Dead," Baudrillard adds that regarding the slaughter of the Bosnian Muslims, the West watches helplessly as "this dirty little job (with international status) is carried out by intermediary mercenaries," the Serbs. One should not fail to note, in relation to the discussion of Giddens versus Baudrillard in the previous chapter, that: (1) Baudrillard contradicts many of Giddens's charges that postmodernity revels in fragmentation of meanings, contextualization of truth claims, and the dissolution of epistemology. Clearly, in the essays cited above, Baudrillard takes a clear stand regarding meaning, truth, and value. (2) Baudrillard's expressed opinions in these essays, not only on Bosnia but also regarding European civilization, globalization, and universality, seem to contradict his assessments on these topics as expressed in his other writings. Thus, Giddens's modernism can dissolve into the postmodernist position he rejects and Baudrillard's postmodernism can come across as modernist in the old-fashioned sense, even traditionalist. The more important point is that Baudrillard's provocative stand helps to expose the vacuousness of both Fukuyama's and Giddens's theories of democracy.

FROM BOSNIA TO RUSSIA

Like Fukuyama and most other Western commentators on post-Cold War developments, Giddens (1994) sees in the end of the Cold War the triumph of democracy. He fails to see, as Anatoly Khazanov (1995) notes perceptively, that the much touted revolution against Communism never really took place. Instead, a nationalism aimed at *fission* – the splintering of nation-states into nations in search of states – as opposed to the modernist nationalism of *fusion* (the creation of vast federations such as the USSR) has replaced Communism as the dominating and state-supported ideology in all of the newly formed independent nations that used to be part of the Soviet Empire. Because Russia dominated the former Soviet Union, it has reacted to this fission by openly seeking to establish its old Empire.

In general, according to Khazanov, "It was hard for Russia to free itself from the legacy of the empire, just as it was difficult for many Russians to free themselves from a certain empire-oriented psychology" (ibid.: 38). Thus, "when Russia declared herself the legal successor to the Soviet Union, and in a more tacit way the legal successor to the Russian Empire, other republics conceived this as her desire to dominate in the commonwealth" (ibid.: 47). Khazanov's conclusion is chilling, but probably more correct than the one reached by Giddens concerning the triumph of democracy:

> The message that Russia is sending to the near-abroad countries is fairly clear. In violation of the Treaty on the Conventional Armed Forces in Europe, Russia is deploying its new 51st army in the North Caucasus. . . . Foreign Minister Kozyrev asserted the Kremlin's right to use direct military force to protect the ethnic Russians living in other ex-Soviet countries. Hitler made similar statements regarding the ethnic Germans. The consequences are well known.
>
> (ibid.: 224)

In general, Khazanov writes, "the Soviet Union was an anachronism, because its creation delayed the disintegration of the former Russian Empire for more than 70 years" (ibid.: 240). Nationalism proved to be a much more powerful social force than the modernist system that Communism was, and also more powerful than the Soviet nation-state. But aren't all nation-states erected on the basis of a dominant national group that oppresses minorities?

Neither Khazanov nor Giddens makes the conceptual connection between what happened after the demise of the Soviet Union and what happened after the demise of Yugoslavia. I contend that Yugoslavia was an empire dominated by Serbs every bit as much as the Soviet Union was an empire dominated by Russia. The collapse of Communism destroyed the nation-states of the Soviet Union and Yugoslavia but also unleashed the emancipatory and nationalistic forces of the submerged nations that were oppressed in the Soviet and Yugoslav Empires. Belgrade's cruel war against the Muslims in Bosnia foreshadowed Moscow's cruel war against Chechnya. Giddens's relevance to these dramatic occurrences is indirect, for he represents the dominant Western response to these events, misconstrued as part of a process of democratization: Western nation-states offered "dialogue" as a moral response to Belgrade-sponsored and Moscow-sponsored terror. In a more inner-directed era fifty years ago, such a response would have been called appeasement. More importantly, I do not see the Russian and Serbian responses to the emancipatory politics of the nations they oppressed as remotely connected to a democratization process. On the contrary, I believe that the road to authoritarianism has been paved.

Insufficient attention has been paid to the role of Islam in the conflicts that Khazanov chronicles. The distinguished anthropologist Akbar Ahmed (1992, 1995) has argued convincingly concerning the coming apocalyptic confrontation between the West and Islam, and warns of the coming Last Crusade. One should note that both Radovan Karadžić and Vladimir Zhirinovsky, the proponent of Greater Russian nationalism, have already made public statements to the effect that their racist policies regarding Muslims in Bosnia and Chechnya, respectively, are a meritorious extension of the unfinished Crusades. Such contemporary references to the Crusades – which involved the wholesale slaughter and expulsion of peoples – constitute the creation of "synthetic traditions" that concern Giddens. Yet Giddens is not mindful of the possibility that synthetic traditions can be used for evil, specifically genocidal, purposes. There is no good reason to suppose that synthetic traditions will be used solely to promote democracy.

Nearly a century after Max Weber's famous thesis in *The Protestant Ethic and the Spirit of Capitalism* ([1904] 1958), there is no study of what might be termed "The Orthodox Ethic and the Spirit of Authoritarianism." In both the Soviet Union and Yugoslavia, the Orthodox Church was frequently supportive of Russian and Serb-sponsored oppression of minorities during the twentieth century (for documentation, see Khazanov 1995 and Cigar 1995, respectively). It seems to be high time for the cultural tendencies of the Orthodox religion to be studied with regard to their impact on Communism and Russian as well as Serbian imperialism. But Giddens does not take seriously Max Weber's study of the *cultural* origins of Western capitalism and liberalism, so that he is not in a position to suggest a similar study of the cultural roots of Communism or the authoritarianism that preceded it, flourished during the Communist era, and is likely to flower again in the post-Cold War era in some portions of the former Soviet and Yugoslav Empires.

These are among the several important phenomena that Giddens omits in his overly felicitous account of the alleged triumph of democracy in the post-Cold War era.

CONCLUSIONS

With regard to politics, Giddens seems to find himself in the following predicament. On the one hand, those who would complete the Enlightenment project (such as Habermas) or who think it has been completed (Fukuyama) seem naive. Giddens seems as naive as Habermas and Fukuyama in many regards, especially in his earlier works on politics

(Giddens 1982b, 1987). Though Giddens never admits the faults of the Enlightenment project as thoroughly as Bauman (1992) does, in his 1994 work, *Beyond Left and Right*, he seems to be somewhat aware of problems with the modernity project. Reflexivity is not sufficient to produce the democratic transformation that he seeks. On the other hand, Giddens consistently refuses to join Baudrillard and the postmodernists in exposing and rebelling against the hypocritical, oppressive, and defunct aspects of the Enlightenment project. He cannot admit that synthetic traditions can be used for frankly authoritarian purposes. He thus attempts to steer what seems to be a middle ground between these two extremes, yet his *via media* is nevertheless modernist. For example, his proposed creation of synthetic traditions to offset modernity's problems in achieving social solidarity is not fundamentally different from many other grand experiments in societal engineering that have been undertaken in the present century. He tones down yet sympathizes with Fukuyama's naive and incorrect proclamations that democracy has triumphed over Communism and Fascism. Giddens offers what he calls dialogic democracy as the remedy for interpersonal as well as trans-national violence.

In sum, Giddens offers a "feel good" political sociology. His program for "radical" social renewal is so "nice" – it has the feel of Marcuse's happy consciousness to it – that it becomes seductive. The happy consciousness automatically negates serious opposition. Yet his program leaves unexamined some fundamental issues that could easily transform his seemingly nice program into yet another modernist program for oppression. He does not prove that the standards that will guide his program for international renewal are universal. He only assumes that they are, and does not consider the role of cultural filters in interpreting democracy, justice, reflexivity, or other phenomena. He does not specify who would be in charge of this proposed program for international societal renewal, who would create the synthetic traditions, which ones, and for what purpose. Yet this is a crucial issue, given the history of dismal transformations of so many social engineering programs into totalitarianism in the present century.

Giddens takes up Bosnia as an illustration of how dialogic democracy could prevent future Bosnias without confronting the mind-numbing fact that modernity failed the victims of genocide in Bosnia. This particular instance of genocide is the best publicized and most televised in history, yet despite so much reflexivity, time-space distanciation, disembeddedness, and other jargon-filled language Giddens uses to capture what is supposedly benign about modernity, the world essentially stood by and watched as heinous crimes were committed in full view of clever, informed agents in the Western world. This failure does not speak well for his proposed program of radical renewal. Bosnians exhibited a naive *faith* in the modern world to live up to the principles enshrined in the UN Charter and other modernist principles. The world failed to deliver on those principles. The result is devastating for a just world order: given that the refrain, "We didn't know," has been exposed as a rationalization, future victims of genocide will have no solid basis for faith in the modernist principles that Giddens espouses.

Giddens's comments on the demise of Communism and on the Soviet Union conveniently fail to address the crucial fact that Soviet Communism was a modernist system. Given the colossal failure of Communism, as well as its cruel "successes" (organized terror, ethnic cleansing, mass deportations, killing off opponents or minority peoples), one might have expected Giddens or any other deep social theorist to confront honestly what went wrong with the modernist project in the Soviet and Yugoslav experiments in rational nation-state building. But Giddens avoids this issue, and spins an idealized vision of democracy and free markets based on a fictitious and postemotional yearning for what the West should, in his view, represent to itself and to the rest of the world.

Giddens never defines or specifies the traditionalist fundamentalists whom he regards as obstacles to democratization. Are they Islamic fundamentalists? Are they the American New Right or evangelical fundamentalists? Can proponents of pure capitalism be regarded as fundamentalists? Moreover, it is not clear how contemporary fundamentalists, of any sort, qualify as traditionalist. In the USA, the New Right fundamentalists do not represent corporate interests characteristic of President Reagan and his crowd, who represented the conservative "fundamentalism" of the rich. The New Right fundamentalists are middle or lower class primarily, and have learned how to use the electronic media to globalize their message. Contrary to his assertions about the feeling of triumph concerning democracy, New Right fundamentalists are openly contemptuous of the present state of democracy in the West. Moreover, Giddens fails to consider that his own assumptions qualify as a watered-down version of Enlightenment fundamentalism. His arguments appeal to the need for *faith* in the Enlightenment project, not to sound reasons for concluding that it is still workable or capable of producing a decent and moral world.

Finally, one should add one more contradiction to the list of many internal contradictions in Giddens's overall thought: his authoritarian depictions of the rigid nation-state as linked with democracy contradicts his other writings on globalization, internationalization, and cosmopolitanism. One cannot have it both ways: a nation of the world necessarily must not take very seriously the sovereignties of various nation-states, while the idea of the nation-state (as depicted by Giddens) cannot allow its sovereignty to be diminished by international communication, the emancipatory drives of its minority peoples, and other factors.

6

GIDDENS'S MODERNISM LITE

> We forget a little too easily that the whole of our reality is
> filtered through the media, including tragic events of the
> past. This means that it is too late to verify and understand
> those events historically, for the characteristic thing about the
> present period, the present *fin de siècle*, is the fact that the tools
> required for such intelligibility have been lost. History should
> have been understood while history still existed.
> — Jean Baudrillard (1993: 90)

We have seen in chapter 5 that with regard to political sociology, Giddens
contradicts himself by promoting social order and a rigidly controlled
nation-state at the same time that he writes about time-space distanciation
and globalization. If one were to take his thoughts on communications and
globalization seriously, and expected him to be consistent, one would have
anticipated his development of a concept of a cyber-nation or some
cosmopolitan equivalent. But as I have indicated in chapter 2, I agree with
Ian Craib and other critics of Giddens who find him "fox-like" and difficult
to follow in general. Giddens really is like quicksilver, or a moving target.
He makes a claim about Comte or Durkheim, and then, a bit later, hedges,
modifies, or even contradicts himself. Or he makes a statement about
modernity, but he qualifies it later. He moves so quickly from topic to topic
– perhaps more "bee-like" in this regard – that his claims seem undeveloped. Whenever he takes up other intellectuals, such as Erving Goffman,
Sigmund Freud, Erik Erikson, or Francis Fukuyama, among others, one gets
the impression that he reads all of them from the narrow vantage point of
how they can be used for his theories. For example, as we have seen in
chapter 4, Giddens's analysis of Freud is *nothing* like Erich Fromm's
ponderous study *Greatness and Limitations of Freud's Thought* (1980). Fromm
criticizes Freud, but clearly tries to understand him with some degree of
empathy on his own terms and the terms of Freud's cultural milieu. Giddens
does not display empathy toward other thinkers, and, given his narrow
understanding of sociology as the study of the modern, he seems unable to

comprehend any non-modernist aspects of other thinkers and theories. Giddens is certainly not easy to characterize as a modernist in the same, heavy-handed way that Parsons was a modernist: Parsons was a still target who made his position on social order very clear. In contrast to Parsons, Giddens seems to sever ties to tradition, yet he seems not to want to enter the realm of the postmodern. Indeed, he wins the sympathy of many readers by playing on their own, latent ambivalence toward the distinction (if there is one) between modernism and postmodernism. It would be one thing if Giddens would just embrace modernism and reject postmodernism. Instead, he invents the term "post-traditional" to account for the modernist and deliberate construction of synthetic traditions. (To repeat: I prefer the term "postemotional" for this process that Giddens calls post-traditional.) His portrait of modernity is every bit as frightening as Baudrillard's – albeit, for different reasons – yet Giddens seems to urge the reader to stick with and even find comfort in modernity. In sum, there is a method to Giddens's mercurial style and to his apparent evasiveness: he is trying to promote modernity lite. In the 1990s, the modern consumer has the choice of opting for "Bud Lite" or the "lite" versions of cheese, potato chips, and other foods. I contend that similarly, Giddens offers the reader Enlightenment-lite, rationality-lite, social control-lite, and other lite versions of modernism.

But again, the more important point is that many people today identify with Giddens's mercurial, ambivalent stand on modernity. One of several reasons for his success is that most contemporary individuals feel torn between a nostalgic longing for the "good old days" of inner-directedness and the seeming promise of freedom offered by other-directedness or the many systems of thought that pass for postmodernism. *Most people seem to feel helpless concerning the course of world events, as David Riesman prophesied and the postmodernists declare, yet they are comforted by Giddens's observations that they can still feel empowered and exercise agency in local milieux.* For example, if no one could do anything to make their elected leaders stop the slaughter in Bosnia or Rwanda, people feel they can still recycle, and make a difference that way. Giddens is popular because he writes about agency and making a difference "in one's back yard," so to speak, at the same time that he proclaims that the course of world events will eventually catch up with a general movement toward democratization and agency.

In this chapter, I intend to analyze some of the ambiguities and contradictions in Giddens's attitude toward modernism and postmodernism. While some analysts have found Giddens's works amenable to postmodernism, I will argue that ultimately, despite (or perhaps because) of his ambiguity and ambivalence, as well as optimistic and authoritarian implications, he is still a modernist of sorts.

Consider, for example, Giddens's argument in *Modernity and Self-Identity* (1991a). On the opening page, Giddens writes that modern institutions must be understood relative to "the degree to which they undercut traditional habits and customs." This is a stereotypical depiction of modernity that goes down like Pepsi on a hot day. Who would think to question it? Moreover, it is entirely consistent with his often-repeated claims that the human agent in modern times is not a cultural dupe or an automaton and that modernity as well as sociology jettison the traditional. Thus, he asserts in *The Nation-State and Violence* that "it is *the* task of 'sociology,' as I would formulate the role of that discipline at any rate, to seek to analyze the nature of that novel world which, in the late twentieth century, we now find ourselves" (1987: 33). Statements such as the ones above qualify to be labelled as modernist. Yet, upon reflection, what could such claims possibly mean? How is it possible for modern institutions to exist *without* a cultural basis, that is, habits and customs? How can the sociologist study the present without confronting constantly residues from the past? If it is only a matter of "degree," will an end point be reached in which social institutions such as the discipline of sociology, the family, church, university, and others have completely severed all ties with tradition? Note that in this regard, Giddens echoes Baudrillard and the notions of the end of culture, end of history, end of the social, and that he echoes other endgame authors as well, including Francis Fukuyama. Giddens implies that modernity begat itself, *a priori*, almost by magic, and sustains itself by magic as well. Yet in his typically ambiguous style, he leaves open the possibility that to *some* "degree" modernity exists by virtue of customs. However, he never bothers to analyze to what degree.

Against one facet of Giddens's ambiguous claim, one could cite Alexis de Tocqueville ([1845] 1945), Oswald Spengler ([1926] 1961), Pitirim Sorokin (1957), Thorstein Veblen ([1899] 1969), and other cultural theorists who argued that modern institutions depend upon a very definite set of cultural habits of the heart, customs, and *traditions* that are every bit as oppressive as those that our traditionalist ancestors endured. Following the Tocqueville trajectory, blended with Erich Fromm's (1955) thought, David Riesman (1950) depicts the anti-traditional, other-directed mode of relating as a form of social character – in other words, as a mode of conformity. Social character is a distant cousin to Durkheim's collective consciousness or Hegel's *Volksgeist*. But Giddens's notion of human agency does *not* seem to be rooted in social character. In any event, modern cultural habits include: the cult of rationalism, the cult of mechanization, the cult of conspicuous consumption, the cult of science, and, for Riesman, the cult of being "nice," among others (Meštrović 1997). None of these modernist phenomena are self-evident, self-begotten, universal, or independent of culture. Rather, each is refracted in a particular way to a particular time and place and culture, and these phenomena are found most often in so-called Western nations. Yet each of these phenomena exerts tremendous constraint on the knowledgeable and skilled agent to conform. A modernist who exhibited excessive emotion on the job, who walked to work instead of driving an automobile, who refused to shop for things he or she did not really need, who believed in voodoo, or who kept the rude mannerisms of the inner-directed era would be regarded as deviant in contemporary Western cultures. Modern institutions and their norms *are* habitual, restraining, and coercive. More precisely, I agree with Keith Tester (1992: 38) that modernists develop "special habits" of their own, but that these still constitute habits, and are still drawn from tradition.

Yet Giddens hedges a little with the claim that "modernity is a post-traditional order, but not one in which the sureties of tradition and habit have been replaced by the certitude of rational knowledge" (1991a:1). (To repeat: he seems to settle on the term "post-traditional" in his latest books, as a comfortable alternative to postmodernism.) He also introduces the concept of "routinization" as a substitute of sorts for "habits of the heart," minus the emotional and cultural components linked with Tocqueville's phrase. Giddens defines "routinization" as "the habitual, taken-for-granted character of the vast bulk of the activities of day-to-day social life; the prevalence of familiar styles and forms of conduct, both supporting and supported by a sense of ontological security" (1987: 376). Despite this, the reader is supposed to believe that modernity undercuts tradition. In *Modernity and Self-Identity*, Giddens has smuggled "certainty" into the discussion, without a cultural or any sort of justification, and implies that our traditional ancestors had a Max-Weber-Protestant-Thesis sort of modern need for certainty. But that is a highly debatable characterization. Traditionalists did not know about actuarial statistics, predicting stock markets, forecasting crops, the Weather Channel, CNN – and apparently did not care about such things. A few magical spells and prayers concerning the weather or crops or having a baby, and so on, seem to have sufficed in traditional societies, but these rites did not guarantee "certainty." Giddens begs the question: What are the *cultural* bases for the "certitude" of rational knowledge? Do scientific findings speak for themselves? Giddens's implicit answer seems to be negative given his overall emphasis on hermeneutics. But if science does not speak for itself, and presupposes faith in science, then science is *not* fundamentally different from religion, and scientific faith cannot be fundamentally different from religious faith. Faith is a throwback to tradition. In fact, as I have demonstrated in chapter 4, this is Durkheim's central argument in *The Elementary Forms of the Religious Life* ([1912] 1965). If Durkheim is correct, and Giddens is not, then the entire distinction between modernist certitude in rational science versus traditional faith in magic and religion is open to question. In that case, so-called Western science is just another totemic system and modernity is deeply rooted in tradition. If Giddens is correct and Durkheim is not, then Giddens must explain how modern institutions can exist without being rooted in traditions. For example, he would have to explain how faith in science is different from traditional faith, and how it arose in modern societies. Giddens evades issues of this sort throughout all his writings because of the radical discontinuity that he posits between modernity and all forms of relating that preceded it (Giddens 1984, 1987).

But in general, the problem with Giddens's smuggling of the notion of traditional "certitude" into this discussion is that he fails to account for the emotions derived from faith that constituted traditional certitude. Clearly, our traditionalist ancestors did not possess our speculative abilities or stock of modernist knowledge. Their so-called "certitude" was not based on modernist foundations – it was based primarily on faith. And modernists may not be capable of reinventing their capacity for faith.

Giddens continues in *Modernity and Self-Identity*: "Modernity institutionalizes the principle of radical doubt and insists that all knowledge takes the form of hypotheses" (1991a: 3). This assertion is true to some extent, but implies that hypotheses can be falsified only. On the other hand, modernity institutionalizes a postemotional sort of faith in the views of opinion-makers, the guarantees made by corporations, the alleged stability of banks, the superiority of the capitalist system over all others, and, in general, in modernity's alleged permanence and supremacy. It would be a very interesting study, indeed, to compare and contrast these modernist attempts at establishing synthetic faith in opinion-makers with traditional faith in the village elders, for example. In any event, the question arises: how does the modern person satisfy the previously held need for certainty (assuming that such a need existed and was met)? Here again, Giddens mirrors Baudrillard and the postmodernists, that modern persons must learn to live with a high degree of uncertainty. Yet Giddens refuses to call himself a postmodernist. His retort is nevertheless unsatisfactory. If modern persons learn to live in this way, they do so with a high degree of cynicism and repressed need to believe in someone or something, a repressed longing for faith. Or, as I have indicated earlier, they learn to compartmentalize their lives such that they are cynical about the "public" sphere, yet exhibit faith in values pertaining to the "private" sphere. The border between public and private varies tremendously across individuals, of course. Nevertheless, such compartmentalization often proves to be unsatisfactory, as proved by an unexpected divorce, the suicide of one's child, or any number of other family tragedies that afflict modern families.

In addition, consider the many examples of Western countries upholding rigorous scientific or ethical principles for "their" citizens while flouting those same principles for non-Western citizens – for the all-inclusive "them." Thus, DDT is banned in the USA, but is sold by the USA to developing countries to contaminate "their" crops and cause illness to "their" citizens. Similarly,

> The United States is paying for experiments in poor countries that
> could allow 1,000 babies to die of AIDS unnecessarily by

withholding a protective drug from HIV-infected pregnant women, the patient advocacy group Public Citizen charged this week. . . . Dr. Wilbert Jordan . . . compared the U.S.-funded foreign research to the infamous "Tuskegee experiment" in Alabama in which the government withheld syphillis treatment from poor black patients. *Also, federal law says U.S. doctors cannot do experiments abroad that would not be tolerated here, the letter added.*[1]

These are a few illustrations among many of the unethical consequences of risk, trust, and hypothesis-testing that do not get adequate attention in modern societies.

According to Giddens (1990), modernity is a risk culture. This claim is meant to demarcate modernity from the certitude of traditional cultures. But were not traditional societies risk cultures of a different sort? For example, the mother in traditional societies risked the possibility that only half of her children might survive past age two. The modernist mother risks that the one or two children she will ever have in her lifetime might be at risk from cancer because of excessive lead in the water they drink, high-voltage power lines near homes, excessive sodium and other substances in the processed food they eat, and other dangers that traditionalists did not know. There is really very little for the modern agent to do about such dangers: only the very wealthy can ensure that they are getting pure water, uncontaminated food, and a safe environment in which to live. To dismiss these systemic dangers in modern living as the "risks" of living in modernity seems cruel.

Giddens claims that in modernity experience is mediated. This sounds very much like Baudrillard's focus on simulation. But did not traditionalists mediate experience through rituals, rites, and all sorts of representations? Giddens also claims that the scientific outlook excludes questions of ethics or morality (1991a: 6). This point seems to be well established, and may constitute a radical departure with tradition. Yet Giddens's vision of modernity crosses the borders established in the well-known yet ferociously debated dogma of value-free science because it is coupled with risk, relativism, uncertainty, and other frightening characteristics. Giddens attempts to put the best modernist face on these traits, writing in *Modernity and Self-Identity*:

> However, I seek to reframe these issues in terms of an institutional account of the late modern order, developed in terms of internal referentiality. The overall thrust of modern institutions is to create settings of action ordered in terms of modernity's own dynamics and severed from "external criteria" – factors external to the social systems of modernity. Although there are numerous exceptions and countertrends, day-to-day social life tends to become separated from

"original" nature and from a variety of experiences bearing on existential questions and dilemmas. The mad, the criminal and the seriously ill are physically sequestered from the normal population, while "eroticism" is replaced by "sexuality" – which then moves behind the scenes to become hidden away. The sequestration of experience means that, for many people, direct contact with events and situations which link the individual lifespan to broad issues of morality and finitude are rare and fleeting.

(1991a: 6)

If science is independent of ethics and morality, what prevents it from degenerating into sadism that cannot be "sequestered?" Nothing, and one could argue that this has been demonstrated by the Holocaust, the Gulags, Hiroshima, genocide from Cambodia and Rwanda to Bosnia, among other widely known immoral events in the world. The mad, the criminal, and the seriously ill are not routinely sequestered. Sometimes the mad and the criminal become political leaders, as in the cases of Stalin, Hitler, and Karadžić. Mad and criminal political leaders now have access to the most destructive fruits of science and carry out their genocidal aims in excruciatingly rationalist ways. In addition, the widespread dominance of the information media ensures that their crimes are not sequestered, but known by almost everyone who lives in a modern country. But then, how can Giddens claim that Westerners are enjoying the fruits of modernity? Consider the phenomena he discusses under the rubric of modernity: industrialization, capitalism, surveillance and the nation-state (see especially Giddens 1987). Without ethics or morality, each of these should be pulverizing the individual who is supposed to be acting as a skilled and knowledgeable agent, and, in fact, one could argue that this is happening. But not for Giddens, for whom modernity, despite its problems and risks, is unquestionably preferable to traditional forms of social relations and is compatible with democracy. In these regards, he needs to be contrasted sharply with Spengler, Toynbee, and Sorokin, who wrote about the cruel face of modernity and so-called civilization. All the classical social theorists, from Marx to Freud, were similarly aware of civilization and its discontents.

Giddens asserts that "the claims of reason were due to overcome the dogmas of tradition, offering a sense of certitude in place of the arbitrary character of habit and custom" (1991a: 21). Note that this claim contradicts completely his earlier claims that traditionalists enjoyed certainty and modernists live in a risk culture. Nevertheless, this last claim is still consistent with his boosterish admiration for modernity. Second, if reason truly acted independently of morality and other traditions, it could never have led to certitude, but Hobbes's war of all against all or a Tower of Babel. This is because the very notions of *society* and *solidarity* presuppose a certain degree of human sympathy, empathetic identification with others, faith in

154

authority, even sentimentality, among the many non-rational, traditional, and deterministic phenomena that Giddens treats with some contempt. In other words, Giddens is not mindful of the fact that he is really promoting, albeit unwittingly, excessive narcissism, which is a threat to the modern social order (a theme treated by numerous authors, among them David Riesman [1980], Christopher Lasch [1979, 1991] and Robert N. Bellah *et al.* [1985]).

Giddens refers with some approval to the disembedding, globalizing tendencies of modernity, partly because he believes these tendencies are compensated with "re-embedding." I suppose one should think of the "disembedded" refugee from Bosnia as "re-embedded," temporarily at least, in Germany or some other country. But I would point out a more subtle process at work: one could argue that modernists are *embedded* in their own provincial cosmopolitanisms despite the outward appearance of globalization. Westerners gaze at the developing world through the eyes of their Enlightenment-based spectacles, thereby remaining *provincial* and *ethnocentric*. They have *not* managed to assume some magical, universalist outlook. This rich irony is evident from the racist characterization of the genocidal war in Bosnia as based on tribalism and "ancient hatreds" that could not have been stopped, to French, British, and other nations' bickering about how to agree on a common currency for the European Union, and the conflict between protectionist trade policies versus a truly global market, among many other ironies in contemporary "globalization." In fact, most so-called "multi-national" corporations are actually subsidized by and work for national interests. In other words, Giddens does not reckon with the well-known problem of ethnocentrism and its survival into the modernist era. Here again, Spengler and Toynbee are good antidotes to Giddens, and serve to remind the reader that there exist many different histories, several distinct processes of the movement from barbarism to modernism, not just the one, Western process that concerns Giddens more than any other. Modernism is a specific belief system which leads modernists to their own distinctive forms of irrationality.

According to Giddens, "to live in the world produced by high modernity has the feeling of riding a juggernaut" (1991a: 28). Several aspects of this metaphor are curious. How does the skilled and knowledgeable agent ride a juggernaut, which is defined as a blind and destructive belief? Isn't this a contradiction that strikes at the heart of Giddens's thought? One rides a juggernaut if one believes in it, has faith in it – otherwise, one resists the juggernaut or gets off. What could Giddens mean, given his previous praise for modernity, rational control, and human agency? Juggernaut also refers in traditional mythologies to a boulder that crushes everything in its path. But Giddens conveniently overlooks and fails to discuss the *resistances* to the modernist juggernaut that many cultures exhibit. For example, many Dutch men and women decry the sprouting of McDonald's restaurants in Holland

and the McDonaldization of society (Ritzer 1992) it entails. Similarly, many French men and women regard with contempt the existence of EuroDisney just outside Paris as an affront to traditional French culture. Russians have exhibited cultural resistance to Western democratization and the imposition of free markets. Akbar Ahmed (1992) has demonstrated convincingly that contemporary Islam may be regarded as genuinely postmodern in its resistance to Westernization. In addition to cultural resistance, Giddens fails to discuss cultural assimilation, best illustrated by Hindu culture. Hindu culture has thousands of years of history which demonstrate an amazing ability to *absorb* foreign cultural traits and the ability to allow them to co-exist side-by-side with domestic cultural icons. Russian and Slavic cultures also exhibit a remarkable ability to *modify* Western cultural imports, material as well as ideational, into new hybrids based on existing cultures. Drawing on Keith Tester's analysis in *The Two Sovereigns* (1992), I contend that Giddens seems to assume that non-modernist cultures are "dead gardens" in which the modernist gardener may do as he or she pleases:

> The imposition of a single design upon the landscape is only possible if, firstly, that landscape is not able to speak for itself, and if all its indigenous resources have either decayed or been destroyed and secondly, if other gardeners can be prevented from peering over the fence and offering their unwanted advice.
>
> (ibid.: 55)

But the non-Western world is not a dead garden, as the failure to "democratize" and impose "pure" capitalism on formerly Communist as well as many Islamic nations suggests. Whatever modernity is, it is certainly not a juggernaut. It has been and will continue to be resisted by many cultures at the same time that it will result in creative forms of assimilation.

Giddens refers to "the existential contradiction by means of which human beings are of nature yet set apart from it as sentient and reflexive creatures" (1991a: 55). Here again, one needs to challenge the philosophers whom Giddens implies for his theoretical scaffolding. What sort of scientist is Giddens to regard humans as "set apart" from animals with regard to "reflexivity"? Hasn't he heard of Darwin? Animals have brains, and they reflect in their own ways. One might even say they form "animal societies," as Alfred Espinas argued over a century ago. The Enlightenment philosophers set humans apart from, even superior to, animals, but anti-Enlightenment philosophers such as Arthur Schopenhauer argued that what animals and humans hold in common is the "will to life." Giddens's Enlightenment-based philosophical assumptions regarding humans are incapable of sustaining the life politics that he advocates. This is because genuine concern for the environment, if it is to become more than the cliché found in Disney's *Pocahontas*, cannot be achieved through the modernist

156

gardener mentality of ordering the world reflexively and rationally as if the world were a garden (or a game preserve). A successful life politics must be based on the sentiment of respect for life and the feeling that humans, plants, and animals all share the same struggle for existence. A system of life politics without emotion and sentiment is frightening.

Giddens seems to imply that rationality with a capital R somehow lies outside of Nature. But for Spengler, Toynbee, and Sorokin, as well as Durkheim and a host of sociologists from the previous *fin de siècle*, up to and including the "human ecology" movement of the Chicago School, human culture is of nature, a living thing, period. Nothing can exist outside of Nature. If they are right, then human rationality, and the well-developed brain upon which it is based, are accidental products of the struggle for existence in Nature. In other words, this is Schopenhauer's position that the *will* gave rise to the mind, not the other way around. Giddens merely assumes, but does not defend against cogent arguments to the contrary, the Enlightenment position regarding the worship of reason and mind.

Giddens writes in *Modernity and Self-Identity*:

> To live in the universe of high modernity is to live in an environment of chance and risk, the inevitable concomitants of a system geared to the *domination of nature* and the *reflexive making of history*. Fate and destiny have no formal part to play in such a system, which operates (as a matter of principle) via what I shall call open human *control* of the natural and social world . . . yet the notions of fate and destiny have by no means disappeared in modern societies. . . . The world is not seen as a directionless swirl of events, in which the only ordering agents are natural laws and human beings, but as having intrinsic forms which relate individual life to cosmic happenings.
>
> (1991a: 109; emphasis added)

Again, Giddens is slippery, and very difficult to pin down. Yet he betrays the typically modernist attitude of the rationalist gardener obsessed with control that is analyzed by Zygmunt Bauman (1991), Keith Tester (1992), and other cogent critics of modernity. According to Tester:

> The word "gardening" is used here as a metaphor. It was coined by Ernest Gellner and extended by Zygmunt Bauman. . . . [I]t refers to conceptual, practical, and strategic landscapes rather than geographical ones. It refers to how the conditions of social life were interrupted during the era of modernity. A garden is a land which is cultivated and managed by specialist human intervention. Gardening itself is predicated upon a sharp lack of any identity between the land which is made and remade, and the person who

does the making. Gardening assumes freedom, and gardens are proof that the landscape is not at all reified.

(1992: 51)

Bauman (1989) makes an important point in claiming that it is a short step from this modernist obsession with rational control to the Holocaust and other efforts to eliminate "weeds" from the modernist garden.

As usual, however, Giddens equivocates. Fate and destiny do not disappear, but are transformed into "intrinsic forms." First, Giddens needs to be contrasted sharply with Spengler, Toynbee, Schopenhauer, and others who wrote about the power of fate and destiny – even for modernists. He needs to be pinned down on his equivocation: what can it possibly mean that natural laws are ordering agents? At best, this is a murky statement. At worst, it is inexplicable. Either fate does or does not exist, albeit it takes different forms. The fate of a child born in the USA in the 1990s is that he or she will inevitably become a consumer, whereas the fate of a child born to "untouchable" parents in India in the 1990s is that he or she most likely will not rise above that caste despite anti-caste laws passed in New Delhi. But Giddens hedges. Note that he is trying to have his cake and eat it too: modernity is problematic, but he subscribes to it nonetheless.

Thus, he maintains his ideology: "Fatalism is the refusal of modernity – a repudiation of a controlling orientation to the future in favour of an attitude which lets events come as they will" (1991a: 110). But this begs the question: Can the human being control the future? Is the modernist dream realistic in any sense of the term? Or is it, itself, an instance of magical thinking that Giddens ascribes to traditionalists? David Riesman is far more convincing in his *Lonely Crowd* (1950) when he claims that the other-directed type becomes an inside-dopester who wants to know everything possible about political events precisely because he or she feels fundamentally powerless to do anything about them. For example, only a small segment of the US population bothers to vote, under the assumption that their vote won't make a real difference regarding who is elected or what US policies will be. This is modernist fatalism. What can the so-called agent *really* do about his or her air, food, water, and environment? Or, to phrase this question differently: Why are air, food, water, and the environment still unsafe for millions of Westerners despite decades of consciousness raising and what Giddens would call reflexivity? Nor is it an either–or question of all modernism and control or total fatalism and submission to fate. Rather, as Durkheim noted, fatalism ([1897] 1951) is a social current that runs through all societies, traditional as well as modern, and it must interact with other social currents, some of which are more optimistic and progressive.

Giddens's discussion wanders through insurance, religious fundamentalism, and controlling the future: "The overriding emphasis of modernity is on control – the subordination of the world to human dominance" (1991a:

144). Because this is a truly ugly face that modernity wears, Giddens hedges immediately:

> The assertion is surely correct, but put thus baldly it needs consid-
> erable elaboration. One thing control means is the subordination of
> nature to human purposes, organized via the colonizing of the
> future. This process looks at first sight like an extension of "instru-
> mental reason": the application of human organized principles of
> science and technology to the mastery of the natural world. Looked
> at more closely, however, what we see is the emergence of *an inter-
> nally referential system of knowledge and power*. It is in these terms that
> we should understand the phrase, "the end of nature." There has
> taken place a marked acceleration and deepening of human control
> of nature, directly involved with the globalization of social and
> economic activity. The "end of nature" means that the natural world
> has become in large part a "created environment," consisting of
> humanly structured systems whose motive power and dynamics
> derive from socially organized knowledge-claims rather than from
> influences exogenous to human activity.
>
> (ibid.)

This is an example of Giddens's modernism lite at its best (or worst). He clearly intends that the second look at control of nature should appear more benign than the first, which has been criticized amply by the Frankfurt School. Yet it is not clear how an "internally referential" system of instru-mental rationality is different from the old-fashioned modernism. It is clear that Giddens's reformulation is in line with the main tenets of structuration theory and its emphasis on the skilled and knowledgeable agent. But in fact, Giddens's reformulation is more frightening than the old-fashioned, inner-directed version of modernity because it implies *total* control of the "garden" of the world, without any influences from traditions, habits, customs, or other constraints on the modernist gardener. What will prevent such total power from degenerating into forms of anomie that Durkheim could not have imagined?

It is true that there is a tendency in modernity toward wanting control, a culture based on a Nietzschean will to power. Hence all the lawsuits, wars, arguments, striving for domination, imperialism, and so on. But Giddens does not seem to consider that this imperialist, colonialist, violent orienta-tion toward the natural world extends to dominating other people, and might lead to genocide and wholesale destruction of cultural achievements that negates his starting premise, that the human agent is in control of nature. Let me reiterate that in his *Introduction to Sociology* (1991b) textbook, Giddens never mentions genocide, not even in the chapter on ethnicity and race. Even with regard to more mundane examples of alleged control and created environments, consider the following counter-example to Giddens. If someone who visits my home might sue me because he or she slipped on the acorns on my walkway, am I in control? True, modern home contracts take into account "risks" such as this one that go along with high modernity, but the amount of insurance built into the contract might not be sufficient. If I'm constantly sweeping up acorns, I will have less time for other modernist risks or pleasures based on control. Multiply this mundane example with the many other risks entailed by high modernity and the actions I will have to perform to address them (dig a well to get pure water, grow my own food, live out in the country away from high-voltage lines, and so on) and the question arises: in what ways am I as a modernist really in control?

Giddens engages in a harsh criticism of Christopher Lasch – who is highly critical of the notion of modern progress – and dismisses his claims concerning the explosion of narcissism in modern societies. In this regard, one might extend the polemic beyond Lasch to include Robert N. Bellah *et al.* (1985) and Allan Bloom (1987), who clearly write in the same conservative vein as Lasch. I agree with Giddens that modernists cannot and should not want to return to some nostalgic golden age: the "good old days" were not all that good for all of the people, after all. But this does not mean that modernists live any more independently of traditions than our ancestors did. Of course, Giddens hedges:

> The case of tradition is complicated, nevertheless, because appeals to traditional symbols or practices can themselves be reflexively organized and are then part of the internally referential set of social relations rather than standing opposed to it. The question of whether tradition can be "reinvented" in settings which have become thoroughly post-traditional has to be understood in these terms.
>
> (1991a: 150)

If I understand Giddens correctly, he seems to be claiming that through the act of rational reflection, the human agent tames tradition and controls it, as opposed to passively succumbing to its control. But if one penetrates beyond this benign rhetoric, the implication seems to be that selected groups of highly skilled rational agents will be able to reinvent synthetic traditions that will then control and oppress other agents. For Giddens's emancipatory goal to work in a democratic way, all agents would have to be equal and agree on the invention of particular traditions. It is impossible to imagine such a utopian state of affairs. It is far more likely that the deliberate reinvention of tradition for the purposes of rational control will lead to a new, neo-Orwellian form of totalitarianism (see Meštrović 1997). What is there in human agency or structure to prevent such a likely outcome?

Most importantly, Giddens is misleading to present only two options: the oppressive submission to traditional forms of social constraint versus the reflexive reinvention of traditions. Other forward-looking options might include a version of modernity based on reconciling the emotions with rationality and of social life based on compassion and justice, not more rationality or reflexivity. In other words, old-fashioned, non-reflexive and spontaneous traditions based on compassion could co-exist with progressive traditions essential to the modernist project. I have argued for other forward-looking options elsewhere (Meštrović 1993a, 1994).

According to Giddens, "apocalypse has become banal" (1991a: 183). Modernity fragments, but it also unites (ibid.: 189). These are unsatisfactory dismissals of some of the apocalyptic themes found in some postmodern literature. It is worth contrasting both Giddens and the postmodernists with Oswald Spengler's insight in *The Decline of the West* ([1926] 1961): precisely when apocalypse has become banal do we find that a culture is obsessed with self-conscious control of its fate and destiny. Toynbee and Spengler both pointed to the late Roman Empire in this regard. Thus, from their perspectives, Giddens's faddish books are *symptoms* of dissolution and apocalypse, precisely because he dismisses the possibility of apocalypse so casually. And from their perspectives, this may be the underlying reason why Giddens is so popular even though his theory offers very little substance: late or high modernists want to believe that they can control almost everything as part of a pathogenic reaction formation in response to the unconscious perception that the world is completely beyond anyone's control.

In summary, I agree with the many commentators on Giddens who find him to be slippery and difficult to follow. As was remarked earlier, Ian Craib (1992) captures this frustration by referring to Giddens's writings as an omelette of ingredients that often seem to have been thrown in haphazardly. But the critical reader should question Giddens's choice of "ingredients" in the omelette. Why does Giddens use Heidegger instead of Schopenhauer? Did he smuggle in a dash of Baudrillard without telling us? Is Durkheim really too old to be used as an ingredient? Why is Toynbee – a very well-known spice – still on the shelf? And so on. I contend that such a critical appraisal leads to the conclusion that Giddens's views on modernity are not the chaotic mix that the word "omelette" implies. On the contrary, he offers the reader a modernity lite omelette that tries to imitate Immanuel Kant's or other Enlightenment thinkers' omelette. It is my contention that Giddens fails in this endeavor. Kant thought that Enlightenment would make the world a better place because it would make humans free, rational, and self-sufficient. Giddens seems to think that the reflexive and deliberate *reinvention* of some Enlightenment-based *traditions* will also make the world a better place because it will empower human agents. But Horkheimer, Adorno, Bauman, and other critics of such misuse of the Enlightenment have already demonstrated how it can lead to totalitarianism. I believe that similar doubts should be raised concerning Giddens's lite version of the Enlightenment project. The deliberate reinvention of traditions and synthetic construction of society are god-like endeavors fraught with dangers. They have nothing to do with Kant's original aims to liberate the individual from custom and tradition.

In fact, Giddens's social program is potentially more dangerous than the old-fashioned Enlightenment project because it has the feel of what Marcuse called the "happy consciousness." Marcuse thought that mass society was one in which people obeyed without thinking and lived in a society without real opposition. Giddens presents a more disturbing vision of agents who will obey *while* thinking because they are convinced that reflexivity has emancipated them. There are risks in modernity for Giddens, but the risks are worth the alleged benefits of increased reflexivity and agency. Modernity is divisive, but in the end, he thinks, modernity will unify humanity. Not surprisingly, Giddens (1982a) tends to be rather dismissive of Marcuse, and especially of the latter's charge that Western, capitalist nations have established their own form of totalitarianism. But Marcuse cannot be easily dismissed.

THE MUTUAL UNAWARENESS OF GIDDENS AND BAUDRILLARD

Edward Tiryakian (1966) has written of the apparent mutual unawareness of two giants of classical social theory, Max Weber and Émile Durkheim. These two intellectuals wrote without referring to each other's works, as if the other did not exist. Did they really not know of each other's works, or did egoism prevent them from acknowledging each other? The benefits to social theory of a hypothetical Weberian critique of Durkheim, or vice versa, would have been immense. A similar state of affairs seems to exist regarding Giddens and Baudrillard. Both intellectuals are considered leading social theorists in the present era, yet they refer to each other infrequently. When Giddens criticizes postmodernism in general, one gets the feeling he is really arguing against Baudrillard, but one cannot be certain. For example, in one of the few allusions by Giddens to Baudrillard, he writes:

> A universe of social activity in which electronic media have a central and constitutive role, nevertheless, is not one of "hyperreality," in Baudrillard's sense. Such an idea confuses the pervasive impact of mediated experience with the internal referentiality of the social systems of modernity.
>
> (1991a: 5)

Similarly, when Baudrillard mocks the modernists, one cannot help feeling that he is aiming his barbs partly at Giddens, but again, this is no more than intuition. In any event, much can be learned from a comparison and contrast of their respective views on modernity and postmodernity.

Contrasting Giddens with Baudrillard is instructive because Baudrillard seems to argue the very opposite of Giddens's emancipatory dogma: modernity and postmodernity enslave agents in ways that we are just beginning to understand. Unlike Giddens, Baudrillard understands that the information media are the key to understanding the modern world. Giddens, by contrast, merely imposes his boosterish rhetoric concerning modernity onto the media: that they globalize, democratize, teach reflexivity, and so on. Given the many fine treatises today on how the media often degenerate into propaganda, Giddens's omission of this important point is practically fatal to any theory of modernity. Furthermore, Baudrillard seems to be warning readers that because of the media and the dominance of the hyperreal, the idea of the emancipated subject is more questionable than ever. Witness the response to genocide in Bosnia: it was the best documented and most covered case of genocide in human history, but human agents – especially Western intellectuals – did not respond by putting a stop to the genocide (Cushman and Meštrović 1996). Instead, most human agents became unwilling spectators and indirect accomplices to slaughter.

In *The Consequences of Modernity* (1990), Giddens distinguishes between postmodernism and postmodernity. According to him, "post-modernism, if it means anything, is best kept to refer to styles or movements within literature, painting, the plastic arts, and architecture" (ibid.: 45). In this regard, Giddens is taking his cue from Daniel Bell and others who distinguish between postmodernism and postmodernity, as well as modernism and modernity. Such distinctions turn out to be little more than pedantic exercises, because they beg the question of how styles in literature and the arts could develop independently of social developments outside the arts. Daniel Bell (1976) posits that society moves and develops in separate spheres, but Giddens neither accepts nor refutes this underlying assumption for the postmodernism versus postmodernity distinction. He simply jettisons postmodernity from the discussion!

Giddens believes that postmodernity refers to something different from postmodernism and also that postmodernity constitutes a radical disjunction with modernity:

> If we are moving into a phase of post-modernity, this means that the trajectory of social development is taking us away from the institutions of modernity towards a new and distinct type of social order. Post-modernism, if it exists in cogent form, might express an awareness of such a transition but does not show that it exists.
>
> (1990: 46)

Let me make it clear that I reject the distinction between postmodernism and postmodernity for the reasons stated above, and shall use the terms interchangeably. Postmodernism could not exist without the cultural base of postmodernity. Conversely, one cannot speak of postmodernity as a break with modernity without acknowledging postmodernism as a coherent set of values and beliefs based on this disjunction. It is impossible to have one without the other if one subscribes to the view that society is held together by culture, as I do. Moreover, let us note that Giddens has no problem with positing a radical disjunction between tradition and modernity so that his refusal to acknowledge postmodernity is apparently not due to some aversion toward entertaining radical breaks in history. Finally, in claiming, against Giddens, that postmodernism and postmodernity are but two faces of the same phenomenon, I do *not* subscribe to the view that either one constitutes a radical break with modernity.

It is necessary to ask why Giddens holds such a dismissive attitude toward postmodernity conceived as a radical break with modernity given that he conceives of modernity as a radical break with tradition. The answer seems to be that because he is a modernist, Giddens cannot tolerate postmodernity's focus on chaos, disorder, and the boundlessness of the social universe. I agree with Keith Tester that

> Post-modernity is the intimation from within modernity of a condition without bounds of modernity. What this means in more concrete terms, of course, is that from the point of view of the certain modern boundaries, post-modernity seems to be directionless, blurred and lacking in rigor. But from the point of view of post-modernity, modernity with its boundaries is a prison of one sort or another towards which the only proper attitude is one of incredulity.
>
> (Tester 1993: 28)

Referring back to the last quotation from Giddens, above, I would note that it is not self-evident that postmodernity represents a new and distinct type of social *order*. This is truly a curious move by Giddens. In the first place, many postmodernists write of *disorder* as the hallmark of postmodern societies. For Giddens to transform the postmodernist focus on *disorder* as a new form of *order* is telling: Giddens's career-long obsession with the Parsonian problem of social order will not allow him to consider the possibility of pure disorder. Yet one need not accept order versus disorder as the only alternatives in discussions of this sort. There are other alternatives, including the simultaneous co-existence of order and disorder in the modernity and postmodernity debate, as argued by Chris Rojek (1995), Keith Tester (1993), Mike Featherstone (1995), and others. But this is different from claiming that postmodernist disorder is a new form of order. Nor should one accept Giddens's claim that postmodernity must be radically something new and distinct in order to exist. Postmodernity could well be a *relatively* new form of some elements in tradition- and inner-directed societies of the past that merges with modernity. (Here again I should note my admiration for David Riesman's [1950] positing that there exist continuities between and among modern and other sorts of societies.) Again, my position in these regards is that contemporary Western societies exhibit traditional, modern, as well as postmodern characteristics simultaneously in addition to hybrids of these ingredients which appear to be relatively new (see Meštrović 1993a). For example, what Giddens calls synthetic post-traditions and I refer to as post-emotions seems to involve the modernist manipulation of traditional emotions.

In addition, postmodernity, according to Giddens, generally means one or more of the following:

> that we have discovered that nothing can be known with any certainty, since all pre-existing "foundations" of epistemology have been shown to be unreliable; that "history" is devoid of teleology and consequently no version of "progress" can plausibly be defended; and that a new social and political agenda has come into being with the increasing prominence of ecological concerns and perhaps of new social movements generally. Scarcely anyone today seems to identify post-modernity with what it was once widely accepted to mean – the replacement of capitalism by socialism.
>
> (1990: 46)

Giddens does not indicate the sources from which he gleams these characteristics of postmodernity, but it seems clear that in his writings he agrees with many of these points in some respects. It is worth contrasting, briefly, Giddens's version of postmodernity with some others. Pauline Rosenau (1992) makes an important distinction between affirmative versus skeptical postmodernism. It seems that many affirmative postmodernists find genuine grounds for hope, belief in progress, and even faith in some sort of truth despite the skeptical aspects of postmodernism upon which Giddens focuses. For Zygmunt Bauman, postmodernity obliterates the notion of culture, such that the term "postmodern culture" is an oxymoron: "Culture is about hierarchy, discernment and evaluation; postmodernity, on the contrary, is about flattening of hierarchies, absence of discretion, and equivalence" (1992: 34). I disagree with Bauman, and have written about "postmodern culture" (Meštrović 1992), because the tenets of postmodernism do constitute a coherent set of cultural values and beliefs. Baudrillad conceives of the postmodern social universe as one of rootless, circulating fictions and simulations that have no origin or referent (Rojek and Turner 1993). Douglas Kellner captures Baudrillard's intent with the line, "a society of simulations governed by implosion and hyperreality" (1989: 13). Bauman seems to summarize Baudrillard's work well with this passage:

> Baudrillard writes of what is not there, what went missing, what is no more, what lost its substance, ground or foundation. The major trait of our time, he insists, is disappearance. History has stopped. So has progress, if there ever was such a thing. Things we live with today are identifiable mostly as vestiges: once parts of a totality which gave them a place and function, but today just pieces condemned to seek a meaningful design in vain and destined for a game without end.
>
> (1992: 149)

In contrast to these postmodernist concerns with simulation and the end of culture, Giddens focuses on epistemological foundations, the notion of progress, and ecological movements in his critique of postmodernity. These are among his chief concerns expressed in his academic career. His early work was centered on epistemological issues; he is an advocate of narrowly defined progress; and his later works focus on life politics and global as well as environmental concerns. Giddens seems to feel, in some ways, that post-modern writers threaten his modernist ambitions. On the other hand, he does not single out for attack or criticism the postmodern claims that society is nothing but simulation, that there is no culture, and that meaning is not grounded in reality. Interestingly, Giddens's work seems to suggest that he shares some postmodern beliefs. He is open to the idea of simulating tradi-tions; he rejects the traditional notions of culture as inimical to agency; and he seems comfortable in a world based on hermeneutic interpretation that can never be proven to be true or false. He is also open to the idea of post-modern decentering. Thus, in *The Constitution of Society*, he writes:

> I acknowledge the call for a decentring of the subject and regard this as basic to structuration theory. But I do not accept that this implies the evaporation of subjectivity into an empty universe of signs.
>
> (1984: xxii)

In some ways, Giddens's modernism overlaps with major tenets of postmod-ernism. In particular, he comes across as Rosenau's (1992) affirmative postmodernist. If this is true, he does not admit it. Instead, he takes the position that there is no need for the term "postmodernity" because its char-acteristics can be captured by what he calls at various junctures in his discussion high modernity, late modernity, or radical modernity.

The converse may also be true to some extent: what is called postmoder-nity may overlap in significant ways with modernity, and does not constitute a decisive break with the Enlightenment project, as I and others have argued elsewhere (Featherstone 1995; Meštrović 1991, 1993a, 1993b, 1993c; Rojek 1995). To phrase this differently: the tendencies toward order and disorder are exhibited in modernism as well as postmodernism. Thus Baudrillard, in particular, might be regarded as a modernist thinker as well as an anti-modernist. Yet Giddens seeks to distance himself from postmodernity, and his criticisms of it are typically evasive and unsatisfactory. His first objection is that "to speak of post-modernity as superseding modernity appears to invoke that very thing which is declared (now) to be impossible: giving some coherence to history and pinpointing our place in it" (1990: 47). This is another one of Giddens's characteristic replies, a logical point. Technically speaking, Giddens is correct, and some postmodernists have set themselves up for criticisms of this sort by positing a total break with modernity. His second objection is that postmodern nihilism is not new because "the seeds of nihilism were there in Enlightenment thought from the beginning" (ibid.: 48). His third objection is that postmodernists cannot speak of the "end of history" since there is no Archimedean point to history. Finally, his overall point is that all of the changes that he believes lie at the core of the postmodernist argument are really modernist trends: "We have not moved beyond modernity but are living precisely through a phase of its radicalization" (ibid.: 51). He refers to this period as one of high or late modernity. Giddens summarizes his main point in *The Consequences of Modernity*:

> The dissolution of evolutionism, the disappearance of historical teleology, the recognition of thoroughgoing, constitutive reflexivity, together with the evaporating of the privileged position of the West – move us into a new and disturbing universe of experience.
>
> (1990: 52)

By deliberately restricting the discussion to points that he can dismantle through the use of logic and rhetorical devices, Giddens appears to absorb postmodernity into modernity. His apparent victory over the postmodernists seems dazzling. If Baudrillard represents the postmodernist position (although we must keep in mind that Baudrillard denies being a postmodernist), Giddens has apparently vanquished him. But the interesting thing about Baudrillard is that his vision of postmodernism carries an *emotional* appeal despite some of the illogical positions that he takes. Rojek and Turner illustrate this well in their book *Forget Baudrillard?*, wherein they refer to Baudrillard as being on "the cutting edge of social and cultural theory," even though many academics dismiss his writings as "ludicrous" (1993: ix). Baudrillard is a disturbing figure who tends to provoke, unsettle, and annoy as he thumbs his nose at logic and rhetoric. Giddens is a soothing figure who tends to settle things down, put matters into their "proper" place, and who ends up reassuring us that order has prevailed over chaos.

Despite Giddens's efforts, however, one cannot forget Baudrillard. His disturbing vision of the contemporary world as chaotic, meaningless, and fake – not to its core, but without a core – resonates emotionally with all too many readers.

Let us suppose that Giddens had admitted *emotions* into the discussion instead of limiting himself to cognitive and epistemological issues; that he had discussed cultural issues vis-à-vis the postmodernism discourse; that he had conceived of progress as simultaneously making life better in some regards at the same time that it creates new problems; and that he had introduced global concerns alongside Balkanization, provincialism, ethnocentrism, and other anti-globalizing tendencies. It would not have been as easy for him to dismiss postmodernity. Baudrillard has a valid point when he claims that emotion seems to have been dried up in the postmodern world that is based on the model of the computer and the television medium. Again, this is a key component of what I call postemotionalism (Meštrović 1996, 1997). Are modernists or postmodernists capable of experiencing authentic emotions any longer? Or is the postmodern world one in which, as Baudrillard claims in *America* (1986), there is no pity or compassion for the have-nots, who must simply "exit"? It is certain that many have-nots *feel* that this is the case. David Riesman (1950) has an equally valid point that other-directedness has freed modernists from the constraints of traditions at the same time that it has made them slaves to the jury of their peers and public opinion. And as I have indicated in chapter 2, the evidence for Balkanization in the West in the present era is overwhelming, despite the rhetoric of globalization. Ethnic cleansing in Bosnia has become a metaphor for our times (Ahmed 1995), as we have argued earlier, and strikes a chord of fear regarding ethnicity that is felt all over the world, including the industrialized West. Quite apart from Giddens's logical or rhetorical rejoinders, these trends seem to constitute radical breaks with the more innocent, spontaneously emotional, and inner-directed eras of the past.

POSTMODERNITY TRANSFORMED
INTO MODERNITY LITE

We have seen that Giddens clings to modernity in the face of the postmodernist challenge by renaming postmodernity as high modernity, late modernity, or radicalized modernity. Apart from these rhetorical maneuvers, Giddens seems be doing something else: implicitly, he agrees with the postmodernists that the old-fashioned modernist project based on the Enlightenment is heavy-handed and out of fashion. If he had joined the postmodernists in rebelling at the "grand narratives" spun from the Enlightenment, Giddens might have become a leading postmodernist theorist. But as I have suggested throughout this volume, Giddens is wedded ambiguously to the very modernist narratives that he has been criticizing throughout his career. Giddens repudiates Parsons's focus on social order, yet is unable to move beyond the terminology of order. Giddens criticizes both Comte and positivism, but is unwilling to explore the non-rational, emotional components of social life. Giddens criticizes Durkheim as Comte's protégé and precursor to Parsons, but is blind to Durkheim as a *fin de siècle* rebel against the Enlightenment. Despite his self-conscious goals and concerns for structuration theory, Giddens's underlying aim seems to be to rescue the Enlightenment project by softening and taming it – by turning it into modernism lite. In all these ways, and others, he appeals to today's mainstream social theorists, who are as ambiguous and ambivalent as Giddens about these phenomena.

This is best illustrated by taking up Giddens's eight points of comparison and contrast between postmodernity (abbreviated by him as PM) and what he calls radicalized modernity (abbreviated as RM), as set forth in *Consequences of Modernity* (1990: 150). I shall take up each of his points in turn, but I shall add the heavy-handed modernist point of comparison that I believe is the implicit but real point of contention for Giddens and his admirers:

1 PM *"{u}nderstands current transitions in epistemological terms or as dissolving epistemology altogether."* The harsh Enlightenment version of epistemology stems from Kant's radical severance of the phenomenon from the noumenon. Only phenomena can be known epistemologically while the noumenon or thing-in-itself is forever out of the reach of knowledge. Descartes achieved much the same modernist break with tradition by positing that valid, scientific knowledge must be disembodied, solely cognitive. A radical rebellion against this modernist claim would follow Schopenhauer's lead and attempt to retrieve the noumenon, renamed the will, which is the site of passions. But neither Giddens nor the postmodernists are prepared to take this radical step. Instead, postmodernists reduce the social world to a cognitive text or claim that the world can never be known in any event. But Giddens's "radical" alternative to PM in this regard is not really fundamentally different from the postmodernist position. The RM position "[i]dentifies the institutional developments which create a sense of fragmentation and dispersal." Identifying such developments in no way resolves the Kantian and Cartesian dilemmas that have plagued the West for centuries. Fragmentation and dispersal might be remedied if the role of the body and of the passions were restored in epistemology. The more important point is that most modernists will probably agree with Giddens that even if one cannot avoid the fragmentation and dispersal of knowledge, one can at least hope to *locate* the source of the disarray. Giddens give the reader hope.

2 PM *"{f}ocuses upon the centrifugal tendencies of current social transformations and their dislocating character."* Whether these tendencies are centrifugal or centripetal depends upon one's point of reference. I prefer the terms "social

169

fusion" versus "fission" to capture the intent of discussions of this sort. The Enlightenment project has been one of promoting social fusion through imperialism, colonialism, empire-building, and federalism. These phenomena were often promoted through brutal and oppressive means. Processes of fission such as secessionism, emancipatory nationalism, and Balkanization have been anathema to modernists. Postmodernists are ambiguous overall on this issue, as they celebrate differences and local sites of power and identity at the same time that some of them celebrate globalization and a utopian dream of world-wide tolerance. A radical break with modernity on this issue would admit that fusion and fission are a dialectical given of the human condition: humans are tied to their families, the soil, and other local sites at the same time that they yearn for cosmopolitanism. How these two opposing tendencies could be integrated would then become an important item on the agenda of social reconstruction. But again, Giddens does not opt for this radical break with modernism, and instead merely softens the PM position into his RM position: "Sees high modernity as a set of circumstances in which dispersal is dialectically connected to profound tendencies towards global integration." Giddens is right about the dialectic, but his position fails to address how these "profound" tendencies toward globalization continue to brutalize cultures that oppose them. As I have stated previously, the most recent example of Western cultural imperialism has been the cruel effort to export "pure" capitalism in the former Soviet Union, which not only failed and caused widespread suffering, but triggered a renewed effort to establish the Russian Empire. But again, the more important point seems to be that Giddens offers the reader a happy version of Balkanization: it will "dialectically" lead to its opposite, globalization. This is a soothing conclusion to draw, and undoubtedly appeals to most contemporary readers.

3 *PM "{s}ees the self as dissolved or dismembered by the fragmentation of experience."* This postmodernist tenet constitutes a genuine break from the inner-directed self of the modernist era, which was rigid, intolerant, and often beset by various psychopathologies. Riesman's *Lonely Crowd* offers the best analysis of this momentous change from tradition and inner-directedness to the tolerant but fragmented, other-directed self. Predictably, Giddens cannot soften the postmodernist position, for it is too radical, and chooses to soften the image of the rigid, inner-directed self of bygone days. Thus, the RM position is fundamentally different: "Sees the self as more than just a site of intersecting forces; active processes of reflexive self-identity are made possible by modernity." Giddens elaborates on this point in his *Modernity and Self-Identity*, which I have already analyzed in this chapter. Using Riesman's terminology, Giddens seems to be promoting an other-directed (tolerant and complex), inner-directed type.

4 *PM "{a}rgues for the contexuality of truth claims or sees them as 'historical'."* This point constitutes another genuine rebellion against the rather arrogant

modernist faith in the universality of rational truths. Again, given his modernist leanings, Giddens cannot join the postmodernists in this rebellion. Despite his apparently harsh criticisms of the Enlightenment project, the model of the natural sciences, positivism, and so on, he must defend yet soften the modernist claims to truth. Thus, the RM position: "Argues that the universal features of truth claims force themselves upon us in an irresistible way given the primacy of problems of a global kind. Systematic knowledge about these developments is not precluded by the reflexivity of modernity." But even if global survival hangs in the balance, it does not follow that there exist universal truth claims. For example, the West's efforts to promote birth control – based on its *provincial* solution to over-population – has been met by stiff resistance in developing countries. Western standards of human rights, which usually involve freedoms of expression, speech, the press, travel, and so on, are met with scorn in developing countries which perceive universal human rights in terms of the fundamental right to a minimum sustenance. Giddens does no more than mute the modernist position without accounting for how Western and non-Western truth claims can accommodate each other. It is my position that this needed accommodation cannot be achieved on a purely rational basis, but must involve some empathetic understanding and other strands of *caritas*.

5 PM *"{t}heorizes powerlessness which individuals feel in the face of globalizing tendencies."* This point also flies in the face of the modernist faith in power based on rationalist principles. But it is not clear that the sense of powerlessness stems solely from globalizing tendencies. Riesman depicted the powerless "inside-dopester" as part of the tendency toward other-directedness. In any event, this PM tenet challenges directly Giddens's pronouncements on human agency and empowerment, and must be neutralized by him. Hence, the RM position: "Analyzes a dialectic of powerlessness and empowerment, in terms of both experience and action." This is a typical, rhetorical solution by Giddens that does not hold much meaning. The widespread recourse to Western cynicism, terrorism, and fragmentation into increasingly smaller group identities that are hostile to each other bespeaks a tendency in the direction of powerlessness rather than a dialectic with empowerment. I would add that the sense of powerlessness is fueled by the increase in the processes of fission as well as global fusion.

6 PM *"{s}ees the 'emptying' of day-to-day life as a result of the intrusion of abstract systems."* It seems to be true that the modernist, Enlightenment project held and to some extent still holds that heightened rationality will save humankind from its many social illnesses. But neither the modernists nor the postmodernists take seriously the alternative of restoring a balance to abstractionism by incorporating emotions and traditions into social life. Instead, both groups, as well as Giddens, write of creating synthetic, abstract traditions. The communitarians, too, write about the rational construction of abstract communities in the vain hope that the emotions

171

pertaining to communal life can be created through abstraction. Thus, this PM tenet exhibits an ambiguous position in relation to the modernist project. Predictably, Giddens's reaction is equally ambivalent, such that RM "sees day-to-day life as an active complex of reactions to abstract systems, involving appropriation as well as loss." Giddens fails to specify that the "loss" extends beyond the loss of meaning to include the loss of emotional life.

7 *PM "{r}egards coordinated political engagement as precluded by the primacy of contextuality and dispersal."* This is not entirely true. Foucault thought that contextuality and dispersal offered more, not fewer, chances for empowerment. Bauman writes of the opportunities for greater political tolerance as the result of postmodernism. Nevertheless, it is true that old-fashioned modernists had faith in political engagement because they were intolerant or unmindful of contextuality and minority opposition. To be consistent, Giddens must take the position that political engagement is possible yet it must not be brutal. The "Velvet Revolution," a term coined by Václav Havel to capture the peaceful collapse of Communism, might be an exemplar of the position that Giddens must promote. RM "[r]egards coordinated political engagement as both possible and necessary, on a global level as well as locally." Yet this claim fails to address the fact that coordinated political engagement in the contemporary context invariably invites indignation from opposing group interests. Recent examples in the USA include the failure to reform health care and consummate the "Republican revolution" promulgated by Newt Gingrich. Without empathetic understanding, coordinated political engagement must resort to brutality or fail. There are increasingly worrying signs that even the "Velvet Revolution" that led to the fall of Communism in Eastern Europe and the Soviet Union may be mutating into new forms of authoritarianism. One reason among many is the decidedly nonempathetic and stingy reaction of the West to countries freshly freed from Communism who wanted to, at least initially, emulate the West.

8 *PM "{d}efines post-modernity as the end of epistemology/the individual/ethics."* It is true that many if not most postmodernists engage in endgames of various sorts that are difficult to defend. This is because social phenomena are continuous, and do not suggest starting or end points. Postmodernity would be much more defensible as a position if it focused on contemporary transformations of epistemology, the individual, and ethics in relation to their historical precedents. Thus, Giddens has a valid point when he claims that RM "[d]efines post-modernity as possible transformations moving 'beyond' the institutions of modernity." Nevertheless, neither Giddens nor the postmodernists are able to jettison completely the modernist vocabulary of linear movement from traditionalism to postmodernity, captured by Giddens's metaphor of the juggernaut. It is worth recalling that Durkheim found modern phenomena such as individualism and cosmopolitanism even among the aborigines in Australia, and, conversely, he pointed to the

persistence of traditional rituals and categories of the sacred even in modern European societies. I contend that tradition, modernity, and post-modernity co-exist.

In summary, Giddens's alternatives to the genuine skepticism he uncovers in postmodernism amount to little more than rhetoric: disembeddedness is to be followed by re-embeddedness; fragmentation can lead to globalization; dispersal can lead to renewed coherence and reflexivity; losses in one area are offset by gains in another, and so on. In concrete terms, Giddens seems to be saying little more than the following: even if the modernist cannot do much about influencing world events, he or she can recycle. Even if the modernist feels like a stranger in the public sphere, he or she can feel embedded at home. If Scotland secedes from the United Kingdom, it can still be a part of the European Union. And so on. These are trite and superficial alternatives to the very real and disturbing tendencies uncovered by Baudrillard and some other postmodernists.

THE ROLE OF THE INFORMATION MEDIA

It is curious that Giddens posits the existence of time-space distanciation brought about by the communication revolution but does not develop this insight to any appreciable degree in any of his writings. In stark contrast to Riesman, Baudrillard, and the postmodernists, who write extensively on television and other communications media, Giddens fails to develop claims such as the following in *The Nation-State and Violence*:

> The separation of communication from transportation which the telegraph established is as significant as any prior invention in human history. . . . My point is to emphasize the significance to the consolidation of the nation-state in the latter part of the 19th and early 20th centuries of the separation of the communication of information from transportation.
>
> (1987: 176)

This insight is developed in relation to the rest of Giddens's thought by John B. Thompson in *The Media and Modernity* (1995). Thus, Thompson claims, along the lines of Giddens's overall argument, that "the development of communication media – from early forms of print to recent types of electronic communication – was an integral part of the rise of modern societies" (ibid.: 3). Furthermore, "in a fundamental way, the use of communication media transforms the spatial and temporal organization of social life, creating new forms of action and interaction" (ibid.: 4). Like Giddens, Thompson dismisses the critical theorists and the postmodernists to argue that "what we need today is not a theory of a new age, but rather a new theory of an age whose broad contours were laid down some while ago, and whose consequences we have yet fully to ascertain" (ibid.: 9). But this is essentially Giddens's position in *The Consequences of Modernity* (1990). Thompson offers a Giddenesque reading of the role of the communication media in the age of high modernity.

The central features of Thompson's Giddenesque take on communication are the following:

1 The communication media lead to "the discovery of despatialized simultaneity" (Thompson 1995: 32).
2 Contrary to the Frankfurt School's depiction of mass society as promoting the passive consumption of imagery, the reception of imagery "should be seen as an *activity*; not as something passive" (ibid.: 39). Thus, "the reception of media products is a *skilled accomplishment*" (ibid.: 40).
3 Individuals involved in receiving media images in high modernity engage "in a process of self-formation and self-understanding" (ibid.: 43).
4 The media promote democracy by promoting visibility, openness, and "publicness" (ibid.: 123).
5 The media promote globalization because "media products circulate in an international arena" (ibid.: 163).
6 The communication media do not obliterate tradition entirely but lead, instead, to the "re-mooring of tradition" (ibid.: 187).

Thompson elaborates on his last point as follows:

> While tradition retains its significance, it has been transformed in a crucial way: the transmission of the symbolic materials which comprise traditions has become increasingly detached from social interaction in a shared locale. Traditions do not disappear but they lose their moorings in the shared locales of day-to-day life. The uprooting of traditions from the shared locales of everyday life does not imply that traditions float freely; on the contrary, traditions will be sustained over time only if they are continually re-embedded in new contexts and re-moored to new kinds of territorial unit. The significance of nationalism can be partly understood in these terms: nationalism generally involves the re-mooring of tradition to the contiguous territory of an actual or potential nation-state, a territory that encompasses but exceeds the limits of shared locales.
>
> (ibid.)

There can be little doubt that Thompson extends faithfully Giddens's thought regarding agency, globalization, self-identity, and the creation of synthetic traditions vis-à-vis the topic of the communication media. But like Giddens, he does not confront the many studies of the media that challenge Giddens's overly felicitous account of the role of the media. One such excellent study is Douglas Kellner's analysis of the media's impact in the Gulf War. In *The Persian Gulf TV War* (1992), Kellner offers scrupulous and extensive documentation to argue that: against the rhetoric of democracy, freedom of expression, and openness, the US Government controlled the movement of journalists as well as their access to information; against the characterization of journalists as agents, most journalists put a slant on information that supported the West's demonization of Muslims in the Gulf War; contrary to the hope that media consumers would be critical and reflexive, most Americans and Western Europeans as well generally accepted the one-sided picture of the Gulf War that was broadcast in the West.

Giddens and Thompson are correct that contemporary American nationalism is, indeed, being reinvented and re-moored: military personnel returning from the Gulf War were treated to a heroes' welcome and American nationalism was palpable. Yet it would be difficult to argue that this particular instance of creating a synthetic tradition was related even remotely to increased reflexivity, democratization, or cosmopolitanism. On the contrary, the aftermath of the Gulf War left most Americans wondering what it was all about, given that Saddam Hussein remained in power following the war; the US Government proved that it could control the flow of information and get away with it; and Muslims were demonized. Moreover, Kellner proves his assertions with hard facts whereas both Thompson and Giddens engage in abstract theorizing without confronting theoretical perspectives that would challenge them, namely, those of the critical theorists and the postmodernists.

Another excellent illustration of how the role of the communication media did not live up to Giddens's and Thompson's expectations is the coverage of the Serb-sponsored genocide against Bosnian Muslims in the 1990s. I demonstrate in *Genocide After Emotion* (1996) that despite the general conclusion reached by the world's respected fact-gathering organizations that Serbs were the overwhelmingly guilty party in this Balkan War, the media tended to present the frame of reference that all sides were equally guilty; that the Croats were demonized as Nazis and the Bosnian Muslims as terrorists whereas sympathy was expressed for Serb fears of Croats and Muslims; that Serbian Nazi collaboration in World War II (documented in Cohen 1996) was almost never invoked in discussing this Balkan War whereas Croatian Nazi collaboration was systematically invoked as explanation for Serb actions; and that the "live" coverage of Belgrade-sponsored genocide did not result in action, mandated by the UN Charter, to put a stop to it. Far from feeling enabled or becoming more reflexive, most Western consumers of the information media felt confused and powerless to do anything to stop the slaughter. Again, as in the Gulf War, nationalism was reinvented and re-moored – in this case, Serbian nationalism – but was not related to democratization.

Despite these two major counter-factual examples, Giddens and Thompson may still be able to demonstrate that their theory is tenable. However, there are other counter-factual examples, such as the coverage of Moscow-sponsored slaughter of Muslims in Chechnya. But in general, the important point, for the purposes of the present discussion, is that Giddens skews his scant comments on communication in the direction of the overly felicitous and unsubstantiated vision of high modernity found in *The Consequences of Modernity* and *Modernity and Self-Identity*. He does not take up the challenges to his theory posed by either the critical theorists or the post-modernists, both of whom write about the new forms of enslavement and non-reflexivity brought on by the communication media.

CONCLUSIONS

In this chapter I have suggested that Giddens's apparently mercurial and fox-like writing style constitutes more than technique. The medium is the message. Ambivalence, ambiguity, evasiveness, vacillation, and so on, are integral to Giddens's vision of radicalized modernity. Ironically, and despite the fact that he appears to reject postmodernity, postmodernists have enshrined these traits as intellectual virtues in the contemporary era. In sharp contradistinction to the rigid inner-directed intellectual of bygone modernist eras, the contemporary intellectual is trained to see as many points of view as possible in every discussion, and not to take a definitive position regarding any point of view. For example, Durkheim was suffi-ciently inner-directed to propose that sociology should be the science of morality in part because he assumed that morality could be defined. No serious contemporary intellectual would dare make such a move. Critics would immediately raise the question, whose morality is being promoted? The morality of the affluent? The morality of women? The morality of heterosexuals? And so on. Postmodernists have not only identified this process of the fragmentation of meaning vis-à-vis *any* contemporary topic or phenomenon; many of them actively promote it as liberating. But if ambiva-lence, ambiguity, evasiveness, and so on, are carried one step further, the contemporary intellectual must wonder whether taking the position that one cannot take a firm position in any discussion is itself rigid. This apparent contradiction is corrected by softening the rigid positions of past modernists. For example, old-fashioned morality is too oppressive, but surely societies need some sort of ethics, so Giddens introduces into his structuration theory the notion of "life politics." This is Giddens's strategy in general: he is postmodernist enough to agree that there is no firm referent in contemporary social life for any phenomenon, yet he is more sophisticated than the postmodernists in avoiding a commitment to postmodern ideology as a firm referent. As a result, he strives to reconcile the rigid stance of the modernists with the equally rigid nihilism of the postmodernists. The result is modernism lite.

Hence, Giddens's evasive stances on a myriad of topics. Yes, the rigid self no longer exists, but a reflexive self does. Yes, truth is not universal, but some versions of truth claims persist. Yes, contemporary individuals feel powerless, but they are also empowered. Yes, the days of imperialism and empire-building are gone, but there is globalization, which achieves similar aims with a softer touch (one could argue that McDonald's and Coca-Cola have established world empires). And so on. There is a methodological, substantive component to Giddens's style.

While Baudrillard provokes rage and ridicule, Giddens evokes sympathy and acceptance. Part of the explanation for Giddens's success is that his writings are in tune with the general social traits of contemporary, Western individuals. Contemporary Westerners, like Giddens, are generally ambivalent about most matters, evasive in their commitments, and quick to spot the ambiguities of modern life. President Bill Clinton exhibits all of these traits in a remarkably consistent way, constantly vacillating in the stands he takes, openly second-guessing his decisions, and consistently eager to accommodate as many points of view as possible. Those Americans who criticize him for these traits do so with minimal conviction, for they realize that he represents most of them. For example, contemporary Americans decry rising crime rates yet resist any notion of a government "crackdown" on crime. They complain about the budget deficit, yet resist Newt Gingrich's efforts to correct it by cutting back social services. They feel terrible about genocide in Bosnia, yet they object to American involvement in putting a stop to it. They decry the use of racial slurs in conversation, yet they support the elimination of Affirmative Action. And so on. Giddens's style as well as content are commensurate with the general characteristics of the contemporary era. He is a man for this season.

But is he a man for all seasons? I realize that such a question carries inner-directed, rigid overtones that are immediately suspect. Nevertheless, the question must be asked for the simple reason that the present state of what Giddens calls radicalized modernity may collapse. Ambivalence and openness to all points of view are virtues only up to a point. Thus, regarding genocide in Bosnia, the West's reactions exhibit all of the traits that I call modernity lite and ascribe to Giddens: in its openness to all points of view, the West took seriously Serbian rationalizations for committing genocide against Bosnian Muslims and negotiated with indicted as well as suspected war criminals. The West was simply unable to distinguish between "good" versus "bad" in Bosnia and generally subscribed to the view that all sides were equally guilty. At the same time, the West had to do something in accordance with its Enlightenment-based principles. It could not simply acquiesce to genocide, as if such a phenomenon no longer held meaning, as many postmodernists might claim. Thus, the West engaged in humanitarian aid and proposed a "peace plan." In other words, the West *feigned* resolve, commitment to moral principles, and adherence to democratic values. Rigid inner-directed types might point out that there is something dubious morally about such ventures, which include treating genocide as if it were a natural disaster and promoting the ethnic partition of a country in the name of peace. Nevertheless, the West tried to find a middle path between rigid adherence to Western moral principles regarding genocide and throwing up its hands at the alleged confusion in distinguishing victimizers from victims. The West has similarly adopted a modernist lite position in relation to many other events and phenomena, from Boris Yeltsin's dictatorial brand of democracy to the sympathy afforded to many convicted criminals. Can such institutionalized ambivalence be sustained in the long run?

A Durkheimian reply might be negative. He considered crime normal, but he also considered the rigid punishment of crime as normal. Modernist lite tolerance toward what used to be intolerable weakens the collective consciousness in the Durkheimian scheme of things, and causes further fragmentation and fission. If Akbar Ahmed is right that ethnic cleansing has become a metaphor for our times, and if the response to ethnic cleansing all over the world continues on its present trajectory of ambivalent tolerance, the end result will not be Giddens's vision of globalization based on reflexivity and agency. Baudrillard's vision of a fragmented, nihilistic world devoid of meaning may be anticipating the cultural season that will follow the present one.

7

UNLIMITED AGENCY AS THE NEW ANOMIE

The will always knows, when knowledge enlightens it, what it wills here and now, but never what it wills in general. Every individual act has a purpose or end; willing as a whole has no end in view. . . . In fact, absence of all aim, of all limits, belongs to the essential nature of the will in itself, which is an endless striving. . . . Every attained end is at the same time the beginning of a new course, and so on *ad infinitum*. . . . Eternal becoming, endless flux, belong to the revelation of the essential nature of the will.

– Arthur Schopenhauer ([1818] 1969a:164)

In chapters 5 and 6, I have touched on the same modernist formula that seems to animate Giddens's theory of the individual as well as the nation-state: both are rigidly bounded, seek order, and operate on an exclusively rationalist basis. In fact, Giddens uses a rhetoric concerned with "clearly bounded systems with an obvious and easily identifiable set of distinguishing traits" with regard to societies, individuals, nations, and even modernity (1984: 201). It appears that one of the reasons he banishes postmodernity is that it seems to promote boundlessness. Giddens banishes the emotional components of human life from his understanding of the nation-state much as he banishes the unconscious as the id from the reflexive individual – emotions are unruly and seek to break through boundaries. To phrase this another way: Giddens's *Transformation of Intimacy* is cut from the same theoretical cloth as *The Nation-State and Violence*. Against Giddens, I contend that much like nationalism is the strongest social force in modern society, and the nation-state's existence is therefore precarious, so the unconscious as the realm of the id and other anomic forces is the strongest force regarding individuals, thereby making modern self-identity precarious. In this chapter, I intend to explore the dimensions of this latter claim by analyzing the problems and vicissitudes associated with what Giddens calls human agency. I shall be leading to the paradox that heightened agency, at least on Giddens's terms, implies diminished agency.

Giddens does little more with regard to developing the concept of human agency than to insist on its existence. For example, he writes in *Central Problems in Social Theory* that agency means that "every social actor knows a great deal about the conditions of reproduction of the society of which he or she is a member" (1979: 5). Similarly, in *A Contemporary Critique of Historical Materialism*, Giddens writes that "social science must elaborate a satisfactory account of the competent and knowledgeable human agent" (1982b: 15). But statements such as these – found throughout Giddens's works, as we have seen already – amount to little more than slogans. He is certainly right that human agency seems preferable to being treated as a cultural dope. But surely a condition of extreme cultural constraint is not the only antipode to agency. Another possibility is the one envisioned by David Riesman: "The inside-dopester knows, but he doesn't care (high competence, low affect)."[1] The hallmark of David Riesman's portrait of modern agents in *The Lonely Crowd* (1950) is that they become relatively powerless consumers of information, but not producers of policy or action.

The contrast between Riesman and Giddens vis-à-vis human agency is worth developing. Both theorists are clearly aware that persons living in the modern era have access to more information and knowledge than their ancestors could have imagined. Consider the proliferation of twenty-four-hour news channels such as CNN Headline News; the many talk shows on television that focus on specific issues; the vast choice of magazines; the easy accessibility of books; and, most recently, the Internet and other knowledge systems that can be accessed through "cyberspace." Whereas Giddens seems to conclude that such unprecedented access to information is enabling and conducive to human agency, Riesman concludes that other-directed types want to know so much to compensate for the rarely admitted perception that they feel powerless to do much about the world. In Riesman's words, the other-directed "inside-dopester may be one who has concluded (with good reason) that since he can do nothing to change politics, he can only understand it" (1950: 181). It would be important to subject these contrasting visions to some sort of empirical verification. Moreover, it could well be that the truth lies somewhere in the middle between Riesman's and Giddens's visions: Giddens may be partly right that contemporary agents have access to information that enables them to change what they dislike about the world, while Riesman may be partly right that contemporary agents feel cynical, fear being taken in, and seek to conform to the "right" opinion as exhibited by the jury of their peers.

For the purposes of this discussion, the more important point is that Riesman perceives ironies in relation to the much touted information revolution whereas Giddens is simplistic and comes across as naive in his faith in knowledge and agency. To be sure, Giddens hedges on his overly felicitous vision of agency by positing agency as a duality in relation to structure: structure does not constrain the agent, but it does create boundaries as well as offer resources. A deeper irony is the following: Giddens's vision of the skillful and knowledgeable human agency who is in control of his or her destiny vis-à-vis an abstract social structure comes across as Riesman's inner-directed type, but for Riesman, the inner-directed type is vanishing. Thus, Giddens's thought is less an illumination of the contemporary scene and more the expression of a wistful nostalgia. Riesman seems to be on target that the contemporary other-directed type fears that "to shine alone, seems hopeless, and also dangerous" (1950: 139). But note that Giddens's skilled and knowledgeable agent comes across as self-centered, much like the hero in any one of Ayn Rand's novels. For Riesman, "the uncertainty of life in our day is certainly a factor in the refusal of young people to commit themselves to long-term goals" (ibid.: 138). But Giddens does not deal with the issue of how the emancipated agent chooses to commit him- or herself to one course of action out of a Milky Way of options. Riesman portrays the inner-directed type as impersonal in his or her pursuit of specific goals, and as relatively unconcerned with the feelings of others. Whereas the other-directed type is necessarily tolerant and attuned to the feelings of other people, the inner-directed type is intolerant and relatively insensitive. Again, it is ironic that Giddens's modern human agent is consistently portrayed in relation to social structure or goals or knowledge or skill, but *not* in relation to other people and their feelings, opinions, and presence.

The important point is this: for Riesman, the contemporary agent's knowledge and skill pertain more to other people than to an amorphous and impersonal structure in the manner depicted by Giddens. Today's politician is concerned with opinion polls whereas yesterday's politician took it for granted that his or her actions might be unpopular. Today's university professor knows that he or she must be liked in order to receive high teaching evaluations, no matter how skilled he or she is in transmitting knowledge, whereas yesterday's professor was not evaluated by students. The contemporary parent must gain his or her child's compliance as well as *good will*. And so on. In every walk of life and in every profession, the premium in contemporary societies is placed on being able to work smoothly with other people and on being able to come across as sensitive and tolerant. Giddens never discusses these other-directed aspects of human agency, and it is simply not true that a successful agent in today's world can be attuned only to societal structure. In fact, Giddens defines structure in strictly impersonal terms: "Structure: Rules and resources, recursively implicated in the reproduction of social systems. Structure exists only as memory traces, the organic basis of human knowledgeability, and as instantiated in action" (1984: 377).

PARTIAL AGENCY

Furthermore, can agents move between states of heightened agency and non-agency in the manner, let us say, of Freud's insistence in *The Psychopathology of Everyday Life* ([1901] 1965) that "normal" people are "neurotic" on a daily basis in their dreams, through their slips of the tongue, and other regular irrationalities? It is curious that in analyzing this book by Freud, Giddens (1984) fails to take up this aspect of Freud's thought, which is clearly the most relevant to Giddens's assertions concerning agency. As I have noted in chapter 4, both Freud and Schopenhauer conceived of something like a will that acts *through* agents and *beyond* the goals and means they set for themselves – in other words, of an agent within an agent. Giddens (ibid.) dismisses such a notion as nonsensical, but can sense be made out of it?

How should a condition of agency be distinguished from partial versus complete non-agency? Is it possible for an agent to act skillfully and knowledgeably in *some* or even most dimensions of daily social life, yet act as if that skill and knowledge were lacking in other dimensions? I believe the answer is yes. Harking back to Riesman's fruitful distinction between inner-directedness and other-directedness, one can envision persons who are highly skilled with manipulating objects and knowledge, but who fail miserably in being liked by their peers – and vice versa. There are other problems that can arise with agency: how can other persons determine when someone is having a problem acting as a human agent in the fullest sense of the term as opposed to having other problems (for example, physical illness, problems in living, bad moods, and so on)? Giddens seems to assume that agency – and he never takes up the issue of problems with human agency – is implicitly universal in modern nation-states, whereas the entire thrust of cultural studies in this century leads one to suppose that agency and problems with agency are assessed through *cultural* filters. This means that what will seem to be normal or problematic agency in one culture may appear entirely different in a different culture or within a subculture. It would be an important task to compare and contrast modern, Western characterizations of human agency from traditional equivalents of agency as enshrined in law, religion, and other social institutions. Yet, by implication, Giddens seems to disavow the possibility of human agency in traditional societies.

On the analytic level of the individual agent as well, it is not at all obvious how individuals determine the relative degree of human agency regarding themselves or other agents. This issue is inherently an other-directed one, because it involves other agents and their perceptions and feelings. How do individuals within a given culture determine that someone is responsible for his or her actions versus the determination that an agent has diminished responsibility for his or her actions? How were such determinations in predominantly inner-directed cultures similar to and different from such determinations in predominantly other-directed cultures? Within a given culture or subculture, such questions arise every day due to stress, intoxication, obsessions, fatigue, and a host of other factors. People determine regularly that someone is "not himself," or "she was just tired," or some similar conclusion. The issue becomes even more complicated when inner-directed agents judge the actions of other-directed agents, and vice versa. One would think that given his career-long concern with agency, Giddens would be interested in offering a Goffmanesque description of *how* agents arrive at such conclusions. But he does not, and cannot, because his theory disavows any and all connections between contemporary (other-directed) and previous (inner-directed, tradition-directed) conceptualizations of human agency.

Finally, given that Riesman's types are meant to be interpreted as Weber's ideal types – real people are mixtures of inner-, other- and tradition-directed traits – the questions with which I began this section become still more complex. For Giddens, the self is a "project," much like the Enlightenment is transformed by Habermas into a "project." The concept of the self enshrined by Giddens is as bounded and rigid as his vision of the nation-state. But if the self is not a project and is instead an amorphous mixture of sometimes conflicting ideal types, then Freud's observation concerning the crossing of boundaries between normalcy and neurosis takes on a fresh new meaning. It could well be that, on a daily basis, modern individuals cross the boundaries of the self pertaining to inner-, other-, and tradition-direct-edness. For example, the contemporary executive must be ruthless and driven on the job, loving and tolerant with his or her family at home in the evening, yet attuned to traditions if he or she is still religious and/or nation-alistic. This schizophrenic-like existence seems to be precisely what is demanded of agents in the contemporary world.

MENTAL ILLNESS AS A PROBLEM WITH AGENCY

These are important issues, but, curiously, Giddens never takes them up. Perhaps the single best focus for such issues is that perplexing condition that nowadays goes by the label of "mental illness." Whatever it is that actually afflicts the mentally ill, it surely seems to be the case that at times, with regard to certain dimensions of their lives, and always vis-à-vis the cultural backdrop of the habits of the heart that envelop them, the mentally ill are not able to put their knowledge and skill to use in a manner that qualifies as human agency in the eyes of significant others. Using Riesman, one would put the emphasis on the opinions of others. Instead, they seem – at least relative to the perception of others – to suffer from inner constraints known as phobias, delusions, compulsions, anxiety, projections, and other phenomena uncovered by Freud and others which often work counter to the goals and means available to agents. Giddens does not raise the problem of mental illness vis-à-vis human agency in his treatises and not even in his treatment of mental illness in his textbook *Introduction to Sociology* (1991b).

In his textbook, Giddens takes the standard approach to mental illness as a form of deviance – namely, as the breaking of social norms. This is an antiquated, inner-directed mode of apprehending mental illness. A generation of other-directed sociologists have taught us that society's rules are socially constructed, negotiated, and fluid, so that the "breaking" of rules and norms is never obvious. In the other-directed society, deviance always involves hermeneutics. In his textbook, Giddens notes that in the past "people we would now regard as mentally disordered were considered 'possessed,' 'unmanageable,' or 'melancholic'" (ibid.: 178). This seems to be true, but the implication of these terms is that the human agent is not an agent in the fullest sense of the term. How can Giddens glide over such a challenge to his theory of agency? Moreover, people are considered as possessed – hence not agents in the fullest sense – by other agents, and not only in the past, but in present-day India, many African countries, and other traditional settings. Western nation-states in the modern era also allow some subcultures within them to subscribe to non-modernist cultural practices. Thus, traditional folk-healing, New Age healing, mysticism, religious healing, and various local superstitions all co-exist in the West alongside a modernist vision of psychiatry (see Cockerham 1981). Furthermore, both notions, "possession" and "mental illness," are special roles established by societies to designate a condition in which persons are exempted from the usual responsibilities for their actions that accompany human agency. Psychiatrists still debate whether the condition that underlies the label of mental illness is actually an organic problem, a problem of living, a myth (as Thomas Szasz [1961] claims), or a spiritual problem. Regardless of how this debate is eventually resolved, I propose that (1) mental illness is also a problem of human agency and (2) these and other determinations are constructed culturally and socially. Furthermore, the social construction of mental illness is more pronounced in other-directed societies than in any other type.

Commensurate with my overall aims in this book, I am less interested in discussing possession or mental illness *per se* and more interested in the consequences of invoking these phenomena for analyzing Giddens's theory of human agency and, by extension, modernist understandings of agency. While it is beyond the scope of this discussion to delve into the historical background for approaching mental illness as a problem of human agency, I will sketch it out briefly. Hegel's *Philosophy of Mind* ([1830] 1971) contains an intriguing chapter on "madness" in relation to what Giddens might call human agency. Schopenhauer ([1818] 1969b: 229–38), too, conceives of "madness" as a problem with remembering and placing one's knowledge into a proper individual life-span as well as cultural context. Thus, the "mad" agent possesses knowledge but is unable to use it effectively. It was a short step from Schopenhauer's assessment to Freud's ([1901] 1965) elaboration that repression – as an act of deliberate *or* accidental "forgetting" – is the fundamental basis for all forms of neurosis and psychosis. For both

Schopenhauer and Freud, mental illness comes down to a problem concerning reminiscences, as I have argued at length in *The Barbarian Temperament* (Meštrović 1993a). Retracing the history of psychiatry in terms of problems with knowledge and skill, the two essential components of what Giddens calls agency, in a *cultural* context, would be a worthwhile endeavor.

But adding Riesman's insights to this portion of the discussion is important as well. It seems that the other-directed type, who is more sociable and gregarious than other character types, will "remember" things primarily in relation to a real or imagined peer group. The portraits of repression offered by Freud come across as much more inner-directed: an individual who struggles against repressed memories in solitude or on the analyst's couch. Today's neurotic is more likely to overcome repression in *group therapy*, and even outside of therapy, by discussing his or her therapy session with his or her spouse and friends. Thus, the "problem of reminiscences" vis-à-vis the agent takes on a substantially new meaning in the contemporary era.

Empirically driven research in the future should be cross-cultural and should compare and contrast the many ways that "normal" as well as "mentally ill" persons in various cultures and vis-à-vis various types of social character behave as non-agents even when they believe they are acting as agents. For example, the researcher might take up contemporary India as a site to confront Giddens, even though Giddens might reply that the harsh, tradition-directed constraints in India are precisely the sort of thing that his emancipatory theory of human agency seeks to overcome. My reply is that much like Durkheim wrote about Australian aborigines in his *Elementary Forms of the Religious Life* ([1912] 1965) to make points about modern, Western societies, India is instructive about the co-existence of modernity and traditionalism even within so-called Western, modern nations. The superstitions and traditions that are obvious targets of Western scorn in Indian society do not differ fundamentally from superstitions and harmful traditions that persist in Western societies – only Westerners turn a blind eye toward modernist irrationalities. To pick one example out of many, the ethnocentric Westerner reacts with horror to the lack of hygiene in India that produces so many unnecessary deaths, especially among young children, yet is not horrified by Western habits such as the love of red meat, excessive sodium, caffeine, and other poisons that also produce too many unnecessary deaths. An Indian child might die if given water from a polluted "sacred" river to drink by his or her mother, yet a Western child might die or suffer brain damage because contemporary mothers are taught not to switch to formula if the child resists breast-feeding. As of this writing, the peer group exhibits tremendous pressure on the mother to breast-feed, unlike the belief in the inner-directed age of the 1940s which taught, through manuals, that bottle-feeding was preferable to breast-feeding. Similarly, Westerners die needlessly because of the widespread cultural penchant for red meat. I do not seek to defend any sort of rationalization for needless death based on cultural practices, only to suggest that it is ethnocentric to criticize the backwardness of non-Western societies without confronting the prevailing "backwardness" of Western societies. In both modern and traditional cultures, human agents act as agents as well as non-agents – albeit in diverse, socially constructed ways – and Freud's discovery that normality and neurosis lie on a continuum should be sociologized: societies enforce all sorts of "collective neuroses" that are destructive to the individual's health, and these cannot be overcome completely by heightened reflexivity. The important point is that Western, modern agents are not as free as Giddens purports; and agency as well as problems with agency are always ascertained through cultural filters.

CAN EXCESSIVE AGENCY LEAD TO ANOMIE?

I have suggested throughout this book that Giddens does not account for the origins of human agency. Is it self-begotten? He argues that the agency–structure linkage must be understood as a duality rather than a dualism, but this claim seems to be little more than rhetoric. For example, he defines duality of structure as follows: "Structure as the medium and outcome of the conduct it recursively organizes; the structural properties of social systems do not exist outside of action but are chronically implicated in its production and reproduction" (1987: 374). But is agency possible without *culture* (not only structure)? Are some humanly constructed cultures or some types of social character more conducive to agency than others? Can agency in certain periods and at certain times in the agent's life and in certain cultural contexts become excessive such that the skilled and knowledgeable agent becomes detached from the social structure and becomes a narcissist? If so, is agency culpable in such a new form of anomie, or are culture and social character also culpable by enabling the agent to become narcissistic? Is the bond that links the agent to structure strictly cognitive, given that Giddens rarely discusses emotional attachments? Most importantly, does agency lay the ground for anomie, which, in turn, diminishes the capacity for agency by subjecting the human actor to the paradox that the more that he/she knows, the more he/she desires, and these desires can never be quenched, and thereby enslave the agent?

As I have suggested already, Giddens's treatment of agency remains superficial, in sharp contrast to the implicit treatment of agency found in works by Simmel, Durkheim, Freud, Veblen, and other classical theorists from the previous *fin de siècle*, because Giddens never addresses the question: what comes after the agent's attainment of a goal? Many social theorists from the previous *fin de siècle* followed Schopenhauer's lead in positing that the will, which acts *through* agents – or, in Giddens's vocabulary, as an agent within the agent – is inherently insatiable. Hence, any attainment of a goal leads to boredom and the unquenchable thirst for new attainment. Enlightenment only exacerbates this human insatiability by expanding the cognitive horizon of objects to be desired, so that modern agents are confronted with a relatively new form of social and individual pathology, anomie as the disease of infinite wanting, insatiable desiring, and relentless consuming, all of which diminish the agent's sense of personal empowerment by enslaving him/her to obsessions. Veblen's writings on the increase of conspicuous consumption in modern times, especially in *The Theory of the Leisure Class* ([1899] 1969), are an important part of this *fin de siècle* vision of the human agent, but Giddens never mentions Veblen. David Riesman's (1950) portrait of the other-directed type as confronted by a Milky Way of choices and objects of desire is another apt characterization of anomie. The implication of Riesman's work seems to be that other-directedness exacerbates anomie precisely because the other-directed type seeks to consume not only material goods but personal relationships. He or she wants to be loved, or at least liked or appreciated, by as many people as possible. Keith Tester's discussion of postmodernity as a condition of relative boundlessness also seems similar to Durkheim's understanding of anomie: "The notion of the intimation of a world without bounds is one very useful way of coming to terms with the status and meaning of the debates on postmodernity" (Tester 1993: 27). The notion that humans are enslaved by constant, relentless, and inexorable desiring as part of the eternal flux of life is to be found in the writings of Nietzsche, William James, Freud, Simmel, Veblen, Durkheim, and a host of writers from the previous *fin de siècle*, and stands in sharp contrast to Giddens's shallow and modernist reading of the human agent as bounded by yet enabled by structure that leads to emancipation. No one can cast an eye on the infinite striving and consumption of modern living, so accurately prophesied by Veblen, for example, and be convinced by Giddens. Schopenhauer's assumption of an infinitely striving will seems to resonate in the present *fin de siècle* more than it did in the previous one.

It is obvious that Giddens regards human agency as a sort of virtue, even an unqualified good. But ever since Plato and Aristotle, philosophers have been aware that excessive virtue of any sort can become a vice. Giddens seems oblivious to this possibility regarding human agency. Yet it is an important issue which I shall analyze by using Durkheim to criticize Giddens. Giddens also seems to imply that all agents in modern societies hold the potential for reflexivity. Against this seemingly happy vision, Tester (1993: 27) seems more correct to claim that most agents seek certainty while only a few are willing to push reflexivity to the point of boundlessness, because of the perceived dangers of radical questioning (anomie, neurosis, loss of security, and so on). The critical reader of Giddens must confront the question: what can go awry in Giddens's rather blithe vision of the human agent's cognitive relationship to structure? My reply shall be that anomie, conceptualized contextually as a state of infinite desiring, is what can and does go wrong. In order to achieve this goal, it shall be necessary to challenge the glib, modernist misreading of Durkheim's concept of anomie as a fictitious state of normlessness and its modernist derivatives.

Discussions concerning Durkheim's concept of anomie tend to be murky. We have seen that Giddens throws out Durkheim's concept of anomie with the bathwater of Parsonian functionalism. The received view is that anomie is a state of "normlessness" or "deregulation" that is generally harmful. It is important to note that Giddens seems to be aware that these received views of anomie are not the same as Durkheim's original version, yet he does not take a stand one way or the other. His discussions of anomie tend to be little more than a recasting of Durkheim into Parsonian and Mertonian views. But the functionalist misunderstandings of anomie are basically inner-directed, hence irrelevant to contemporary times: normalcy is assumed to consist of following norms within a bounded system (not in relation to other people) and anomie is assumed to be an abnormal state of lack of norms that can be fixed with more norms. The inner-directed type might have lived and worked under such assumptions, but the other-directed type's emotional insatiability will not be cured by adding more norms into a social system. More norms, for the other-directed, means that he or she is more likely to be confused in trying to sort out which norms are worthy of allegiance or commitment, and will therefore become *more* anomic. But Giddens has no feel for such ironies. For example, he writes in *Durkheim*:

> The more recent literature in which the concept of anomie has been taken over from Durkheim and elaborated by other authors indicates how the notion can be developed in different directions. Some have used "anomie" as equivalent to "normlessness". . . . [S]uch a view tends to treat social conflict as the result of incomplete moral consensus, and to trace the sources of "deviance" to "imperfect socialization" or incomplete moral development. Others have tended towards the second type of interpretation, using "anomie" to mean "normative strain" rather than "normlessness": i.e., a situation where the moral values or norms which are accepted by the members of a group are not matched by the possibilities of realizing the goals thus affirmed. Each of these versions of the idea of anomie is present in *The Division of Labor*, and although in his later writings Durkheim tried to resolve the difficulties which this created for his analysis of the emergence of the modern industrial order, he did not manage successfully to do so.
>
> (Giddens 1978: 108)

This is the typical Giddens strategy of dealing with an idea he dislikes: evasiveness, contradiction, and ambiguity. For if subsequent theorists changed Durkheim's understanding of anomie, how can the misunderstood concept be found in his work? If these modernist misunderstandings pose conceptual difficulties, how could Durkheim be expected to have anticipated and resolved them? Giddens reasons that if the division of labor produces solidarity, it cannot simultaneously produce anomie. To be sure, this is a problem for progressive theories such as functionalism, but it is not an inherent flaw in Durkheim's anti-modernist theory. Giddens responds to the discourse on anomie with logic devoid of intuition. He cannot grasp what Durkheim was trying to achieve with the concept of anomie nor the reasons why the functionalists misinterpreted him.

Similarly, in *Capitalism and Modern Social Theory*, Giddens reasons that Durkheim contradicted himself by claiming that with the progress of modernity, the collective consciousness disappears and individualism and anomie increase: "Modern societies do not thereby collapse into disorder" (Giddens 1971: 79). Giddens the modernist seems unable to conceive of a society simultaneously experiencing order and disorder. Yet, as noted previously, Chris Rojek (1995) as well as many other contemporary theorists demonstrate that this state of affairs seems to be the hallmark of modernity.

We have already established that Giddens aligns Durkheim – albeit, in an ambiguous way – with the functionalist focus on social order. It seems to be the case that because Giddens rejects the problem of social order, he rejects the concept of anomie, misunderstood as a key component of the functionalist paradigm. At least two significant consequences follow from Giddens's move. One is that Giddens's theory of the agent remains a progressive and utopian scheme in which the agent is not subject to anomie or its equivalents. The other is that Giddens does not challenge the functionalist, inner-directed misunderstanding of anomie, and thereby robs sociological theory of a concept that could counter-balance its overly felicitous, progressive ideology. Functionalist misunderstandings of anomie continue to reverberate in social theory. As Ernest Wallwork put it: "Anomie or normlessness, as the term itself implies, is due to insufficient normative control whereas fatalistic suicide is the result of excessive group surveillance and lack of individuation" (1972: 49). But modern societies seem to exhibit more surveillance and more norms in contrast to traditional societies, yet anomie does not seem to be decreasing. La Capra defines anomie as "a state of complete normlessness and meaninglessness of experience attendant upon institutional and moral breakdown" (1972: 159). A state of complete meaninglessness is itself meaningless. There is always some meaning in social structures. Dohrenwend also refers to the "absence of norms altogether" in anomie (1959: 472). Some theorists have noted that there cannot be a total lack of norms if one is going to speak of society, so they refer to anomie not as normlessness but as a state of "multiple, contradictory normative standards with which the actor must contend" (Dudley 1978: 107). Merton's (1957: 131–60) goals–means schema of anomie also

189

falls under this latter rubric though it rests on his incorrect assertion that "as initially developed by Durkheim, the concept of anomie referred to a condition of relative normlessness in a society or group" (ibid.: 161). Merton's view, of course, is but an echo of the definition of anomie put forth by Parsons: "Anomie is precisely this state of disorganization where the hold of norms over individual conduct has broken down" (1937: 377). According to Parsons, "the breakdown of this [normative] control is anomie or the war of all against all" (ibid.: 407). Let me repeat that all of these mistaken views of anomie come across as inner-directed, hence hopelessly old-fashioned. The contemporary other-directed type orients him- or herself toward other people in his or her peer group, not just an impersonal structure of norms. Giddens (1976) has hinted that the Parsonian view is completely unsubstantiated by Durkheim's writings, yet he also accepts the false Parsonian view, does not offer an alternative understanding, and does not incorporate any form of equivalent for anomie regarding structuration theory.

Not one of the above-mentioned theorists quotes Durkheim to support the claim that anomie is normlessness. It is impossible to find such support because Durkheim never wrote anything like it. The view that anomie is normlessness is an inner-directed misconception that is irrelevant to our other-directed and post-other-directed era. As I will demonstrate shortly, Durkheim conceptualized anomie as a state of unlimited *desires* that afflicts the core of society, not its alleged deviants. Durkheim's characterization is seemingly other-directed and relevant to contemporary times, and also entirely commensurate with similar assessments of social life at the previous *fin de siècle* made by his colleagues, such as Thorstein Veblen ([1899] 1969), who focused on incessant consumerism and consumption, and with the works of Georg Simmel (1971), who was concerned with how "life" breaks through "forms," as well as other theorists from that era.

Let me turn to a possible objection on the part of some readers at this point in the discussion: if Durkheim lived and wrote in what was presumably an inner-directed era, how could he have envisioned anomie in a manner that is relevant to other-directedness? A question of this sort presupposes that Giddens is right in his claims, previously discussed, that there exists a radical disjunction between the most recent era and the past. But I have argued throughout this book (and elsewhere) against this and similar assumptions by Giddens: the present *fin de siècle* and the previous *fin de siècle* exhibit some remarkable cultural overlap; there exist continuities regarding sociological concepts such as anomie; and Durkheim's genius is to be found in his remarkable ability to prophesy future developments. Moreover, Riesman's brief comments on anomie are illustrated by quoting literature from Durkheim's era, and they contain intriguing linkages between anomie and other-directedness.

Riesman's brief discussion of adjustment, anomie, and autonomy in *The Lonely Crowd* is among the least developed by him as well as other sociologists, yet is extremely relevant for the present discussion. In summary, Riesman believes that all three of his character types are subject to specific forms of adjustment, anomie, and autonomy:

> In each society those who do not conform to the characterological pattern of the adjusted may be either anomic or autonomous. Anomic in English coinage from Durkheim's *anomique* (adjective of *anomie*) meaning ruleless, ungoverned. . . . The "autonomous" are those who on the whole are capable of conforming to the behavioral norms of their society – a capacity the anomics usually lack – but are free to choose whether to conform or not.
>
> (1950: 241)

Note that "autonomy" is not the same as Giddens's agency. Giddens's free and knowledgeable agent can easily become "ruleless" or, in Durkheim's vocabulary, *déréglée* (he uses *dérèglement* as a synonym for anomie). In fact, Riesman's description of an anomic type comes across very much like the caricature of the reflexive agent put forth by Giddens. Riesman writes:

> The anomics include not only those who, in their character, were trained to attend to signals that either are no longer given or no longer spell meaning or success. They also may be, as has just been said, those who are overadjusted, who listen too assiduously to the signals from within or without. Thus we have seen that in a society dependent on inner-direction there may be oversteered children and oversteered adults, people of too tight super-ego controls to permit themselves even the normal satisfactions and escapes of their fellows. Likewise, among those dependent on other-direction, some may be unable to shut off their radar even for a moment; their over-conformity makes them a caricature of the adjusted pattern – a pattern that escapes them because they try too hard for it.
>
> (ibid.: 244)

I agree with Riesman that anomie varies with social character. Riesman's brief analysis is pregnant with meanings and full of ironies that are not to be found in Giddens's simplistic rebellion against the functionalist misunderstanding of anomie as normlessness, and his equally simplistic vision of the bounded, reflexive self as agent. In the remainder of this chapter, I intend to explore some of the subtleties in Riesman's approach to anomie by re-examining and recontextualizing Durkheim's comments on anomie in contrast to Giddens's thought.

LAYING THE GROUNDWORK FOR A RECONTEXTUALIZED READING OF DURKHEIM'S CONCEPT OF ANOMIE

Translated into Giddens's terminology, Durkheim seemed to claim that human agency itself is the result of structure, that structure can enable human agency. In *Suicide*, for example, Durkheim writes that "man has become a god for men," but that "this cult of man is something, accordingly, very different from the egoistic individualism . . . which leads to suicide" ([1897] 1951: 336). This is because "the cult of man" is a *collective* representation, and is not derived from the individual but is derived from society (see especially Durkheim [1893] 1933: 407; [1912] 1965: 271–2). According to Durkheim, humanity in the abstract has become the new secular religion in modern times, but "the religion of the individual was socially instituted, as were all known religions" ([1924] 1974: 54). Elsewhere, Durkheim phrased this insight as follows: "It is not this or that individual the *State* seeks to develop, it is the individual *in genere*, who is not to be confused with any single one of us," and "this cult, moreover, has all that is required to take the place of the religious cults of former times" ([1950] 1983: 69). Obviously, Giddens is wrong to claim that Durkheim fails to find enabling functions in social structure. As an important aside, let me note that Giddens contradicts his harsh verdict on Durkheim as a clone of Parsons with other, much more sympathetic (and accurate) passages such as the following from *Durkheim on Politics and the State*:

> Individualism, or the "cult of the individual," is founded upon sentiments of sympathy for human suffering, a desire for equality and for justice.
>
> (1986: 14)

> Examination of Durkheim's writings on the growth of moral individualism, on socialism, and on the State, in the context of the social and political issues which he saw as confronting the Third Republic, shows how mistaken it is to regard him as being primarily "conservative" in his intellectual standpoint.
>
> (ibid.: 23)

In any event, Durkheim's point seems to be that humans are not born with human rights or agency. If the societies into which they are born do not hold a tradition of human rights, these agents will have a difficult time sustaining their individualisms. Previously, I have shown that Giddens fails to explain how agents come to perceive social structure. The other side of this criticism is that Giddens also fails to explain how agency originates if not through the enabling powers of society. For Giddens, human agency seems to be self-begotten, a sort of "natural rights" doctrine in social theory. Such *a priorism* is a curious stand for a sociologist to take.

In contrast to Durkheim, Giddens offers no subtlety in his theory concerning human agency. Giddens has jettisoned positivism and the natural sciences model as exemplars for sociology, but, ironically, his work remains in the shadow of Parsons's problem of social order. Giddens assumes that the freedom of the agent and his or her ability to use structure for enabling purposes are an unqualified good, in large measure, it seems, because he finds Parsons's vision too constraining. Yet Giddens neither speculates on nor conducts research into the possibly *disabling* properties of excessive enablement. The enablement of the human agent is a good thing, but can one have too much of a good thing? Giddens seems to assume that modernity and enablement are commensurate with each other (with some negative consequences that can be overcome). It is more realistic to suppose that modernity enables as well as disables human agents.

Another approach to anomie is found whereby it is treated as a feeling of "meaninglessness" on the psychological level. This is what Srole's anomia scale purports to capture, according to Merton (1957: 164–6). La Capra (1972: 160) also refers to the "psychological expression of anomie" in the individual as the expression of anxiety and frustration. There are many problems with this received and not sufficiently examined view beside the fact that it misrepresents Durkheim's position. First, Srole's anomia scale consistently correlates with low social status such that the lower the person's occupational prestige, level of education, and income, the higher such person's score on anomia. But in Durkheim's classic study of suicide ([1897] 1951), anomie was not associated with lower social class; rather, it was associated with what one would consider to be indicators of high social standing, namely, being male, Protestant, well educated, literate, and urban, indeed, with civilization and its attendant progress. These are the categories of agents who are able to make skillful use of society's enabling rules. In Giddens's terminology, anomie was associated with power and enablement. This is one of Durkheim's most counter-intuitive insights, that those social strata who enjoy luxuries and seem to have the most ontological security are paradoxically the most vulnerable to anomie. Even if Western intellectuals seek to ignore this aspect of Durkheim's work – because it is a direct affront to the assumptions of the Enlightenment project – the fact remains that in the 1990s the least amount of anomie as well as suicide is to be found in the poorest countries and social strata of the world. Dodder and Astle (1980: 334) are correct that rather than regard the Srole anomia scale as a measure of anomie, one ought to regard it as a measure of "a general dimension of despair," or at least a qualitatively different form of unhappiness than that which afflicts the upper strata of society.

There is no good reason to expect that the individual agent will be able to feel anomic or otherwise to know that he or she is disabled. Like his contemporaries – including Freud – Durkheim made extensive use of the concept of the unconscious (Meštrović 1988). He accepted without question that psychic phenomena occur within agents even though agents do not apprehend them ([1924] 1974), that agents can be subject to illusion when they try to determine the reasons for their acts ([1897] 1951: 43), and that, in general, "social life must be explained not by the conception of it formed by those who participate in it, but by the profound causes which escape their consciousness" (in Lukes 1982: 171). Of course, every one of these claims by Durkheim goes against the grain of Giddens's (1984) use of the concept of the unconscious (previously discussed) and of his theory of human agency. Yet in reworking Freud's conceptualization of the unconscious along modernist assumptions – and neglecting the many contemporaries of Freud who subscribed to the concept of the unconscious (see Ellenberger 1970) – Giddens fails to account for the very human phenomenon of the agent not always being able to give an adequate account for what he or she does or feels.

In general, none of the received views of anomie prevalent in the literature use Durkheimian texts to support the view that anomie is normlessness or meaninglessness, though they misattribute these meanings to him.[2] In the remainder of this chapter, I intend to (1) retrieve Durkheim's original understanding of anomie, (2) show its continued relevance, (3) and use it to criticize Giddens's thought extended to modernism in general. Contrary to functionalist misreadings of Durkheim, he did not link anomie with crime and deviance – which he regarded as "normal" phenomena in all societies – but did link it with modern progress. This anti-progressive strain in Durkheim's thought may be the underlying reason why his concept of anomie has been and continues to be obfuscated. Yet it is vitally important for exposing the shallowness of Giddens's writings.

For Durkheim, a part of society is always invisible so that some offenses against it are something other than normative transgression. By contrast, Giddens's structure seems to be clearly visible to agents at all times. To be sure, Giddens makes passing references to the unconscious, as we have seen in chapter 4 (in relation to Giddens's *The Constitution of Society* [1984]), but he reconceptualizes the unconscious in a modernist way so that it cannot threaten the core of his theory. Similarly, in *Central Problems in Social Theory*, Giddens makes his well-known claims about the knowledgeable human agent, and adds:

> There are various modes in which such knowledge may figure in practical social conduct. One is in unconscious sources of cognition: there is no reason to deny that knowledge exists on the level of the unconscious. Indeed, a case can be made to the effect that the mobilization of unconscious desire normally involves unconscious cognitive elements. More significant for the arguments developed in

this book are the differences between practical consciousness, as tacit stocks of knowledge which actors draw upon in the constitution of social activity, and what I call "discursive consciousness," involving knowledge which actors are able to express on the level of discourse. All actors have some degree of *discursive penetration* of the social systems to whose constitution they contribute.

(1979: 5)

Elsewhere in this same book, Giddens waters down the concept of the unconscious further:

> The whole weight of psychoanalytic theory suggests that motivation has an internal hierarchy of its own. I shall argue . . . that a conception of the unconscious is essential to social theory, even if the resultant schema I shall develop departs in some ways from classical Freudian views. *But the unconscious, of course, can only be explored in relation to the conscious: to the reflexive monitoring and rationalization of conduct, grounded in practical consciousness.* We have to guard against a reductive theory of institutions in respect of the unconscious: that is, against a theory which, in seeking to connect the forms of social life to unconscious processes, fails to allow sufficient play to autonomous social forces − Freud's own "sociological" writings leave a lot to be desired in this respect. But we must also avoid a reductive theory of consciousness: that is, one which, *in emphasizing the role of the unconscious, is able to grasp the reflexive features of action only as a pale cast of unconscious processes which really determine them.*

(ibid.: 58; emphasis added)

When all is said and done, Giddens has effectively reversed and neutralized Freud's, Durkheim's, and other understandings of the unconscious from the previous *fin de siècle* into a modernist version. For Giddens, the id as the source of desire has been transformed into a storage bin of cognitive categories. If human action is not the reflex of unconscious forces, then − despite Giddens's rhetoric − the unconscious is no longer the unconscious as originally conceptualized in the previous century. Nor should one overlook the fact, demonstrated by Henri Ellenberger in *The Discovery of the Unconscious* (1970), that plenty of intellectuals other than Freud held to some version of the concept of the unconscious, which was foreshadowed by Schopenhauer.

Giddens's attempt to keep some version of the concept of the unconscious at the same time that he seeks to keep his ideological stand on the knowledgeable agent is inconsistent and unconvincing. Contemporary society is so vast and complicated that no agent could possibly account for all of its rules and enabling functions at all times, even if the unconscious is conceived as a storage bin for cognitive knowledge that is not always at hand. Clearly, many if not most of these rules and enabling functions lie beyond the horizon of consciousness most of the time. In fact, it would be important to study when and how rules and enabling functions are called up, constructed, and retouched by the agent.

To be sure, Giddens attempts to remedy this problem in *The Constitution of Society* (1984) by distinguishing among practical consciousness, discursive consciousness, and the unconscious. He defines the two forms of consciousness as follows:

> [*Practical consciousness:*] What actors know (believe) about social conditions, including especially the conditions of their own action, but cannot express discursively; no bar of repression, however, protects practical consciousness as is the case with the unconscious.
>
> (ibid.: 375)

> [*Discursive consciousness:*] What actors are able to say, or to give verbal expression to, about social conditions, including especially the conditions of their own action; awareness which has a discursive form.
>
> (ibid.: 374)

But this does not solve the problem I have presented above. Regarding both the practical and discursive forms of consciousness, Giddens treats the agent's beliefs as knowledge. He does not seek out "real" motives or knowledge as contrasted with apparent knowledge. Against Giddens, I am claiming that the agent can never be certain about what he or she really knows, not only because of unconscious motives, but because conscious motives and knowledge are constantly retouched, modified, and rationalized by the agent.

But there is another problem with Giddens's vision, namely, what constitutes rule violation? For Durkheim, because collective representations are not material "stuff," one does not have to "do something" to violate them. They can be violated by a wrong attitude or "spirit," even when one follows the letter of the law. Theology has been well aware of this in its concern with the problem of evil, but sociology has not. Giddens concentrates so much on behavior and on the phenomenon of *doing* or *knowing* something on the part of the agent that he neglects the issue of anti-social sentiment.

ANOMIE AS SECULAR SIN

We have seen that Giddens eschews both religion and tradition as subjects for analytic study. Given that I have challenged him on his assumption that sociology is the study of only modern societies, the following question

196

arises: what are the traditional antecedents of anomie conceived as a state of infinite desires? If it is true that modernity exacerbates anomie by expanding the horizon of desires for the individual, it must also be true that anomie, in less acute forms, was conceptualized in some way by members of traditional societies. It seems that it was conceptualized as sin. Thus, this discussion turns to a search for other-directed equivalents of one of the most traditional concepts to be found, namely, sin.

To conceive of anomie as the mere transgression of norms is as naive and insipid as conceiving of sin as the mere breaking of religious prescriptions. In fact, as Lyonett and Sabourin (1970) point out in their analysis of the notion of sin, the early Christian fathers referred to what we now call "sin" as "anomia." Anomia corresponds to twenty-four Hebrew words in the Old and New Testaments. Not one of these meanings refers to the mere breaking of God's commandments. They imply, rather, that in sin "God in some way, at least in the intention of the sinner, is hit, grieved, and, as it were, hurt" (ibid.: 14). Sin is also conceived as a debt, a disease to be healed (ibid.: 26), "not as a specified sinful deed, but as a power which governs men and inspires their conduct" (ibid.: 27). Anomia, as sin, is therefore "the secret quality, the spirit, the tendency, which inspires the sinful actions and provokes them" (ibid.: 30). It is "a general state of hostility against God" (ibid.: 33). In the parable of the prodigal son, for example, the sin is not a visible, external transgression; "rather, the prodigal son has offended his father by refusing to be son, to receive, that is everything from his father's love, by pretending to be his own master, like Adam in Eden" (ibid.: 37).

Therefore, "to commit sin is not only to make a bad action, it means to commit also 'iniquity,' to reveal, that is, the sinner in his innermost, as a son of the devil, as he who opposes God and Christ, as he who accepts Satan's rule" (ibid.: 43), so that "to sin is to follow one's fancy, unrestrained by the law of God" (ibid.: 43). Sin is therefore the "rejection of light, acceptance of darkness," and leads to death (ibid.: 43). Sin "is the inward dynamism of evil leading to and manifesting itself in sinful actions," so that "man cannot be liberated from the tyranny of sin except by receiving a new dynamism, the life-giving Spirit, who works in man his reunion with God" (ibid.: 291).

Some of these theological meanings of anomia as sin could not have escaped Durkheim, who was descended from a long line of rabbis and whose classical education could scarcely by excelled. It is as impossible to find Durkheim ever making the claim in any of his writings that anomie is normlessness or the breaking of norms as it is to find sin defined anywhere in the Bible as the mere transgression of divine law or the absence of such law. Rather, Durkheim seems to use "anomie" as the secular equivalent of "sin." It is, therefore, an inversion of the sacred and the profane, a domination not by the "devil" but by its secular equivalent, by what is personal, egoistic, materialistic, transitory, and sensual. The sacred in modern times, as he makes clear in "The Dualism of Human Nature and Its Social

Conditions" ([1914] 1973), is comprised of conceptual thought, the impersonal, altruism, idealism, collective ideals, and intellectual values. The profane is comprised of "the body," sensations, anything personal, egoism, and sensory appetites. Anomie as sin is the *condition* of rebelling against the sacred such that the profane is treated as if it was sacred, and vice versa.

Curiously, Giddens does not seem to be overly concerned in his writings with contemporary developments of secular sin. Parsons's oversocialized vision of the human agent is apparently so disturbing to him that he overcompensates for it by positing a skilled and knowledgeable agent who can use structure to enable him- or herself without any negative consequences. Yet it should be obvious that a skilled and knowledgeable agent can use his or her talents for crime or other anti-social acts. And if the agent does not become an overt lawbreaker, his or her over-confidence in human agency can become a sort of megalomania. This narcissistic megalomania seems to constitute a new form of anomie which is as damaging to society as Durkheim's depiction of more traditional forms of anomie. For if the agent cynically uses structure solely for his or her enablement, he or she must necessarily do so at the expense of other agents, many of whom will be bent on doing the same. Such concerted albeit individualistic megalomania must eventually erode social structure.

Consider Durkheim's comments on anomie in book three and the second preface to *The Division of Labor*. He is concerned with anomie in government, economics, and science. If one considers, for brevity's sake, only his comments on science and anomie as illustration, it is obvious that he does not so much as breathe the notions of "normlessness" or "deregulation." Rather, he discusses the "concrete and living" part of science which "is even its best and largest part" because "otherwise, one will have the letter, but not the spirit" of science (Durkheim [1893] 1933: 362). Durkheim is making a clear allusion to the Bible and is criticizing, in a direct and searing fashion, the tendency for scientists merely to follow a paradigm (the letter of the law). Scientists are in a state of anomie when they focus so exclusively on "some propositions which have been definitively proved" that they lose sight of the sacredness of their task. In a word, the anomic scientist works in the equivalent of a state of "sin," but this condition may be caused by following too closely the norms of one's profession.

To update Durkheim's discussion of the anomic scientist, one could speculate that the overly other-directed scientist is anomic when he or she becomes obsessed with the opinion of his or her peers, publishing in mainstream journals, or pursuing research projects that are "fundable," and therefore convey status and prestige. In such a case, the scientist may believe that he or she is an emancipated agent, but is actually enslaved by excessive worry about the opinion of peers.

Elsewhere in *The Division of Labor* Durkheim states outright that "it is not sufficient that there be rules, however, for sometimes the rules themselves are the cause of evil" (ibid.: 374). Clearly, the frequently alleged "normative regulation" that is purported to be the obverse of anomie is regarded by Durkheim as one of its possible causes. This Durkheimian insight holds consequences for Giddens's acceptance of part of the Parsonian vision of social order that some constraint based on social rules is necessary for social functioning. Giddens does not distinguish between benign versus destructive rules in his notion of social constraint. Structure is always somehow constructed by human agents, and there is no good reason to suppose that humans always produce structures that are either constraining or enabling: some structures are evil.

What, then, does Durkheim truly regard as necessary for the division of labor to function normally? He claims that what is needed above all is "justice" (ibid.: 388). Justice is a fascinating sociological concept – albeit, neglected by Giddens as well as other prominent social theorists – because it presupposes that all rules are not created equal. Only those rules that are deemed worthy of respect by most of society's members will be regarded as just, and of course, every society will have standards of justice peculiar to it in addition to some standards that might be termed universal. But rules that are not deemed worthy of respect are perceived by agents as repressive, odius, cruel – in a word, unjust. How do human agents arrive at the notion of just versus unjust rules, cross-culturally and relative to tradition-, inner-, and other-direction? When do they suffer in silence under unjust rules and when do they rebel? These are additionally important questions that Giddens fails to address in his glib vision of the agent as constrained by seemingly neutral rules and the agent as the evader of rules. The important point is that constraint by just rules is welcomed whereas constraint by rules regarded as unjust is unbearable for most agents.

As with the concept of the unconscious, Giddens mentions justice in passing, but clearly does not develop this concept or take it seriously. For example, in *Modernity and Self-Identity,* Giddens claims that "emancipatory politics makes primary the imperatives of justice, equality, and participation" (1991a: 212). He adds:

> The basic conditions governing autonomy of action are worked out in terms of a thematic of justice; Rawls provides a case for justice as an organizing ambition of emancipation. Yet how individuals and groups in a just order will actually behave is left open.
>
> (ibid.: 213)

Giddens does not pose or answer questions such as the following: what is the origin of the imperative of justice? Is justice solely a matter of emancipation or does it have repressive aspects? Is justice primarily a rationalist phenomenon, as Rawls claims, or does it involve feelings, habits of the heart, and other irrational phenomena? Can a just social order simultaneously produce injustice? Giddens's quick references to justice amount to little more than rhetoric.

Durkheim's use of "justice" resonates in part, of course, with his Judaic cultural heritage, as noted previously. It is also akin, in many ways, to the classical notions of justice found in the writings of Plato and Aristotle in which justice is the cardinal virtue that puts the other virtues into a proper balance. Durkheim writes:

> We are thus led to the recognition of a new reason why the division of labor is a source of social cohesion. It makes individuals solidary, as we have said before, not only because it limits the activity of each, but also because it increases it.
>
> ([1893] 1933: 395)

How Giddens could have concluded that Durkheim made no allowance for enabling functions in social structure is truly mysterious. The above quotation from Durkheim clearly illustrates, again, his sensitivity to the enabling functions of structure. Moreover, Durkheim's assessment is far removed from the Parsonian implication that justice is the mere imposition of a normative structure. (Anyone familiar with the classics will note the affinity between the modern vision and the view of Thrasymachus in *The Republic*, which Socrates attacks.) The division of labor inhibits individuality at the same time that it makes it possible because of the proper balance of forces that comprise *homo duplex*. Durkheim reiterated this point eloquently in an article published in *L'Année sociologique*: "The division of labor is the only process which allows us to reconcile the necessities of social cohesion with the principle of individualism" (1980: 102). Conversely, the anomic division of labor is a "sinful" state in which these opposing forces are not in harmony, in which "justice" has not been achieved.

Durkheim seems to have been keenly aware of the implicit parallel between this conception of anomie as a replacement for sin and that of the relationship of Christianity to Judaism. *The Division of Labor* ends with the thought that "the collective conscience is becoming more of a cult of the individual" ([1893] 1933: 407). According to Durkheim, it is Christianity, in contradistinction to Judaism and Greek religions, that essentially worships the individual:

> By contrast, the Christian religion had its seat in man himself, in his very soul. . . . [T]o sum up, with Christianity the world loses its primitive unity and becomes divided into two parts, two halves, to which very different values are ascribed.
>
> ([1925] 1961: 283)

The reference to the "two halves" refers to the Christian version of *homo duplex* as two irreconcilable poles of human existence. Yet Durkheim treated *homo duplex* as an antagonistic *unity*. Durkheim reiterates this point many times, as in *Moral Education*, wherein he writes that Christianity is "an essentially human religion since its God dies for the salvation of humanity. Christianity teaches that the principal duty of man toward God is to love his neighbor" (ibid.: 6–7).

It is worth posing the question: is Giddens's theory of structuration a caricature of a basically Christian set of ideas or does it resonate with non-Christian traditions? Despite his rhetoric of seeking to overcome Parsons's dualisms in favor of a duality, Giddens fails to examine how agency and structure may be reconciled or how the relationship between them can go awry. In other words, he posits no equivalent to Durkheim's notion of justice as the principle of reconciliation and he ignores the problem of anomie to account for how the relationship between agency and structure can go wrong.

According to Durkheim, with the aforementioned shift in focus in the object of worship there occurs a shift in the focus of sin. Sin in traditional religions was essentially a violation of specific rites and norms, whereas in Christianity, according to Durkheim, "the place they [rites] occupy and the importance attributed to them continue to diminish" (ibid.: 7). Rather, in Christianity,

> Essential sin is no longer detached from its human context. True sin now tends to merge with moral transgression. No doubt God continues to play an important part in morality. . . . But He is now reduced to the role of guardian. Moral discipline wasn't instituted for His benefit, but for the benefit of men.
>
> (ibid.)

The mere breaking of rules is not sufficient for anomie because that would imply a very traditional or inner-directed morality. Modern anomie requires a veneration of the individual to such an extent that it is believed that the individual is capable of choosing a state of moral transgression. In other words, anomie presupposes the existence of Giddens's skilled and knowledgeable agent.

Even Durkheim's famous discourse on anomie in chapter 5 of *Suicide* refers to "deregulation" not as the absence of norms but as the absence of "justice" (Durkheim [1897] 1951: 249). He illustrates this lack of justice with regard to economics, such that in trade and industry anomie is "in a chronic state" (ibid.: 254) because both religion and government have become the "tool and servant" of business (ibid.: 255). It is more true in the present *fin de siècle* than in Durkheim's *fin de siècle* that churches and governments are run as businesses; moreover, that they seek to market the masses in order to increase revenue. This is the "injustice" of anomie, so similar to the iniquity of sin. Thus, Durkheim writes:

The longing for infinity is daily represented as a mark of moral distinction, whereas it can only appear within unregulated consciences which elevate to a rule the lack of rule from which they suffer. . . . Since this disorder is greatest in the economic world, it has most victims there.

(ibid.: 257)

Can there be any doubt that Durkheim's reference to a rule that is really the lack of rule means something other than "normlessness"? The longing for infinity is the hallmark of modernist progressivism and Durkheim clearly felt that this insatiable desire had to be restrained. One has to strain language to an absurd degree to conceive of a norm of normlessness. But the rule of lacking rule is intelligible as a contemporary version of sin. Durkheim's description also bears an uncanny resemblance to Riesman's descriptions of the other-directed type who is seduced by the Milky Way.

A section of *Suicide* is rarely discussed by scholars, the one pertaining to "conjugal anomy" (ibid.: 384–6). Had Durkheim truly possessed the strong normative streak often ascribed to him, surely he would have agreed that "the only way to reduce the number of suicides due to conjugal anomy is to make marriage more indissoluble" (ibid.: 384). But having offered stricter divorce laws as a "solution," Durkheim proceeds to ask: "Must one of the sexes necessarily be sacrificed, and is the solution only to choose the lesser of two evils?" (ibid.). He answers, no – "For man and woman to be equally protected by the same institution [marriage], they must first of all be creatures of the same nature" (ibid.: 386). The mere passage of laws to promote equality or make divorce difficult will only result in what the calls "juridical equality." As in *The Division of Labor*, in *Suicide* Durkheim calls for the "spirit of the law" and not just the letter of the law as the solution to anomie.

In his neglected work, *Professional Ethics and Civic Morals*, Durkheim continues the attacks on business that he began in *The Division of Labor* and *Suicide*. He makes the charge that in business, considered as a profession, "no professional ethics exist" (Durkheim [1950] 1983: 9) and that both capitalism and socialism "do no more than raise a *de facto* state of affairs which is unhealthy, to the level of a *de jure* state of affairs" (ibid.: 10) because "it is not possible for a social function to exist without moral discipline" (ibid.: 11). According to Durkheim, "it is precisely due to this fact that the crisis has arisen from which the European societies are now suffering" (ibid.). Even military, governmental, and religious functions have been made subordinate to business. Thus, "this amoral character of economic life amounts to a public danger," and "the unleashing of economic interests has been accompanied by a debasing of public morality" (ibid.: 197). It is certainly true that since Durkheim's time most societal institutions and professions have been made subordinate to economic self-interest, including medicine, research, academia, and the law. Yet in Giddens's terms, this anomic state of affairs (from Durkheim's point of view, because self-interest, not justice, has been enshrined as the central principle of social activity) is commensurate with individual agents making skilled use of the social structure to enable themselves. Durkheim adds that,

> In fact it is a general law of all living things that needs and appetites are normal only on the condition of being controlled. Unlimited need contradicts itself. For need is defined by the goal it aims at, and if unlimited has no goal – since there is no limit.
>
> (ibid.)

This is a far cry from Merton's use of "goals" and "means" with regard to anomie. Durkheim seems to rely on the classical notion of goals as "the Good" which "rational principles" must enable persons to attain. The goals must be sacred to begin with, and the means must be commensurate with them. Durkheim continues:

> As there is nothing within an individual which constrains these appetites, they must surely be constrained by some force exterior to him, or else they would become insatiable – that is, morbid. . . . This is what seems to have escaped Saint-Simon. To him it appears that the way to realize social peace is to free economic appetites of all restraint on the one hand, and on the other to satisfy them by fulfilling them. But such an undertaking is contradictory.
>
> (ibid.: 199)

This insight seems to have escaped Giddens as well. The rest of chapter 6 of *Professional Ethics and Civic Morals* is a detailed criticism of Saint-Simon, pursuing the theme that, contrary to Saint-Simon, "the problem is to know, under the present conditions of social life, what moderating functions are necessary and what forces are capable of executing them" (ibid.).

In his conclusion, Durkheim accuses Saint-Simon of trying to get "the most from the least, the superior from the inferior, moral rule from economic matter" (ibid.: 240). In essence, Durkheim accuses Saint-Simon of advocating anomie. I contend that, similarly, Giddens and many other modernists try to get the most from the least, moral rule from human agency.

Note that Durkheim is essentially objecting to the inversion of what has for centuries been considered an unbridgeable gap between the sacred and profane as the essence of anomie. That is, the economic structure was traditionally considered profane because it emphasized personal egoism and material well-being (this observation enters into Max Weber's thesis in *The Protestant Ethic and the Spirit of Capitalism*). Society, on the other hand, was traditionally considered sacred because it involved that which transcends personal egoism and is essentially spiritual, a system of ideas. Thus, according to Durkheim, "it could not be a question of building one to the other – still less of mingling them," so that "the very idea of such fusion was revolting – like sacrilege" ([1928] 1958: 41). Durkheim's repugnance at this treatment of money as something sacred when it is really profane is clearly expressed in the second preface to *The Division of Labor*, the conclusion of *Suicide*, and, of course, the works on ethics and socialism already cited. Similarly, Marcel Mauss's thesis in *The Gift* is "that the whole field of industrial and commercial law is in conflict with morality" (Mauss 1967: 64). He echoes Marx and Durkheim, when he claims that in losing the collective representation of gift-giving, man "became a machine – a calculating machine" (ibid.: 74). Both Parsons and Giddens seem to lift the notion of the human agent as a calculating machine solely in economic spheres of life and generalize it to all of social life.

One of the most ponderous claims Durkheim makes in *The Elementary Forms of the Religious Life* occurs immediately following the presentation of his thesis of *homo duplex*:

> This duality of our nature has as its consequence in the practical order the irreducibility of a moral ideal to a utilitarian motive and in the order of thought, the irreducibility of reason to individual experience.
>
> (Durkheim [1912] 1965: 16)

The reduction of morality to utilitarianism and of rationalism to empiricism are, in fact, the two forms of anomie that concerned Durkheim the most. It is this sense that law, morals, and even scientific thought were considered by him to be of *religious origin* (ibid.: 70). In their "just" versions, they uphold a moral social structure, but when inverted, they represent sin. In *The Division of Labor*, he attacked anomie in all its forms, but prior to 1912, he seems to have emphasized sin "in the practical order," in the business world. After 1912, he turned his attention more toward the sin of reversing the premises of rationalism, as in his critique of pragmatism.

The connection between anomie and sin may be a key to resolving the ambiguities of *Suicide*. Note that in Durkheim's treatment of the four suicidal currents, egoism and anomie are treated as one pole of *homo duplex* and altruism and fatalism as the other pole. He also claims that all four currents are virtues in certain social settings. (Indeed, he even saw anomie as a virtue, for without it societies would remain mired in tradition and would never progress.) But all four virtues, in the extreme, are prototypes of "sin" as it has been discussed here. Note that egoism is a state "in which the individual ego asserts itself to excess in the face of the social ego and at its expense" (Durkheim [1897] 1951: 209). And altruism, "where the ego is not its own property" (ibid.: 221), also violates the proper relationship of *homo duplex*, as does the excessive regulation of fatalism (ibid.: 276). Anomie is referred to as "the spirit of progress" or rebellion. In effect, overall societal "virtue" depends on the proper balance of four virtues that can easily become vices when they are excessive – a classical model, beyond a doubt (compare *Suicide* to Aristotle's *Nicomachean Ethics* or Plato's *Republic*). It is no wonder that Durkheim concludes that "suicide is a close kin to genuine virtues, which it simply exaggerates" (ibid.: 371).

My conclusion is that Giddens's notion of reflexive agency, too, is a virtue that can become pathological when exaggerated. Moreover, Giddens's writings on agency seem to emphasize egoism and anomie and tend to neglect altruism and fatalism. Nowhere in his writings does Giddens write of the agent's compassion or self-sacrifice for other agents, and he argues against fatalism. Yet without the balance of altruism and fatalism, there is nothing to restrain the agent, as depicted by Giddens, from becoming a megalomaniac.

Finally, it would seem that Riesman's other-directed type suffers from excessive altruism and fatalism. He or she is overly concerned with the feelings and needs of others, and succumbs to a new and contemporary form of fatalism when confronted with too many choices or demands by others: the other-directed type shuts off his or her feelings as a defensive mechanism and becomes indifferent:

> We have seen, for example, the effort of the other-directed person to achieve a political and personal style of tolerance, drained of emotion, temper, and moodiness. But, obviously, this can go so far that deadness of feeling comes to resemble a clinical symptom.
>
> (Riesman 1950: 244)

CONCLUSIONS AND IMPLICATIONS

In this chapter I have contrasted Giddens and Riesman in relation to agency, broadly speaking (for Riesman does not use this term), and with Durkheim as a backdrop. This way of reading Giddens leads to the realization that his claims about agency amount to little more than rhetoric, clichés, and slogans. He simply fails to compel the reader to believe that the agent is knowledgeable and able all or even most of the time. On the other hand, Riesman's ironic twist on the agent as someone who knows much but feels little seems to resonate with the existence of widespread cynicism in the present era. Giddens portrays the agent in relation to an abstract structure of rules, whereas Riesman is more compelling in his claim that the other-directed agent confronts other *people* in addition to if not more than structure.

What Giddens refers to as agency seems to correspond in some ways to what Riesman calls autonomy. Whereas Riesman allows that some form of autonomy is possible in tradition-, inner-, as well as other-directed societies, Giddens restricts agency to modern societies. Whereas Riesman is sensitive to the complexities of life such that autonomy and anomie are perilously close to each other, Giddens rejects the concept of anomie along with the rest of functionalism. Of course, in making this move, Giddens fails to appreciate the contemporary relevance of Durkheim's non-functionalist vision of anomie.

In sum, this chapter leads to the conclusion that an other-directed understanding of anomie is vital for understanding contemporary social problems: overconformity, compassion fatigue, cynicism, the manipulation of self and others, curdled indignation coupled with a sense of powerlessness, the desire to know many things as a compensation for feeling fatalistic about making a real impact upon others, and so on. Conversely, Giddens's vision of the reflexive agent is really a nostalgic throwback to inner-directedness that cannot account for the times in which we live.

8

CONCLUSIONS

Life can express itself and realize its freedom only through forms; yet forms must also necessarily suffocate life and obstruct freedom.

— Georg Simmel (1971: 391)

I cannot here withhold the statement that *optimism*, where it is not merely the thoughtless talk of those who harbor nothing but words under their shallow foreheads, seems to me to be not merely an absurd, but also a really *wicked*, way of thinking, a bitter mockery of the unspeakable suffering of mankind.

— Arthur Schopenhauer ([1818] 1969a: 326)

I have demonstrated that Giddens's slipperiness, evasiveness, and ambivalence, noted by Craib and other students of Giddens, is actually more subtle, complicated, and significant for what it betrays about his readers than such adjectives would imply. The subtlety is that despite his "fox-like" qualities, Giddens remains an ambivalent Enlightenment modernist, and thereby appeals to many modernists today who are equally ambivalent. The complexity is that despite his disavowal of postmodernity, Giddens actually holds many assumptions in common with the postmodernists. Ambivalence might have been a reproach a generation ago, but in the 1990s, ambivalence has been enshrined as an intellectual virtue in academia as well as in much of social life in general. In fact, in chapter 7, I have pinpointed Giddens's ambivalence as stemming from a nostalgic yearning for the inner-directed-ness of yesteryear (hence, his rhetoric concerning social order, agency, clear boundaries, and so on) coupled with a moralistic defense of contemporary other-directedness (hence, his rhetoric concerning dialogue, life politics, engagement, and so on). Throughout this book, I have maintained that Giddens's popularity is premised on a similar, widespread ambivalence in contemporary Western societies. Most modernists are as uneasy as Giddens in choosing between modernity and postmodernity, social order and chaos, inner-directedness and other-directedness, and other distinct choices. The contemporary intellectual in sociology is an especially ambiguous creature, and Giddens speaks for him or her.

Yet this realization has not softened my conclusion that such ambivalence is unsatisfactory. In the moral realm, it has led to an agonized indifference regarding recent crimes against humanity from Bosnia to Rwanda and Zaïre. In politics, it has led to movements toward respecting emancipatory drives in various nations at the same time that Western nation-states have insisted on the Helsinki Accords and the inviolability of borders. In law, modern societies boast of getting "tough on crime" at the same time that "cultural defenses" for crimes are increasingly being admitted into trial proceedings. In methodology, it has resulted in social scientists going through the motions of positivism at the same time that everyone recognizes the inevitability of hermeneutics. With regard to concepts of the self, it has led to an appreciation of sorts concerning tolerance at the same time that an inner-directed, rigid self is required to succeed in the world. The modernists keep writing about social systems and boundedness while the postmodernists keep writing about the absence of boundaries, chaos, and meaninglessness. How these and other contemporary tensions will be resolved is an open question.

At this concluding point in the discussion, some readers might be expecting me to present a manifesto or a newer set of rules to offset Giddens's "non-functionalist manifesto" (1979:7) and new rules of sociological method. Such readers would have missed the gist of my critique of Giddens's work: sociology does not need yet another manifesto or more rules. Sociology should not be made into a modernist "project." By this I mean that it should not be modernist in the sense of amputating the legacies of Durkheim, Weber, Marx, Simmel, Veblen, and other thinkers from its not so remote past. After all, sociology is only about a hundred years old, and that is young relative to other disciplines. It should also not relegate the study of traditional forms of association to anthropology because traditions persist into modernity. But it should also not be made into any sort of "project," that is, a reflexive, self-conscious attempt to make it a "garden" (from Bauman 1991) in which the "weeds" have been plucked out. Whatever constitutes modernity as well as sociology, both have – at least had until recently – a spontaneous aspect to them that continues to defy social engineering. This is the gist of Simmel's (1971) claim that "life" always breaks through humanly constructed forms. Similarly, and still against the grain of Giddens's approach, there is no need to "reinvent" a Durkheimian or Simmelian or Marxist or any other tradition to correct what many call the chaotic state of sociological theory. Why not simply reread Durkheim or any other classical sociologist in the context of the present? Much of what Veblen, Durkheim, Simmel, and other sociologists wrote about still resonates with contemporary times. And ironically, what binds these and other classical social theorists together is not any paradigm but a deeply held conviction that life is in constant flux. They thought of modernity as one stage in this flux, not anything like a static project amenable to conscious control. I will conclude this book with a call to allow sociology to be spontaneous and wild, and with an overview of my criticisms of Giddens as the spokesperson for modernity in sociology.

Closely related to my criticisms of Giddens for attempting to remake sociology into a modernist project is the conviction that neat and tidy divisions between sociology and the other disciplines should not matter. Veblen was and still is perceived widely as an economist, yet his relevance to sociology is not diminished by this fact. Marx also lends himself to economic analysis, and Weber is more of a political scientist than a sociologist. Simmel saw himself as a philosopher and was not absorbed into sociological discourse until recently. Marcuse and Fromm were right to grasp the sociological import of Freud's writings even though Freud has been claimed by psychologists. In fact, the only one of the founders of sociology who was a *bona fide* sociologist was Émile Durkheim, and even this observation must be qualified by noting that he held a chair in education and sociology. At its inception, sociology was one of the "moral sciences" along with disciplines that have come to be known later as psychology, political science, anthropology, and economics. Giddens's attempt to sever sociology from its wild and amorphous beginnings is unnecessary and artificial at best, and damaging at worst. If sociology cannot draw from and in turn be used by the other social sciences, its relevance is severely circumscribed. Of course, Giddens seeks to circumscribe sociology tightly vis-à-vis its origins as well as the other social scientists because he is a modernist.

Twentieth-century sociology also defies Giddens's neat and tidy divisions. Robert Park, one of the founders of the Chicago School, was a journalist by training, and the world's first sociology textbook by Park and Burgess (1921) draws on the whole spectrum of the social sciences and humanities. It is really a manifesto for the liberal arts. David Riesman was a lawyer by training who held a chair in the social sciences, not sociology, at Harvard University. His works draw upon and have been used by a wide range of theories and theorists concerned with society. Some of sociology's leading theorists in the twentieth century, from Daniel Bell to Seymour Martin Lipset, have become great "sociologists" by not restricting themselves narrowly to the type of sociology envisioned by Giddens.

To put the matter differently, from its inception until the rise of Anthony Giddens's reputation in the present *fin de siècle*, sociology was a wild discipline that was kept alive mostly by amateurs or non-sociologists who came to the discipline from other fields. There were very few *bona fide* sociologists until recently. By wild I mean that sociology as a discipline was not well organized and took what it needed from the humanities, natural sciences, and the other social sciences in order to make sense of the social world.

Sociologists prior to World War II had not really learned the rules of socio-logical method in a formal way, and had not studied the history of the discipline. Except for the Chicago School, there were few sources of sociology to master – and the Chicago School was eclectic in any event, drawing far and wide for the sources of "sociology." Judging by sociology journals during that wild era, sociologists were studying anything and everything, arguing about the meanings of basic concepts such as "society" and "social interaction," and drawing extensively on the theories and works in neighboring disciplines such as philosophy, anthropology, psychology, and economics. Sociologists thought that they could solve or at least make an impact upon social problems without worrying unduly whether they were scientists in the positivistic sense, whether they should or should not encroach on the "turf" of other disciplines, or whether they should be concerned with the long list of concerns offered by Giddens: that the classical theorists are no longer relevant, that studies of pre-modern societies are no longer relevant, that sociology must subscribe to specific views on human agency, and so on.

The rise of "grand theory" with Parsons – who came to sociology from economics, let us note – signaled the beginning of the end of sociology's collective wilderness. Parsons was sociology's first great systematizer, and I do not mean that as a compliment. Giddens is the second major system-atizer. In addition, Giddens's grand theory marks the beginning of the *institutionalization* of the end of sociology's state of wilderness. Sociology's founders were amateurs, by necessity, because sociology was too young at the time for any of them to know what it was. Most of them were philosophers by training who made a living in various fields, but were dissatisfied with the pure abstractionism of philosophy. Those who read Simmel, Veblen, Durkheim, Freud, or other classical social theorists without trying to force them into Parsons's, Giddens's, or any other paradigm will most likely conclude that in their writings they sought to make sense of the contradic-tions, restlessness, and wilderness that constitute modernity. They conceived of the apparent order of modernity, when it was perceived in this way, as ephemeral and temporary in the great stream of constant historical and social flux. In place of today's sophisticated empirical methods, Simmel, Veblen, Durkheim, and the rest did little more than "go out and look" at the society around them. Today's sophisticated methodologists who criticize them for this innocence should be reminded that at least the classical social theorists were curious about the world and were capable of making discov-eries about society. By contrast, today's tendency toward modernist organization and deductive reasoning within sociology results in reification and has a stultifying effect on curiosity. Ritzer (1992) has a point when he claims that sociology has been McDonaldized along with most of Western society.

To capture what this previous state of wilderness was and what its loss entailed, consider what it might have meant for a sociologist to pick up a book by Durkheim or Simmel or any other founding figure prior to Parsons's systematization of the origins of sociology. The pre-Parsonian sociological neophyte had few if any guides for understanding or interpretation. He or she was mostly on his/her own – a theoretical frontiersman or frontierswoman. The neophyte was forced to be creative and original in interpreting sociology if for no other reason than that there were so few other sociologists or sociology books to tell him or her what to think. To be sure, after 1921, but before the rise of Parsons, there was Park and Burgess's *Introduction to the Science of Sociology*. But this book, the world's first sociology textbook, is really a wonderful compendium of quotations and commentaries drawn from an incredibly diverse field of thinkers. Park and Burgess end every chapter with a list of thought-provoking questions, not assertions. The thinkers upon whom Park and Burgess draw include Schopenhauer, Simmel, Worms, Durkheim, Mead, Freud, Sumner, Thorndike, Binet, Dewey, Rousseau, Gumplowicz, Darwin, Watson, and many other intellectuals from a vast field of knowledge. The diversity and range of thinkers is breathtaking, and the result is that the reader's imagination soars. Park and Burgess give the student a sampling of sociology's richness, and do not restrict his or her vision to any one set of concepts or paradigm.

But following Parsons, sociology's founders were forced into a single paradigm. The many contributors to sociology are narrowed down to a very short list of contributors vis-à-vis action theory. A generation of post-Parsonian sociologists read Parsons *instead* of reading Durkheim, Marx, Simmel, Pareto, or the other founders. This did not stop them from believing that they understood Durkheim and the other classical thinkers through Parsons. One might call this attitude the conceit of innocence. It is innocent in its provincialism and amateurism, yet is really a pretentious, fake innocence because it assumes that reading Durkheim or Marx second-hand is as good as – if not better – than reading them directly.

Giddens has taken this modernist tendency toward systematization and the loss of innocence several steps further. He also reads Durkheim and other founders of sociology through Parsons, and then rereads them through his own neo-Parsonian attempt to establish yet another neat and tidy, imperialist, grand theory. Giddens also uses a very narrow canon of thinkers to construct social theory (simply contrast his list of thinkers with the seemingly unending list used by Park and Burgess). But instead of questioning Parsons's interpretation of the origins and meaning of sociology, Giddens concluded that Parsons's goal was worthwhile, only that Parsons failed at implementing it. Giddens would succeed where Parsons failed. Giddens would force sociology into another paradigm, but this time, it would "work." Giddens would solve the riddle of agency versus structure that baffled Parsons and that supposedly concerned Durkheim and other theorists from the previous *fin de siècle*. The 1990s graduate student in sociology is likely to be introduced to Durkheim and the other originators of the discipline through reading Giddens (because Parsons is passé). The irony is that Giddens reads Durkheim through Parsons, and then throws out Durkheim with the bathwater of Parsonian functionalism. Giddens lays out how sociology should be read and understood so as to avoid the chaos of competing interpretations. As indicated in chapter 2, many of Giddens's sharpest critics conceive of this tendency toward second- and third-hand knowledge as progress.

There is no way to argue effectively against such sentiment because it is a sentiment, hence immune to rational arguments; and it is a *modernist* sentiment, hence part of that great tide that continues to force most everyone into the direction of systems, artificiality, and mechanization. George Orwell saw the tide coming in *The Road to Wigan Pier* ([1937] 1958): mechanization becomes a social habit such that everything, even thought, has to be systematized. Orwell linked the origins of totalitarianism to the twentieth-century modernist love of the machine, a stark linkage that Henry Adams, Veblen, and other rebels against mechanization were too innocent to imagine. Yet Orwell's vision of totalitarianism stopped with the concept of thought. Giddens carries matters further by positing the need to reinvent and create artificial traditions, which involve feelings as well as thought. One is not better able to justify or explain effectively the opposing sentiment of horror at this incessant tendency toward systematization and artificiality than the sentiment for mechanization itself. It comes down to a matter of taste: those who prefer a healthy home-cooked meal, despite all the inconveniences experienced by the modernist in preparing it, versus a McDonald's "happy meal," containing high levels of sodium, cholesterol, and fats; those who prefer the majesty of diverse interpretations in Park and Burgess's 1921 textbook versus Giddens's manifesto; those who prefer the wilderness of emotions and competing interpretations to a neat and tidy garden. Giddens serves up a processed "happy meal" of social theory. He reduces the richness and depth of sociology as a springboard for *questioning* the world to a set of trite formulas and sayings: the agent is knowledgeable, structure is enabling, tradition needs to be reinvented, and so on.

I am well aware that Giddens's admirers will flinch or scoff at the suggestion that Giddens's program holds any potential for a new form of totalitarianism. I stated at the beginning of this volume that Giddens comes across as ever gracious and kind, and his emancipatory politics is clearly in tune with the surface sentiments of the times in which we live. Yet throughout this book I have also pointed to Giddens's authoritarianism, penchant for social order, rhetoric concerning boundaries, dismissal of postmodernity (probably because it questions boundaries), contradictions, and arrogant attitude toward classical theorists (probably because of their antimodernist outlook). After so many dismal failures in societal engineering in the present century (see Bauman 1989, 1991), there is no good reason to suppose that the next experiment will "work." Giddens's happy conscious-ness makes opposition unlikely, but it does not hide the fact that his writings are modernist treatises on social order, control, power, and societal engineering. It really is high time for sociologists to confront seriously and deeply the failures and dark side of the Enlightenment project. Bauman indicts modernity with the gruesome failures and horrors of Communism and Nazism. I maintain that, as of this writing, the West's complicity in the genocide in Bosnia is the most serious indictment of the goals and values that Giddens holds dear (see Meštrović 1996, 1997). Reflexivity, dialogue, and the rhetoric of emancipation did nothing to stop the bloodshed. In fact, in his comments on Bosnia, Giddens, the writer on emancipatory politics, never mentions Bosnia's yearning for and right to emancipation from Greater Serbia as this project was disguised in the rhetoric of a federal Yugoslavia.

But again, my polemic is not aimed at Giddens personally but at Giddens as the vehicle for a much larger "happy consciousness" in Western societies. In addition to Bosnia, contemporary Western countries do impose cruelties on the rest of the world despite their collective rhetoric of democracy, agency, freedom, and so on: cigarette companies seek markets outside the USA as the USA becomes more "reflexive" concerning the dangers of smoking; economic sanctions by the USA and other democracies against scores of countries hurt millions of innocent civilians who are simply unable to overthrow the dictatorial regimes under which they must live; various poisons banned in the USA (such as DDT) are routinely sold to developing countries; Western countries sell weapons to governments and factions throughout the world who use these weapons to kill literally millions of people in the numerous "small wars" that occur constantly around the globe. This list of evils could be extended, but the point has been made: a "nice" rhetoric concerning agency and democracy in the West cannot efface the real cruelties of the world, some of which could surely be ameliorated by the West if it would only confront them.

MIXING METAPHORS

I began this book by approaching Giddens's work via Ian Craib's metaphor of the omelette, and shifted gradually to Bauman's and Tester's metaphor of the modernist as gardener. Though some readers will fault me for mixing metaphors – an untidy, unmodernist thing to do – I did it deliberately. The omelette metaphor captures Giddens's slipperiness, ambiguity, ambivalence, and other fox-like qualities, but does not capture his modernist tendencies that lie beneath these surface appearances. The omelette metaphor was a good point of departure for discussion, but no more than that. But just as there are different kinds of cooks (those who prefer natural fare versus artificiality), there are different kinds of gardeners. Giddens is the orderly, modernist gardener as opposed to the dying breed of natural gardeners who tried to cultivate flowers in a natural and wild context. Regarding sociology as a garden, Giddens plucks out Durkheim and Veblen as if they were weeds. Simmel is not allowed to grow in Giddens's garden. The many colleagues of Durkheim that are found in Park and Burgess's text never have a chance to sprout in Giddens's garden. In addition, Veblen, Riesman, Baudrillard, Wundt, and Sorokin effectively do not exist. Giddens keeps Comte in a hothouse away from the garden, as an exotic plant and icon, useless but prestigious. Marx and Weber are pruned, for if left to develop, these two plants can become quite unmanageable and wild. He cultivates Garfinkel, Schütz, Wittgenstein, Winch, Heidegger (see Giddens 1993), and a few other favorite plants – but he makes sure not to dig to their roots. (For how Heidegger can be used in a Giddens-style theory of modernity is really inconceivable.) The end result is an orderly garden, an alternative to the "chaos" in social theory that Giddens feels afflicted the sociological garden after the 1960s. Structuration theory gives sociology order and design. It is now a well-manicured, well-arranged, *modern* garden.

To repeat: Giddens's harshest critics concede that he brought order to sociology. They find faults here and there with his structuration theory as well as his theory of modernity, but not with his intentions. Few sociologists read Park and Burgess's text any longer, and if they do, they are put off by its wildness. Despite this tendency toward respectability and order, sociology has replaced economics as the dismal science in the 1990s. Sociologists look to their neighboring gardens such as psychology and political science and economics and find them so much more attractive in appearance than sociology. The graduate student who pursues psychology has a laid-out path waiting for him or her. For example, don't pursue Jung (he was a mystic), do pursue experimental or cognitive psychology (these are scientific); don't try to find affinities between Jung and Durkheim (that's messy), do study psychology as a cognitive science, and so on. Sociology students, despite Giddens's popularity and success, still have many options to pursue: there are still weed-covered trails in sociology that graduate students might pursue if they do not choose to stay in Giddens's garden and have the courage to defy their mentors. For example, a sociology graduate student *can* "get away" with a doctoral dissertation on affinities between Jung the wild psychologist and Durkheim the wild sociologist. A graduate student in today's psychology cannot.

The gardener metaphor is powerful, but it needs to be completed by invoking its opposite: the uncultivated, natural field or forest. I contend that despite Giddens's rhetoric of freedom and agency, his structuration theory is ironically and actually stultifying. While sociology was still innocent, one was able to make discoveries precisely because sociology was so untamed and wild. Recall from chapter 3 Durkheim's original depiction of sociology as a science of discoveries. In Giddens's sociological garden, there is no room for discovery because everything has been pre-arranged *a priori*: the idea of agency, the notion of structure, the movement toward globalization, the tendency toward heightened reflexivity, and so on. These are assumed to be universal, and not subject to cultural filters. Giddens goes as far as positing the need to create synthetic traditions. Nothing is left to chance, or questioning. Giddens's theory even comes pre-packaged with a specialized vocabulary (see Giddens 1984), to demarcate it from the vulgar vocabulary of those few sociologists who still work in the wilderness.

Giddens's success is an accomplished fact, and I think it is due more to the need of his admirers for order in a world that postmodernists characterize as meaningless and chaotic than actual substance in his theory. With traditional social theory on one side and the provocative postmodernists on the other, mainstream sociologists find Giddens's version of modernism lite comforting: it avoids the alleged "chaos" of the postmodernists, yet is softer than the rigid Enlightenment project, which has come under so much scrutiny and attack that it can no longer be embraced uncritically without inviting scorn. Giddens is able to come across as both a critic of modernism and as a modernist thinker. There is precious little substance in his structuration theory or theory of modernity, as his critics have already made clear. Giddens misunderstands Marx, Durkheim, and Weber. That he can ignore Simmel is shocking. That he can get away with ignoring Veblen shows how narrow his thought really is. His blissful insistence that human agents are not cultural dupes becomes an article of faith, not fact. (For surely all agents conform some of the time and do not behave as agents at all times. And then thee are all those millions of people suffering from compulsions, anxiety disorders, and other psychiatric manifestations of non-agency.) His theory does not lend itself to empirical research. (One could soften this claim: intellectuals have to struggle to find ways to apply his theory, and prefer to talk and write about his theory rather than apply it.) His arguments are more rhetorical than carefully thought out discourses supported by evidence. For example, his claims about globalization are contradicted by his insistence on the viability of the nation-state, and his writings on human emancipation are contradicted by his clinging to the idea of social order. Meanwhile, the harsh realities of contemporary ethnic cleansing, Balkanization, and the rise of nationalism render his writings obsolete. His claims about dialogic democracy fall flat in the face of the West's shameless behavior in Bosnia and elsewhere in the world – and this despite global information, reflexive knowledge, and all the other ingredients that should lead agents to moral actions. His cheery pronouncements that Communism is gone and democracy triumphed are already open to question given Russia's and Serbia's turn toward new forms of authoritarianism. His writings on modernity fail to confront the fact, noted by Cushman (1995), Bauman (1991), Tester (1992), and others, that Soviet Communism was a modernist system that became totalitarian despite its early emancipatory rhetoric.

CONTEMPORARY SOCIOLOGISTS AS THE LEISURE CLASS

Despite the superficiality of his writings, Giddens's appeal and influence are immense in sociology in the 1990s. Given that Giddens's theory is not useful for understanding Durkheim or predicting the persistence of Communism or understanding genocide in Bosnia, and so on, how can one explain the prestige he enjoys? This observation boils down to the fact that contemporary sociologists have lost the innocent drive toward finding new frontiers and making discoveries, and have settled down to a lifestyle of what Veblen called the leisure class – now extended to everyone in the middle class in the West, thanks to globalization, including sociologists in academia. Veblen ([1899] 1969) showed that the leisure class is inherently conservative and favors inertia over "chaotic" change; it pursues status, prestige, and useless ostentation; and it wants to be seen by others as reputable. Contemporary sociology has taken on this character of the "lifestyle of the rich and famous." Consider, for example, that in recent years the annual conventions of the American Sociological Association have been held in luxury hotels in large metropolitan centers, thereby making the conventions too expensive to attend for "ordinary" sociologists who work in small teaching colleges instead of hugely endowed research universities – not to mention graduate students, many of whom live in poverty as they pursue their graduate studies. Whereas law students edit most of the journals of the legal profession, and certainly the significant ones, graduate students in sociology (not to speak of undergraduates) have no chance to act as editors of sociology journals. That would make learning sociology too practical, too direct, hence lower sociology's "prestige." One presents papers or attends sessions at these meetings increasingly less for motives of exposing one's ideas to criticism or learning something new, and more for the honorific motive of being able to say that one presented in or attended the meetings. (This is the academic version of Baudrillard's observation about "I did it" T-shirts.) Additionally, the fact that one presented a paper at these meetings pads one's vita.

Giddens's writings are tailor-made for this new intellectual leisure class because the central tenets of his theory are the central tenets of the leisure class lifestyle. He offers *order* over chaos; he promotes theoretical *inertia* by modifying and softening extreme positions, as opposed to the radicals who are looking for genuine alternatives to the modernist project; he develops his own glossary of terms and an esoteric vocabulary so as to set himself and his followers apart from other sociologists, and so on. To write clearly and distinctly, using an ordinary vocabulary, is to mark one's self as not belonging to the leisure class, which thrives on what is pretentious and useless. Hence, the trouble Giddens's readers have in trying to understand him, decipher his jargon, and agree on what he means. Yet, the new leisure class is satisfied with this lack of clarity, for it means that those who say they have read and understood Giddens have achieved an honor reserved for the very few.

Veblen ([1899] 1969) does not write about gardens, but he does write about lawns. For the purposes of this discussion, his ideas on this subject are close enough to the gardening metaphor to be relevant. Veblen observes that the middle-class lawn springs up with the advent of modernity as an attempt to emulate the leisure class pasture. The lawn must be well manicured; it must not have any weeds; much money and effort must be expended to keep it looking like a pasture. This is an important point vis-à-vis Giddens's claims about the reinvention of tradition: the lawn is a reinvented, fake, artificial "pasture." Yet it serves no useful purpose other than vicarious consumption of labor, for it does not sustain livestock or produce food. The prestige comes from its well-ordered uselessness. Veblen wrote that, in general, the useless becomes prestigious in all walks of life, for one can display to the world that one has the resources to waste on what serves no useful purposes for bettering humankind. Veblen's description of the lawn is not far removed from Bauman's and Tester's description of the modernist garden.

But again, it comes down to a question of taste or value. Let me make it clear that I am making the analogy that Giddens's work is like Veblen's well-manicured but useless, leisure class lawn. By contrast, the works of Simmel, Durkheim, and other prior thinkers up to and including Park and Burgess are the wilderness – their works are full of weeds! Today's average middle-class Westerner will not tolerate weeds in the lawn, and today's average sociologist will not tolerate weeds in sociological theory. Giddens's stature in sociology is assured so long as these generalized, modernist habits of the mind pertaining to order persist. Giddens is the last modernist.

SUMMARY

In *The Consequences of Modernity* (1990) and some other works, Giddens recognizes that modernity and the Enlightenment project have shortcomings and carry significant risks. But he is not prepared to embrace the postmodernist critique of modernity, nor is he prepared to reconcile the Enlightenment worship of reason with emotions. Instead, he urges the reader to ride the juggernaut of modernity and offers more proposals at social engineering to make the ride smoother. Yet modernity is not a juggernaut: it is constantly resisted, especially by the Islamic world in the 1990s, as Akbar Ahmed (1992, 1993) demonstrates convincingly, but also by many other cultures and subcultures. And to offer further suggestions for social engineering is really to succumb to the modernist faith in the final triumph of rationality over what Simmel called "life." For this reason among many that have been discussed in this book, I refer to Giddens as a modernist despite his sometimes cogent criticisms of modernity.

Furthermore, Giddens's critique of modernity is neither novel nor incisive when compared with the classical social thinkers from Simmel to Veblen. Is Giddens original? I think not, because Simmel, Freud, Durkheim, Veblen, and the other founders of the social sciences all preceded him in criticizing modernity. Yet Giddens obfuscates this fact by transforming them – and especially Durkheim, Marx, and Weber – into modernists. He does this by elevating the low status of Comte into a sacred icon; misrepresenting the focus on induction and metaphysics in nineteenth-century science; and misreading the classical social theorists through the distorted, modernist lens of Parsons. As I have stated throughout this volume, it is important to note the thinkers and concepts that Giddens ignores, obfuscates, or chooses not to incorporate into his writings. Simmel is devastating for Giddens's thought, so Giddens virtually ignores him. What is devastating about Simmel for Giddens includes the following: Simmel subscribed to Schopenhauer's belief that the will to life acts through human agents and ultimately leads to no goals despite the short-term goals of individual agents. Life is restless, aimless, and in constant flux. For Simmel, life is the realm of emotion and produces culture, but then destroys cultural forms as well. Simmel's sociology could never be incorporated into either Giddens's structuration or modernity theories.

Durkheim's *emotional* sociology – all that writing on sentiments, passions, effervescence, and feelings – does not fit into Giddens's abstract thought, so Durkheim is transformed by Giddens into a Parsonian functionalist. Again in line with Schopenhauer's anti-Enlightenment writings, Durkheim's concept of anomie as the infinity of desires captures the fact that human agents are never satisfied for long with the goals that they attain. Giddens makes no room for the anomie concept in his thought.

Simmel's teachers, Lazarus and Steinthal, their establishment of *Völkerpsychologie* and its further development by Wilhelm Wundt, are all threatening to Giddens's system. so he neglects them. This is because the *Volksgeist* or collective consciousness is based on habits and emotions, not rational agency.

I invoked Arthur Schopenhauer's philosophy as an antidote to Giddens's overestimation of Comte and of cognition in general. As Simmel makes clear in his neglected work *Schopenhauer and Nietzsche* ([1907] 1986), Schopenhauer was the intellectual superstar of the previous *fin de siècle*. The focus on Schopenhauer exposes the fact that Giddens ignores passions, emotions, and culture. This is because Schopenhauer's concept of the "will to life," which was refracted into Simmel's concept of "life" in opposition to forms, and Durkheim's concept of anomie as the infinity of desires (*not* normlessness), suggests that human passions are wild and unruly. The human agent is not constrained only by social structure, as Giddens admits, but is also enslaved by the passions coming from within, which Giddens never acknowledges. Introducing Schopenhauer into sociological discourse may finally point to a third way between modernism and postmodernism: the engagement of the passions with abstractionism. This is the way that I have already sketched out in my *The Barbarian Temperament* (1993a).

Moving from classical social theory to the present, it was important to contrast Giddens with Baudrillard, whom he also neglects. Giddens accepts and promotes the idea of the emancipated human agent. He betrays a certain naiveté in believing that agents, in the end, win out over constraint. Baudrillard is important because his work suggests that modernity or post-modernity enslaves human agents in mysterious ways that are still only dimly and imperfectly understood. Baudrillard's depiction of the "iron cage" is not constructed of unruly, anomic emotions, as it was for many classical social theorists, but is also not based on social structure, as it is for both Parsons and Giddens. Rather, the new form of slavery depicted by Baudrillard is based on humanly constructed hyperreality that robs human agents of the capacity to infer meaning. Unlike Marxists and critical theorists who believed that in the end heightened rationality could break through this new hybrid of reification, Baudrillard offers no such solace. Despite my reservations about some aspects of Baudrillard's vision (particularly his neglect of culture conceived as emotional habits of the heart), I contend that he is an anti-modernist who deserves to be taken seriously. Yet Giddens barely mentions Baudrillard by name and does not take Baudrillard's sociology seriously. To take Baudrillard seriously would be devastating for Giddens's theory, because Baudrillard is the theorist of a new form of slavery, in direct opposition to Giddens's theory of emancipation.

Against Giddens, Baudrillard, the modernists, as well as the postmodernists, I contend that the concept of culture, conceived as "habits of the heart," continues to offer promise as well as peril in the contemporary world. The promise is that there exist benign habits of the heart, such as compassion, which can resist the cruel indifference, even sadism, of the modernist project. There is no such thing as a universal standard of compassion, yet some variant of *caritas* is clearly the social "glue" that holds families and societies together in all of the world's diverse cultures. Without some version of *caritas*, mothers and fathers would not sacrifice for their children, soldiers would not give up their lives for their homelands, individuals would not curb their egoisms for the greater good, and so on. For example, despite all the reflexivity, rationality, rationalization, monitoring, surveillance, and dialogue thrown by the West at the genocide in Bosnia, the crimes against humanity continued unabated in full view of the television-viewing public comprised of supposedly emancipated human agents. Missing from the picture was some form of compassion at the sight of innocents being slaughtered without mercy for no reason other than their ethnicity. As for the peril, Communism may well stage a dramatic comeback in the former Soviet Union in a new form of anti-democratic authoritarianism, because Communism, although a modernist system, was rooted in perverse habits of the heart that have not been extinguished (Meštrović 1993b, 1993c). The many Far Right and New Right movements found throughout Western countries are thriving in an age devoid of *caritas*, for their messages of hate resonate with many individuals and are not countered by opposing emotions. Rationality and dialogue cannot stamp out hatred. On the contrary, it is easy to disguise hatred in rationality and dialogue.

Throughout this book, I have suggested that rather than think of modernity as a juggernaut, it is more realistic to conceive of traditionalism, modernity, and postmodernity as co-existing. For example, the United Kingdom offers the interesting spectacle of a modern nation that cherishes its monarchy and still exhibits many of the postmodern tendencies that Baudrillard describes in his books. Similarly, the USA is still as populist as it was at its inception, yet is clearly a modern nation that in many ways resonates with Baudrillard's portrait in *America* (1986). Modernity is not a juggernaut: modernity is resisted by tradition and also by its own postmodern fruits. Simmel (1971) anticipated this state of affairs with his portrait of a modern *culture* that seems to devour itself by the forms it creates.

The concept of modernity fails to account for the persistence of habits of the heart in so-called modern societies, while the term "postmodern" does not seem to refer to anything in particular, except, perhaps, the voyeuristic consumption of images through the information medium or a general sense of dissatisfaction with the orderliness and boundedness of modernity. (This may be one reason among many that Baudrillard rejects the label of postmodernist at the same time that he is seen by many as postmodernity's high priest.) I prefer the term "postemotional" to refer to the uneasy blend of traditionalism, modernity, and what is called postmodernity. Postemotionalism refers to situations which once would have evoked emotion (in traditional societies), but emotion is now choked off by modernist tendencies, allowing detachment from contemporary issues by people who are, in a way, voyeuristic consumers of other people's trials, tribulations, and emotions. I have outlined the parameters of postemotionalism in *Genocide After Emotion: The Postemotional Balkan War* (1996) and *Postemotional Society* (1997), and referred to it briefly in the present volume only to suggest how my position differs from that of Giddens.

The significance of postemotionalism is that it exposes how global humanity in the latter half of the twentieth century is turning its emotional energies from agency aimed at the future to a nostalgic form of slavery that focuses on the past. In the latter half of the twentieth century, postemotional yearnings for the past are apparent all over the world: the Ayatollah Khomeini tried to bring Iran back to the seventh century; Shining Path guerillas in Peru tried to reinstate some sort of "pure" culture based on the Incas; the Serbs in the 1990s focused their emotional energy on the events of 1389; militias in the USA have made 19 April 1789 a sacred icon in their rebellion against the federal government; popular culture recycles the cultural creations of previous generations; Disney World tries to capture the "magic" of an ideal childhood – and so on.

The important point is that Giddens's modernist theory, although popular in academia, is already obsolete. Giddens does not take emotions, culture, and habits of the heart seriously. Yet these phenomena have not disappeared from the social world that he characterizes as one of high or radical modernity. On the contrary, as illustrated by the case of nationalism, these phenomena are becoming noisier than ever. An emotion revolution may well be forming in its nascent stage in the current *fin de siècle*, but, unconstrained by *caritas*, it may turn out to be extremely destructive. For example, I have indicated already my agreement with Akbar Ahmed that ethnic cleansing has become a metaphor for our times. And Giddens does not take the information media and the phenomenon of voyeurism seriously either, not even in his superficial criticism of postmodernity. His exclusive focus on modernity and emancipatory rhetoric are out of sync with the many resistances to modernity and the new forms of enslavement found throughout the world. The supreme irony is that his works are popular in sociology even as sociology's popularity and relevance to world events are plummeting.

Of course, it is an open question whether and for how long the modernist habits of thought that Giddens champions and that sustain him within academia will persist. Despite Giddens's faith in radicalized or high modernity, the legacy of the Enlightenment must finally come to an end one day. Giddens hedges on his bet that it will persist by introducing the possibility of reinventing it if it finally seems to be in its death throes. But the prospects of reinventing communities, traditions, and other projects is ominous. There is absolutely no good reason to suppose that the state of collective morality in the West ensures that the social engineers in charge of this construction will be able to avoid totalitarianism.

NOTES

1 INTRODUCTION

1 See, for example, Giddens's remark in *Central Problems in Social Theory*: "The theory of structuration elaborated in the present book could be read as a *non-functionalist manifesto*" (1984: 7).

2 ANTHONY GIDDENS: THE LAST MODERNIST

1 "Clinton's Words on Mission to Bosnia: 'The Right Thing to Do,' " *New York Times*, 28 November 1995: A6.
2 In the sense that Giddens criticizes the very notions of function and functionalism. But note, that like Parsons, Giddens often writes in terms of the magical "fours" that inform Parson's writings. Thus, Giddens (1990) refers to *four* institutional fields, *four* drives, *four* high-consequence risks. Why not three or five or whatever?
3 For example, Bryant and Jary (1991); Clark *et al.* (1990); Cohen (1989); Craib (1992); Featherstone (1982–3); Held and Thompson (1989).
4 "America's Grade on 20th Century European Wars: F," *New York Times*, 3 December 1995: E5.
5 Dave Barry, "Don't Know Much 'Bout History," *Bryan-College Station Eagle*, 10 December 1985: D1.
6 One of the finest accounts of the importance of Lazarus, Steinthal, and Wundt is to be found in Kalmar (1987).
7 For a fuller discussion see Kaern *et al.* (1991).
8 The books he reviews are *Intimations of Postmodernity* (Bauman 1992), *Post-Modernism and the Social Sciences* (Rosenau 1992), and *Modern Conditions: Postmodern Controversies* (Smart 1991).
9 Namely, that he prefers to speak of radical or "high" modernity rather than postmodernity.

3 THE NEW VERSUS THE OLD RULES OF SOCIOLOGICAL METHOD

1 I have dealt with the role of Wilhelm Wundt's relationship to these issues at length in *Durkheim and Postmodern Culture* in a chapter entitled "Postmodern Language as a Social Fact," and raise them here only for the sake of contextualizing Giddens's work (see Meštrović 1992: 69–90).
2 Discussed at length in Meštrović (1994).

3   André Lalande (1960: 23) notes that Durkheim was so enamored with Schopenhauer's philosophy that his students named him "Schopen." This is not surprising given the vast literature that demonstrates the importance of Schopenhauer's philosophy for turn of the century culture as a whole (see Bailey 1958; Baillot 1927; Bloom 1987; Durant 1961; Ellenberger 1970; Fox 1980; Lukács 1980; Magee 1983; Meštrović 1988).

4   Here I am relying on Zygmunt Bauman's (1991) metaphor for the modernist as gardener who seeks to create a perfectly ordered garden without weeds. Bauman's metaphor also holds affinities with Ritzer's (1992) notion of McDonaldization.

5   Durkheim also adds that social facts are things, but not necessarily material things ([1895] 1938: xliii).

4   THE ROLE OF DESIRE IN AGENCY AND STRUCTURE

1   Giddens devotes a sentence here or there to repression in his discussions of Freud, Habermas, and Norbert Elias (see Giddens 1979: 144, 176–8, 192; 1984: 52–7). But he does not define repression nor take seriously its centrality in Freud's thought.

2   Durkheim writes:

On the one hand, [society] seems to us an authority that constrains us, fixes limits for us, blocks us when we would trespass, and to which we defer with a feeling of religious respect. On the other hand, society is the benevolent and protecting power, the nourishing mother from which we gain the whole of our moral and intellectual substance and toward whom our wills turn in a spirit of love and gratitude.

([1925] 1961: 92)

5   GIDDENS'S POLITICAL SOCIOLOGY

1   Giddens expresses this thought elsewhere in the book as follows:

What makes the "nation" integral to the nation-state in this definition is not the existence of sentiments of nationalism, but the unification of an administrative apparatus over precisely specified territorial bounds (in a complex of other nation-states). . . . I shall define "nationalism" as the exis-tence of symbols and beliefs which are either propagated by lite groups or held by many of the members of regional, ethnic or linguistic categories of a population, and which imply a communality between them. . . . Nationalistic sentiments do not necessarily converge with citizenship of a particular nation-state, but very often they *have* done so.

(1982b: 190)

2   Clyde H. Farnsworth, "Canada's Coat of Arms Spurs Disunity," *Houston Chronicle*, 11 December 1995: 11A.

3   He elaborates elsewhere in the book: "'Society' has often been understood by sociologists, implicitly or otherwise, as a clearly bounded system with an obvious and easily identifiable set of distinguishing traits" (1987:17).

4   Steven Lee Myers, "Converting the Dollar into a Bludgeon," *New York Times*, 20 April 1997: E5.

5   Specifically, Giddens writes:

Violence is a destructive reaction to the waning of female complicity. Save in conditions of war, men are perhaps today more violent towards women than they are towards one another. . . . Women are quite often physically violent towards men in domestic settings; violence seems a not uncommon feature of lesbian relationships, at least in some contexts. Studies of female sexual violence in the US describe cases of lesbian rape, physical battering, and assault with guns, knives and other lethal weapons. . . . [M]any men who regularly visit prostitutes wish to assume a passive, not an active role, whether or not this involves actual masochistic practices. Some gay men find their greatest pleasure in being submissive, but many are also able to switch roles.

(1992b: 122–3)

6 All three essays were translated into English by James Petterson of Wellesley College and are reprinted in Thomas Cushman and Stjepan G. Meštrović, *This Time We Knew* (1996: 79–89). The essays are entitled, "No Pity for Sarajevo," "The West's Serbianization," and "When the West Stands in for the Dead."

6 GIDDENS'S MODERNISM LITE

1 Lauran Neergaard, "U.S. HIV Experiments Criticized as Unethical," *Houston Chronicle*, 24 April 1997: 20A.

7 UNLIMITED AGENCY AS THE NEW ANOMIE

1 From *Time* magazine, 27 September 1954.
2 One sociological voice in all this contemporary wilderness – that of David Riesman (1950: 244) – had caught the correct spirit of Durkheim's writings, though it is almost never referenced.

REFERENCES

Adams, H. ([1900] 1983) The Dynamo and the Virgin. In H. Adams (ed.), *The Education of Henry Adams*. New York: Viking: pp. 1068–75.

Ahmed, A. (1992) *Postmodernism and Islam: Predicament and Promise*. London: Routledge.

—— (1993) *Living Islam: From Samarkand to Stornoway*. London: BBC Books.

—— (1995) Ethnic Cleansing: A Metaphor for Our Time? *Ethnic and Racial Studies* 18(1): 2–25.

Ahmed, A. and Shore, C. (eds) (1995) *The Future of Anthropology: Its Relevance to the Contemporary World*. London: Athlone Press.

Alpert, H. ([1939] 1961) *Émile Durkheim and His Sociology*. New York: Columbia University Press.

Arnason, J.P. (1987) Review Essay: The State and Its Contexts. *Australian and New Zealand Journal of Sociology* 23(3): 433–42.

Bailey, R.B. (1958) *Sociology Faces Pessimism: A Study of European Sociological Thought Amidst a Fading Optimism*. The Hague: Martinus Nijhoff.

Baillot, A. (1927) *Influence de la philosophie de Schopenhauer en France (1860–1900)*. Paris: J. Vrin.

Baudrillard, J. (1981) *Critique of the Political Economy of the Sign*, translated by C. Levin. St Louis, MO: Telos Press.

—— (1986) *America*, translated by C. Turner. London: Verso.

—— (1993) *The Transparency of Evil*, translated by J. Benedict. London: Verso.

Bauman, Z. (1987) *Legislators and Interpreters: On Modernity, Post-Modernity, and Intellectuals*. Ithaca, NY: Cornell University Press.

—— (1989) *Modernity and the Holocaust*. Ithaca, NY: Cornell University Press.

—— (1991) *Modernity and Ambivalence*. Ithaca, NY: Cornell University Press.

—— (1992) *Intimations of Postmodernity*. London: Routledge.

Bell, D. (1976) *The Cultural Contradictions of Capitalism*. New York: Basic Books.

Bellah, R.N. (1967) Civil Religion in America. *Daedalus* 96: 1–21.

Bellah, R.N., Madsen, R., Sullivan, W.M., Swidler, A. and Tipton, S.M. (1985) *Habits of the Heart*. Berkeley: University of California Press.

Berger, P. and Luckmann, T. (1967) *The Social Construction of Reality*. New York: Doubleday.

Bernard, C. ([1865] 1957) *An Introduction to the Study of Experimental Medicine*, translated by H.C. Green. New York: Dover Press.

225

Bernstein, R.J. (1986) Structuration as Critical Theory. *Praxis International* 6(2): 235–49.

Bloom, A. (1987) *The Closing of the American Mind*. New York: Simon & Schuster.

Blumer, H. (1969) *Symbolic Interactionism*. Englewood Cliffs, NJ: Prentice-Hall.

Bryant, C.G. and Jary, D. (1991) *Giddens' Theory of Structuration: A Critical Appreciation*. London: Routledge.

Brzezinski, Z. (1989) *The Grand Failure: The Birth and Death of Communism in the Twentieth Century*. New York: Scribner's Sons.

Callinicos, A. (1985) Anthony Giddens: A Contemporary Critique. *Theory and Society* 14(2): 133–66.

Challenger, D. (1994) *Durkheim Through the Lens of Aristotle: Durkheimian, Postmodernist, and Communitarian Responses to the Enlightenment*. Totowa, NJ: Rowman & Littlefield.

Cigar, N. (1995) *Genocide in Bosnia-Herzegovina*. College Station, TX: Texas A & M University Press.

Clark, J., Modgil, C. and Modgil, S. (1990) *Anthony Giddens: Consensus and Controversy*. London: Falmer Press.

Cockerham, W. (1981) *Sociology of Mental Disorder*. Englewood Cliffs, NJ: Prentice-Hall.

Cohen, I. (1989) *Structuration Theory: Anthony Giddens and the Constitution of Social Life*. New York: St Martin's Press.

Cohen, P.J. (1996) *Serbia's Secret War: Propaganda and the Deceit of History*. College Station, TX: Texas A & M University Press.

Comte, A. ([1855] 1974) *The Positive Philosophy*. New York: Columbia University Press.

Craib, I. (1992) *Anthony Giddens*. London: Routledge.

Cushman, T. (1995) *Notes From Underground: Rock Music and Counterculture in Russia*. Albany: SUNY Press.

Cushman, T. and Meštrović, S.G. (1996) *This Time We Knew: Western Responses to Genocide in Bosnia*. New York: New York University Press.

Dallmayr, F.R. (1982) Agency and Structure. *Philosophy of the Social Sciences* 12(4): 427–38.

Davy, G. (1927) *Émile Durkheim*. Paris: Louis-Michaud.

Deploige, S. (1921) *Le conflit de la morale et de la sociologie*. Paris: Nouvelle Librairie Nationale.

Dodder, R.A. and Astle, D.J. (1981) A Methodological Analysis of Srole's Nine-item Anomie Scale. *Multivariate Behavioral Research* 15: 329–34.

Dohrenwend, B.P. (1959) Egoism, Altruism, Anomie, and Fatalism: A Conceptual Analysis of Durkheim's Types. *American Sociological Review* 24(3): 466–73.

Doubt, K. (1996) *Towards a Sociology of Schizophrenia*. Toronto: University of Toronto Press.

Douglas, J. (1967) *The Social Meanings of Suicide*. Princeton, NJ: Princeton University Press.

Dudley, C.J. (1978) The Division of Labor, Alienation, and Anomie: A Reformulation. *Sociological Focus* 11: 97–109.

Durkheim, É. ([1893] 1933) *The Division of Labor in Society*, translated by G. Simpson. New York: Free Press.

—— ([1895] 1938) *The Rules of Sociological Method*, translated by A. Solovay and J.H. Mueller. New York: Free Press.

—— ([1895] 1982) The Rules of Sociological Method. In *Durkheim: The Rules of Sociological Method and Selected Texts on Sociology and Its Method*, edited by S. Lukes. New York: Free Press: pp. 31–163.

—— ([1895] 1983) *Les Règles de la méthode sociologique*. Paris: Presses Universitaires de France.

—— ([1897] 1951) *Suicide: A Study in Sociology*, translated by J.A. Spaulding and G. Simpson. New York: Free Press.

—— ([1897] 1963) *Incest: The Nature and Origin of Taboo*, translated by E. Sagarain. New York: Stuart Lyle.

—— ([1906] 1978) Review of Marianne Weber. In *Émile Durkheim and Institutional Analysis*, edited by M. Traugott. Chicago: University of Chicago Press: pp. 139–44.

—— (1908) L'inconnu et l'inconscient en histoire. *Bulletin de la Société Française de Philosophie* 8: 217–47.

—— ([1912] 1965) *The Elementary Forms of the Religious Life*, translated by J. Swain. New York: Free Press.

—— ([1914] 1973) The Dualism of Human Nature and Its Social Conditions. In *Émile Durkheim on Morality and Society*, edited by R. Bellah. Chicago: University of Chicago Press: pp. 149–66.

—— ([1924] 1974) *Sociology and Philosophy*, translated by D.F. Pocock. New York: Free Press.

—— ([1925] 1961) *Moral Education*, translated by E.K. Wilson and H. Schnurer. Glencoe, IL: Free Press.

—— ([1928] 1958) *Socialism and Saint-Simon*, translated by C. Sattler. Yellow Springs, OH: Antioch Press.

—— ([1950] 1983) *Professional Ethics and Civic Morals*, translated by C. Brookfield. Westport, CT: Greenwood Press.

—— (1980) *Émile Durkheim: Contributions to L'Année sociologique*, edited by Y. Nandan. New York: Free Press.

—— (1986) *Durkheim on Politics and the State*, translated by W.D. Halls and edited by A. Giddens. Oxford: Polity.

Durkheim, É. and Mauss, M. ([1902] 1963) *Primitive Classification*, translated by R. Needham. New York: Free Press.

Ellenberger, H. (1970) *The Discovery of the Unconscious*. New York: Basic Books.

Featherstone, M. (ed.) (1982–3) *Symposium on Giddens. Theory, Culture & Society* 1(2): 63–106.

—— (1995) *Undoing Culture*. London: Sage.

Fox, M. (1980) *Schopenhauer: His Philosophical Achievement*. Totowa, NJ: Barnes & Noble.

Freud, S. ([1901] 1965) *The Psychopathology of Everyday Life*, translated by J. Strachey. New York: W.W. Norton.

—— ([1913] 1950) *Totem and Taboo*, translated by J. Strachey. New York: W.W. Norton.

Frisby, D. (1986) *Fragments of Modernity: Theories of Modernity in the Works of Simmel, Kracauer and Benjamin*. Cambridge, MA: MIT Press.

—— (1992) *Sociological Impressionism: A Reassessment of Simmel's Social Theory*. London: Routledge.

Fromm, E. (1955) *The Sane Society*. Greenwich, CT: Fawcett.

—— (1956) *The Art of Loving*. New York: Harper.

—— (1962) *Beyond the Chains of Illusion: My Encounter with Marx and Freud*. New York: Simon & Schuster.

—— (1980) *Greatness and Limitations of Freud's Thought*. New York: HarperCollins.

Fukuyama, F. (1992) *The End of History and the Last Man*. New York: Free Press.

Gellner, E. (1992) *Postmodernism, Reason, and Religion*. London: Routledge.

Geyer, G.A. (1996) *Buying the Night Flight: The Autobiography of a Woman Foreign Correspondent*. Washington, DC: Brassey's.

Giddens, A. (1971) *Capitalism and Modern Social Theory*. Cambridge: Cambridge University Press.

—— (1974) *Positivism and Sociology*. London: Heinemann.

—— (1975) American Sociology Today. *New Society* 33(676): 633–4.

—— (1976) Classical Social Theory and the Origins of Modern Sociology. *American Journal of Sociology* 81(4): 703–29.

—— (1978) *Durkheim*. Hassocks: Harvester Press.

—— (1979) *Central Problems in Social Theory*. Berkeley: University of California Press.

—— (1982a) *Profiles and Critiques in Social Theory*. London: Macmillan.

—— (1982b) *A Contemporary Critique of Historical Materialism*. Berkeley: University of California Press.

—— (1984) *The Constitution of Society: Outline of the Theory of Structuration*. Berkeley: University of California Press.

—— (1987) *The Nation-State and Violence*. Berkeley: University of California Press.

—— (1990) *The Consequences of Modernity*. Stanford, CA: Stanford University Press.

—— (1991a) *Modernity and Self-Identity: Self and Society in the Late Modern Age*. Stanford: Stanford University Press.

—— (1991b) *Introduction to Sociology*. New York: W.W. Norton.

—— (1992a) Uprooted Signposts at Century's End. *The Times Higher Education Supplement*, 17 January: 21.

—— (1992b) *The Transformation of Intimacy*. Stanford: Stanford University Press.

—— (1993) *New Rules of Sociological Method*. Oxford: Polity .

—— (1994) *Beyond Left and Right: The Future of Radical Politics*. Stanford, CA: Stanford University Press.

—— (1995) Epilogue: Notes on the Future of Anthropology. In A. Ahmed and C. Shore (eds), *The Future of Anthropology: Its Relevance to the Social World*. London: Athlone Press: pp. 272–7.

Gilligan, C. (1982) *In a Different Voice*. Cambridge, MA: Harvard University Press.

Gouldner, A. (1958) Introduction. In É. Durkheim, *Socialism and Saint-Simon*. Yellow Springs, OH: Antioch Press: pp. v–xxviii.

Halbwachs, M. (1918) La Doctrine d'Émile Durkheim. *Revue Philosophique* 85: 353–411.

Hamlyn, D. (1980) *Schopenhauer*. London: Routledge.

Hegel, G.W.F. ([1830] 1971) *Hegel's Philosophy of Mind*, translated by A.V. Miller. Oxford: Clarendon Press.

Held, D. and Thompson, J.B. (eds) (1989) *Social Theory of Modern Societies: Anthony Giddens and His Critics*. Cambridge: Cambridge University Press.

Hirst, P.Q. (1975) *Durkheim, Bernard, and Epistemology*. London: Routledge & Kegan Paul.

Horowitz, I.L. (1987) *Disenthralling Sociology*. New Brunswick, NJ: Transaction Press.

James, W. ([1890] 1950) *The Principles of Psychology*. New York: Dover Press.

Janik, A. and Toulmin, S. (1973) *Wittgenstein's Vienna*. New York: Simon & Schuster.

Johnson, D.P. (1990) Security Versus Autonomy Motivation in Anthony Giddens' Concept of Agency. *Journal for the Theory of Social Behaviour* 20(2): 111–30.

Kaern, M., Philips, B.S. and Cohen, R.S. (eds) (1990) *Georg Simmel and Contemporary Sociology*. Boston: Kluwer Academic Publishers.

Kalmar, I. (1987) The *Völkerpsychologie* of Lazarus and Steinthal and the Modern Concept of Culture. *Journal of the History of Ideas* 48: 671–90.

Kant, I. ([1788] 1956) *Critique of Practical Reason*. Indianapolis, IN: Bobbs-Merrill.

Kellner, D. (1989) *Jean Baudrillard: From Marxism to Postmodernism and Beyond*. Stanford: Stanford University Press.

—— (1992) *The Persian Gulf TV War*. Boulder, CO: Westview Press.

Khazanov, A.M. (1995) *After the USSR: Ethnicity, Nationalism, and Politics in the Commonwealth of Independent States*. Madison: University of Wisconsin Press.

Kohlberg, L. (1981) *Essays in Moral Development*. San Francisco: Jossey-Bass.

La Capra, D. (1972) *Émile Durkheim: Sociologist and Philosoopher*. Ithaca, NY: Cornell University Press.

Lalande, A. ([1926] 1980) *Vocabulaire, technique et critique de la philosophie*. Paris: Presses Universitaires de France.

—— (1960) Allocution. In *Centenaire de la naissance d'Émile Durkheim*. Paris: Annales de l'Université de Paris.

Laplanche, J. and Pontalis, J.B. (1973) *The Language of Psychoanalysis*. Baltimore: Johns Hopkins University Press.

Lasch, C. (1979) *The Culture of Narcissism*. New York: Norton.

—— (1991) *The True and Only Heaven: Progress and Its Critics*. New York: Norton.

Littré, É. (1963) *Dictionnaire de la langue française*. Vols 1–9. Paris: Gallimard.

Lukács, G. (1980) *The Destruction of Reason*, translated by P. Palmer. Atlantic Highlands, NJ: Humanities Press.

Lukes, S. (1982) *Durkheim: The Rules of Sociological Method and Selected Texts on Sociology and Its Method*. New York: Free Press.

—— (1985) *Émile Durkheim: His Life and Work*. Stanford, CA: Stanford University Press.

Lyonnet, S. and Sabourin, L. (1970) *Sin, Redemption and Sacrifice: A Biblical and Patristic Study*. Rome: Biblical Institute Press.

McLennan, G. (1984) Critical or Positive Theory? A Comment on the Status of Anthony Giddens' Social Theory. *Theory, Culture & Society* 2(2): 123–9.

Magee, B. (1983) *The Philosophy of Schopenhauer*. New York: Oxford University Press.

Marcuse, H. ([1964] 1991) *One-Dimensional Man*. Boston: Beacon.

Mauss, M. (1967) *The Gift*, translated by W.D. Halls. New York: W.W. Norton.

Merton, R.K. (1957) *Social Theory and Social Structure*. New York: Free Press.

Meštrović, S.G. (1988) *Émile Durkheim and the Reformation of Sociology*. Totowa, NJ: Rowman & Littlefield.

229

—— (1991) *The Coming Fin de Siècle: An Application of Durkheim's Sociology to Modernity and Postmodernism*. London: Routledge.

—— (1992) *Durkheim and Postmodern Culture*. Hawthorne, NY: Aldine de Gruyter.

—— (1993a) *The Barbarian Temperament*. London and New York: Routledge.

—— (1993b) *The Road From Paradise: Prospects for Democracy in Eastern Europe*. Lexington, KY: University Press of Kentucky.

—— (1993c) *Habits of the Balkan Heart*. College Station, TX: Texas A & M University Press.

—— (1994) *Balkanization of the West: The Confluence of Postmodernism with Postcommunism*. London: Routledge.

—— (1996) *Genocide After Emotion: The Postemotional Balkan War*. London: Routledge.

—— (1997) *Postemotional Society*. London: Sage.

Mill, J.S. ([1865] 1968) *Auguste Comte and Positivism*. Ann Arbor: University of Michigan Press.

Mills, C.W. (1959) *The Sociological Imagination*. New York: Oxford University Press.

Mouzelis, N. (1989) Restructuring Structuration Theory. *The Sociological Review* 37: 615–35.

Moynihan, D.P. (1993) *Pandaemonium*. New York: Oxford University Press.

Nietzsche, F. (1968) *The Portable Nietzsche*, translated by W. Kaufmann. New York: Viking Library.

Orwell, G. ([1937] 1958) *The Road to Wigan Pier*. New York: Harcourt Brace.

Park, R.E. and Burgess, W.E. (1921) *Introduction to the Science of Sociology*. Chicago: University of Chicago Press.

Parsons, T. (1937) *The Structure of Social Action*. Glencoe, IL: Free Press.

Renouvier, C. (1892) Schopenhauer et la metaphysique du pessimisme. *L'Année philosophique* 3: 1–61.

Riesman, D. (1950) *The Lonely Crowd*. New Haven, CT: Yale University Press.

—— (1980) Egocentrism. *Character* 1(5): 3–9.

—— (1995) *Thorstein Veblen*. New Brunswick, NJ: Transaction Press.

Ritzer, G. (1992) *The McDonaldization of Society*. Newbury Park, CA: Sage.

Rojek, C. (1995) *Decentring Leisure*. London: Sage.

Rojek, C. and Turner, B. (1993) *Forget Baudrillard?* London: Routledge.

Rosenau, P.M. (1992) *Post-Modernism and the Social Sciences: Insights, Inroads, and Intrusions*. Princeton, NJ: Princeton University Press.

Schopenhauer, A. ([1818] 1969a) *The World as Will and Representation*, translated by E. Payne, vol. 1. New York: Dover Press.

—— ([1818] 1969b) *The World as Will and Representation*, translated by E. Payne, vol. 2. New York: Dover Press.

—— ([1841] 1965) *On the Basis of Morality*. Indianapolis, IN: Bobbs-Merrill.

—— (1899) *On the Fourfold Root of the Principle of Sufficient Reason and On the Will in Nature*. London: G. Bell & Sons.

Simmel, G. ([1900] 1990) *Philosophy of Money*, translated by T. Bottomore and D. Frisby. London: Routledge.

—— ([1907] 1986) *Schopenhauer and Nietzsche*, translated by H. Loiskandl, D. Weinstein and M. Weinstein. Amherst: University of Massachusetts Press.

—— (1971) *On Individuality and Its Social Forms*, edited by D.N. Levine. Chicago: University of Chicago Press.

Smart, B. (1991) *Modern Conditions: Postmodern Controversies.* London: Routledge.

Smith, J.W. and Turner, B.S. (1986) Constructing Social Theory and Constituting Society. *Theory, Culture & Society* 3(2): 125–33.

Sorokin, P. (1957) *Social and Cultural Dynamics.* New York: American Book Company.

Spengler, O. ([1926] 1961) *The Decline of the West.* New York: Alfred A. Knopf.

Stinchcombe, A.L. (1986) Review Essay: Milieu and Structure Update. *Theory and Society* 15(6): 901–14.

Szasz, T. (1961) *The Myth of Mental Illness.* New York: Dell.

Tester, K. (1992) *The Two Sovereigns: Social Contradictions of European Modernity.* London: Routledge.

—— (1993) *The Life and Times of Post-Modernity.* London: Routledge.

Thompson, J.B. (1995) *The Media and Modernity.* Stanford, CA: Stanford University Press.

Tiryakian, E. (1966) A Problem for the Sociology of Knowledge: The Mutual Unawareness of Emile Durkheim and Max Weber. *European Journal of Sociology* 7: 330–6.

Tocqueville, A. de ([1845] 1945) *Democracy in America*, vol. 1, translated by P. Bradley. New York: Viking Press.

—— ([1856] 1955) *The Old Regime and the French Revolution*, translated by S. Gilbert. Garden City, NY: Doubleday.

Tönnies, F. ([1887] 1963) *Community and Society*, translated by C. Loomis. New York: Harper & Row.

Toynbee, A. (1978) *Arnold Toynbee: A Selection From His Works*, edited by C. Tomlin. Oxford: Oxford University Press.

Veblen, T. ([1899] 1969) *The Theory of the Leisure Class.* New York: Penguin.

Wallace, W. (1971) *The Logic of Science in Sociology.* Chicago: Aldine.

Wallwork, E. (1972) *Durkheim: Morality and Milieu.* Cambridge, MA: Harvard University Press.

Weber, E. (1986) *France, Fin de Siècle.* Cambridge, MA: Harvard University Press.

Weber, M. ([1904] 1958) *The Protestant Ethic and the Spirit of Capitalism*, translated by T. Parsons. New York: Scribner's.

Wistrich, R.S. (1976) *Revolutionary Jews From Marx to Trotsky.* London: Harrap.

Znaniecki, F. ([1934] 1968) *The Method of Sociology.* New York: Octagon Books.

231

INDEX